Seven years ago we published the first volume of the great Hungarian bishop's meditations. It sold out and for some years remained out of print. The demands for a further edition have been so steadily maintained, and even in the last year or so increased, that we have decided not merely to reprint the first volume, but also to issue for the first time the second and third volumes which complete the work. We quote some Press opinions of the first volume :

" Contains passages of exquisite simplicity."—*Guardian*.

" The thoughts are strong and original, well coloured with sentiment without being in the least sentimental, and above all searchingly spiritual."—*Universe*.

MEDITATIONS ON
THE GOSPELS

MEDITATIONS ON THE GOSPELS

By the Right Reverend

OTTOKAR PROHÁSZKA

Bishop of Székesfehérvár

*Authorised translation
from the Hungarian*

by

M. DE PÁL

Foreword by C. C. Martindale, S.J.

VOLUME II

LONDON

SHEED & WARD

MCMXXXVIII

NIHIL OBSTAT :

REGINALDUS PHILLIPS, S.TH.D.
CENSOR DEPUTATUS

IMPRIMATUR :

✠ JOSEPH BUTT, VIC. GEN.

WESTMONASTERII, DIE 22ND JANUARII 1937

Second Impression January 1938

PRINTED IN GREAT BRITAIN BY
LOWE AND BRYDONE PRINTERS LIMITED, LONDON, N.W.10

CONTENTS

	PAGE
BAPTISM OF JESUS IN THE JORDAN. I - - -	1
BAPTISM OF JESUS IN THE JORDAN. II - -	3
THE FULFILMENT OF JUSTICE - - - -	6
FASTING AND TEMPTATION OF JESUS - - -	9
THE SECOND TEMPTATION - - - -	10
THE THIRD TEMPTATION - - - -	12
THE CALLING OF THE FIRST DISCIPLES - - -	14
THE FIRST MIRACLE OF JESUS AT CANA - -	15
NICODEMUS COMES TO JESUS BY NIGHT - - -	17
THAT WHICH IS BORN OF THE SPIRIT, IS SPIRIT -	19
THE MOVEMENT OF THE SPIRIT - - - -	22
FOR GOD SO LOVED THE WORLD - - - -	23
JESUS AT JACOB'S WELL - - - - -	25
JESUS AND THE RULER - - - - -	29
THE NECESSITY OF FAITH - - - - -	32
THE CALLING OF SIMON AND ANDREW - - -	34
JESUS TAUGHT AS ONE HAVING POWER - - -	36
JESUS HEALS SIMON'S WIFE'S MOTHER - - -	37
ALL SEEK FOR THEE - - - - - -	39
JESUS TEACHES THE MULTITUDE OUT OF THE SHIP -	42
"LAUNCH OUT INTO THE DEEP" - - - -	44
THE MIRACULOUS DRAUGHT - - - - -	47
HEALING OF A LEPER - - - - - -	49
HEALING OF ONE SICK OF THE PALSY - - -	50
THE CALLING OF MATTHEW - - - - -	52
JESUS EATS WITH PUBLICANS AND SINNERS - -	53
THE PHARISEES REBUKE OUR LORD - - -	55
THE HEALING OF THE MAN WHO HAD BEEN INFIRM FOR THIRTY-EIGHT YEARS - - - -	58
JESUS SPENDS THE NIGHT IN PRAYER. I - -	60
JESUS' SPENDS THE NIGHT IN PRAYER. II - -	63

                                                        PAGE
JESUS CHOOSES TWELVE APOSTLES -   -   -   -   65
THE EIGHT BEATITUDES   -   -   -   -   -   66
BLESSED ARE THEY THAT SUFFER PERSECUTION   -   70
LIGHT AND SALT OF THE EARTH -   -   -   -   72
JESUS CAME NOT TO DESTROY THE LAW. I -   -   74
JESUS CAME NOT TO DESTROY THE LAW. II -   -   76
ANGER   -   -   -   -   -   -   -   -   78
THE LAW OF CHASTITY. I -   -   -   -   -   80
THE LAW OF CHASTITY. II -   -   -   -   -   83
SIMPLICITY OF SPEECH -   -   -   -   -   -   86
DO NOT YOUR JUSTICE BEFORE MEN   -   -   -   87
FAST NOT AS THE HYPOCRITES   -   -   -   -   88
PRAY IN SECRET -   -   -   -   -   -   -   90
THE OUR FATHER -   -   -   -   -   -   91
THE EYE THE LIGHT OF THE BODY   -   -   -   96
"BE NOT SOLICITOUS"   -   -   -   -   -   97
THE COMMAND TO LOVE OUR ENEMIES -   -   -   100
THE BLIND CANNOT LEAD THE BLIND -   -   -   101
THE NARROW GATE AND THE BROAD WAY   -   -   103
WARNING AGAINST FALSE PROPHETS   -   -   -   105
WE MUST DO THE WILL OF OUR FATHER   -   -   107
THE CENTURION OF CAPHARNAUM   -   -   -   109
HEALING OF A LEPER -   -   -   -   -   -   111
JESUS RAISES THE YOUNG MAN OF NAIM   -   -   113
JOHN SENDS TWO OF HIS DISCIPLES TO JESUS   -   116
ANSWER OF JESUS TO JOHN'S DISCIPLES -   -   -   117
JESUS PRAISES JOHN THE BAPTIST. I   -   -   -   119
JESUS PRAISES JOHN THE BAPTIST. II -   -   -   122
MARY MAGDALEN   -   -   -   -   -   -   124
JESUS INEXORABLE IN THE FULFILMENT OF HIS
    MISSION   -   -   -   -   -   -   -   126
PARABLE OF THE SOWER   -   -   -   -   -   128
PARABLE OF THE COCKLE   -   -   -   -   -   130
PARABLE OF THE MUSTARD SEED --   -   -   -   132
PARABLE OF THE LEAVEN   -   -   -   -   -   134
PARABLE OF THE HIDDEN TREASURE   -   -   -   135
LEAVE ALL TO FOLLOW CHRIST   -   -   -   -   138
THE TEMPEST AT SEA -   -   -   -   -   -   140
JESUS HEALS TWO THAT WERE POSSESSED OF DEVILS 142
JESUS RAISES THE DAUGHTER OF JAIRUS   -   -   145

PAGE

HEALING OF THE WOMAN WITH AN ISSUE OF BLOOD.   I   147
HEALING OF THE WOMAN WITH AN ISSUE OF BLOOD.   II 149
JESUS IN THE SYNAGOGUE AT NAZARETH   -   -   151
PERSECUTION OF THE CHOSEN   -   -   -   153
FEAR NOT THEM THAT KILL THE BODY   -   -   154
JESUS BRINGS NOT PEACE BUT A SWORD   -   -   156
BEHEADING OF JOHN THE BAPTIST   -   -   -   157
" COME APART "   -   -   -   -   -   -   -   159
FEEDING OF THE FIVE THOUSAND   -   -   -   161
JESUS WALKS ON THE SEA   -   -   -   -   -   163
PROMISE OF THE EUCHARIST   -   -   -   166
" I AM THE LIVING BREAD "   -   -   -   168
" MY WORDS ARE SPIRIT AND LIFE "   -   -   169
" HE THAT EATETH ME SHALL LIVE "   -   -   171
THE HEART THE FOUNT OF EVIL   -   -   -   172
THE WOMAN OF CANAAN   -   -   -   -   -   174
HEALING OF THE DEAF AND DUMB   -   -   -   176
BEWARE OF THE LEAVEN OF THE PHARISEES -   -   178
WHOM DO MEN SAY THAT THE SON OF MAN IS ?   -   181
PETER THE ROCK   -   -   -   -   -   -   -   183
THE HOLY CHURCH OF CHRIST   -   -   -   185
CALL TO FOLLOW JESUS   -   -   -   -   -   187
" HE THAT WILL SAVE HIS LIFE SHALL LOSE IT "   190
VALUE OF THE SOUL.   I   -   -   -   -   -   191
VALUE OF THE SOUL.   II -   -   -   -   -   193
THE TRANSFIGURATION   -   -   -   -   -   197
LORD, IT IT GOOD TO BE HERE   -   -   -   -   199
JESUS HEALS THE DUMB.   I -   -   -   -   -   200
JESUS HEALS THE DUMB.   II   -   -   -   -   203
" UNLESS YOU BECOME AS LITTLE CHILDREN "   -   204
TRUE CHILDHOOD   -   -   -   -   -   -   206
THE CHURCH TEACHES TRUE CHILDHOOD   -   -   208
GOD'S ANGEL ACCOMPANIES US   -   -   -   -   210
PARABLE OF THE CRUEL SERVANT.   I   -   -   -   211
PARABLE OF THE CRUEL SERVANT.   II -   -   -   214
THE SENDING OF THE DISCIPLES   -   -   -   -   216
THE COMMAND OF LOVE.   I   -   -   -   -   -   218
THE COMMAND OF LOVE.   II -   -   -   -   -   221
MARY HAS CHOSEN THE BETTER PART   -   -   -   223
CHRIST AND THE WOMAN TAKEN IN ADULTERY   -   225

	PAGE
CHRIST'S WITNESS TO THE TRUTH	226
HEALING OF THE MAN BORN BLIND	228
WORK WHILE IT IS DAY	231
RETURN OF THE DISCIPLES	232
BLESSED ARE THE EYES THAT SEE THE THINGS WHICH YOU SEE	234
COME TO ME	236
PRAYER IN THE NAME OF JESUS	237
LORD, TEACH US TO PRAY	239
" HE CASTETH OUT DEVILS BY BEELZEBUB "	241
WARNING AGAINST COVETOUSNESS	242
BLESSED ARE THOSE WHOM THE LORD SHALL FIND WATCHING	244
BE YOU READY	246
EXHORTATION TO PENANCE	247
GOD AND THE SINNER	249
THE FIRST SHALL BE LAST	251
HEALING OF THE MAN THAT HAD THE DROPSY	254
PARABLE OF THE SUPPER	256
THE GOOD SHEPHERD	258
THE PRODIGAL SON. I	262
THE PRODIGAL SON. II	264
THE UNJUST STEWARD	267
BE FAITHFUL	269
NOBODY CAN SERVE TWO MASTERS	271
THE RICH MAN	273
HELL. I	275
HELL. II	277
HOPE, WITHOUT OVER-CONFIDENCE	279
THE RAISING OF LAZARUS	280
AT THE GRAVE OF LAZARUS	284
JESUS HEALS TEN LEPERS	286
ONLY ONE PRAISES GOD FOR HIS CURE	287
THANKSGIVING AFTER CONFESSION	289
PARABLE OF THE UNJUST JUDGE	290
THE PHARISEE AND THE PUBLICAN	292
CHRISTIAN MARRIAGE	293
VIRGINITY AND CELIBACY	296
THE DIVINE FRIEND OF CHILDREN	298
THE SPIRIT OF DEVOTION	300

	PAGE
JESUS AND THE RICH YOUNG MAN - - -	302
THE REWARD OF THOSE WHO LEAVE ALL FOR THE	
LORD - - - - - - - - ·	305
PARABLE OF THE WORKERS IN THE VINEYARD -	307
THE GREATER AMONG YOU, LET HIM BE YOUR MINISTER	311
THE SONS OF ZEBEDEE - - - - - -	312
THE BLIND BEGGAR - - - - - -	314
JESUS AND ZACHEUS - - - - - -	316
PARABLE OF THE TEN POUNDS - - - -	318
THE ANOINTING OF JESUS IN BETHANY - - -	320

*" And there went out to him all the country of Judæa . . .
and were all baptized by him in the river of Jordan. . . ."*
(*Mark* i. 5.)

(*a*) We take direction towards rivers on the shores of
which our souls would revive. God flows along the
world; we are not allowed to be dried up; therefore we
take direction towards Him. We stand in a finite world,
both in space and time; the opinion of the changing ages
develops and their view of the world also varies on this or
the other point. We have very little real and true knowledge; we walk amongst philosophers from whom we do
not learn much; but some sort of realism characterises
our nature, which assures us that reality is no play;
our mind finds no peace in materialism, and loses itself
in the pantheism which denies the I, ego. Therefore we
escape from the stagnant waters of philosophy to the
running waters coming from the mountains; the running
water of divine revelation rolls along history. These
are fresh, forceful streams; here we come with humility
and are cleansed from our sins. Here it is that we
progress and develop. Here we do not sit on the edges
of ditches to view our sad face therein. Oh, our dear
Lord, draw us, help us, guide us, cleanse us! Thou sayest:
if we listen to Thee, our lives will be like the swelling
stream. Oh that it might be so; let it be so. We hate the
marsh-fever, and if we do not turn to Thy streams we shall
catch that fever.

(*b*) " *And Jesus, being baptized, forthwith came out of the water : and behold a voice from heaven, saying : This is my beloved Son, in whom I am well pleased.*" (*Matt.* iii. 16, 17.)

Humanity develops in the course of history, and this is where God also approaches it.   He showed Himself to us in Christ ; reality, truth, beauty, and grace revealed themselves to us in Him ; " *plenus gratiæ et veritatis,* filled with grace and truth."   Man should look at Him and be attached to Him ; and should not descend from the heights of history to a mechanical way of life, and should not come down into the chaos of personal impressions and uncertain opinions from out of the glory of the divine face of God. How good for us that beside our speculations and views we possess Christ, from whom we can derive world-conquering evidence.   Through Him and in Him our faith cuts its way through the night of heresy and says : we know in whom we have believed ; our code of faith is : we believe in Christ !   This is our light and sunshine : this is where our soul grows and our disposition becomes sweetened ; it will neither be dark nor without force !   Christ is to our soul as the Himalayas ; the longing for heights carries us towards Him !   The longing for heights out of the depths. We have our sins and we seek for grace.   Jesus is the Redeemer from our sins ; this is Christianity.   Through Him and for His sake the Lord forgives us ; this is the Gospel which is never out of date.

(*c*) By our faith we stretch beyond the world, and this reality of the celestial world we find in Christ ; He descended to us ; thus we build our life according to Him, and shape our faith according to Him.   We shall not dispute and doubt, but live. . . . We doubt a great deal, for we live but little by the light of truth.   Mougel writes of Dionysius the Carthusian : " He wished to know much, so as to be able to love a great deal. He belongs to those saints of the past to whom to know means as much as to love." This same Dionysius writes : " Let us therefore read and learn, not for the purpose of killing time or loading our memory, but for refreshing our spirit and kindling our heart to divine love." . . . We dispute much for we cannot as yet enjoy the truth ; he who enjoys, or rather lives deeply, does not dispute much ; who has treasures does not lament, but rejoices. Our soul also needs air and sunshine ; this our faith gives ! We will neither doubt nor dispute, but live !

BAPTISM OF JESUS IN THE JORDAN. II

" *Now it came to pass, when all the people were baptized, that Jesus also being baptized and praying, heaven was opened and the Holy Ghost descended in a bodily shape, as a dove, upon him ; and a voice came from heaven : Thou art my beloved Son ! In thee I am well pleased."* (Luke iii. 21-22.)

(*a*) With deep humility and holy joy Jesus approached the camp of the great baptizer, the groups on the shores of the river Jordan expecting the Messias ; He was shaken by this fiery, humble zeal of public repentance ; for all' were expecting Him, these fiery longings and this holy ardour were all meant for Him. The consciousness of His mission fills Him with enthusiasm, He steps before John and in humbleness is baptized by him ; but the spiritual eyes of the baptizer open and it is he who longs to be immersed in the depths of Jordan before the Lord ; he wishes Christ to baptize him. Baptism is the beginning of Christ's public life ; the installation ceremony. He begins this life in humility with the penance of John the Baptist.   Let us awake in ourselves the feelings of baptism as an absorption into the new world, as a consecration to new life, and the feelings of completely surrendering our whole soul.   Oh, how few of us live in the consciousness of having been baptized !

(*b*) " *And praying, heaven was opened* " ; otherwise it was closed.   Who goes up to heaven ? is what the ancients questioned in dismay ; we know already who it is who opens the heavens to us.   Others open worldly ways, Jesus opens the celestial one.   Unrivalled are this road-maker and the road.   " Show, O Lord, thy ways to me and teach me thy paths."   (*Psalm* xxiv. 4.)   How many stand outside and argue and criticise and fade away !   Oh, these do not seem to hear the beating of the dove's wings and its inspiration.   Those who feel it, arise ; they step through the open door, look into the face of Christ and revive. Upon the steps of heaven a wrinkled, sharp-eyed hag is sitting : criticism.   It is squabbling and futile.   The loving souls, heroes, artists, and saints see it sitting there, but do not stay to talk to it ; they follow their hearts ! This is what we too should do !

(*c*) The gate of the open heaven is the heart ; the *pure heart* which is anointed and hall-marked with truly divine feelings.   Purification is a long process, an evolution out of selfishness and violence.   Then the gate of heaven is the *loving heart*, which feels by the force of its love that it is the child of God ; this is the soul which " giveth testimony to our spirit, that we are the sons of God." (*Romans* viii. 16.)   Finally it is *the heart living in holy unity of friendly fellow-feeling*, which does not arise from the force of the law but out of longing to be in conformity with

Jesus, and is incapable of acting otherwise, just because it has Jesus for a friend.

(d) "And the Holy Ghost descended . . . as a dove upon him." The flight of the dove implies swift hope; as soon as the heaven opens the dove appears. This dove found a resting-place in Jesus; it brought Him a blossoming olive twig; it flew around Him and kissed Him. O sublime God-man, "filius columbæ," the son of the dove; Thy hopes are swift and Thou livest from divine inspirations; both these we have to tend and enjoy: hope and inspiration.

(e) "Thou art my beloved Son." Thou seemingly sinful, repenting man, Thou true man, Son-of-God, Thou model and teacher of true holiness; according to Thee everyone should be shaped. Each separate man should feel his own insufficiency and seize in Thy grace the force of life which pleases God. Through Christ and through the grace achieved by Him do we become complete men. Out of our own strength and from ourselves we cannot prosper, but through Him we become complete, strong, and happy beings. It is in this son of His that God loves the God-child created after his image: I love my Son, dearly beloved is He to me, and I love those who walk in his footsteps! This shall lift us indeed; from this we should derive consolation and consciousness that we must never let ourselves stray. Does not Christ love us more than the whole world? He poured out his soul upon us; we also are his "filii columbae." At our baptism also the heavens opened, the Holy Ghost descended, and we became the sons of God. Since then, much strength has lain dormant in our souls, the energies óf superior feelings, the veiled traits of God; these we have to develop in Christlike life. The baptized soul is like the dewy meadow, it is fresh, rested and full of magic strength, which the sunshine of grace awakens, and practice develops and perfects.

THE FULFILMENT OF JUSTICE

" *Then cometh Jesus from Galilee to the Jordan unto John, to be baptized by him. But John stayed him . . . And Jesus answering, said unto him : Suffer it to be so now, for so it becometh us to fulfil all justice.*" (*Matt.* iii. 13-15.)

(*a*) The programme of every life is to accomplish every truth, that is to live it with what we owe to God, to our fellow-men, and to ourselves. What else is this than an orientation towards God, ourselves, and the world? From this balance, harmony, peace and joy are derived ; this is the truth expounded in feeling, will, and life. It is the recognition of the " *veritas* " in ourselves, in our talents and our sins ! " *Justitia* " is the transference of this knowledge to our will ; " *veritas* " is the recognition of the reign of God and His sublimity ; " *justitia* " is the will according to this knowledge. " *Veritas* " is the recognition of the world and life ; " *justitia* " is the right way of taking one's position in it. The demands of " *veritas* " must evoke from us acts of " *justitia* " ; truly felt reality and existence shaped in harmony is what we want. The great reality rests around us ; let us touch it with the touch of the soul, and " *pax* " and " *gaudium*," peace and joy, will come of it. We have to be the sculptors of our world ; by our virtues we must create light and sunshine, harmony and beauty. Do not let us await this from anyone else, for the soul is not passivity but active, shaping force.

(b) Towards God our position becomes complete, absolute homage; we owe Him faith with our brain, sacrifice with our hearts; our tears, our strength, and our struggles are also His due. We do not claim anything, but we wish to possess Him. We serve Him wholeheartedly and do not imagine that we have special grace and a special vocation; the love of Christ suffices us. We do not expect manifestations. We have sufficient riches when He looks into our eyes. We do not await for apparitions, why should we? Has not Christ appeared to our soul, "*illuxit in cordibus nostris.*" He places us amongst souls, which shine like grains of quartz upon the sands; they peep out into the world as flowers from out of the edge of the forest into the wilderness. We wish to look upon infinity with clear open eyes; we know that we carry a body for a while, and then escape into another world.

(c) We have to be "*justus*" towards the world; we have to see in it the strength as well as the good, for it is divine; but we also have to see the evil and the danger, for the system is meant for development and the clashing of forces. The world's strength is for the perfecting of man's immortal soul. We therefore have to make use of this divine world for the shaping of our forces and our talents; but at the same time the earth should be our fertile soil and not our grave! Strength comes to us from the world as to a tree from the earth; it belongs and is meant to be under our feet, but our feet are rather roots; they suck strength! We should not be afraid, not disgusted, but we should make use of the earth and pick out from the chaff of earthly

existence the golden grain ; otherwise the sons of the
world would be cleverer than we. And that would be a
pity !

(*d*) We will be "*justus*" towards ourselves, if we do
not expect too much or too little from ourselves. We
have to be moderate in everything, even in dissatisfaction
with ourselves. Those who wish something quickly
and have no patience, those who do not regard the flow
and development of nature, and who because of certain
faults, which are the outcome of their natures, suffer a
hindrance in their perfecting and therefore heap com-
plaints upon the world, those do not comprehend the
"*justitia.*" To these also belong those who kill nature
with the supernatural and the supernatural with nature :
the strict, dark, fanatical zealots whom it hurts to have a
body, although God wished it to be so : or at the other
extreme the weak, incapable, squeamish, soft creatures !
Oh, let us understand ourselves ! We feel a great deal, but
we cannot help it. Just as much as our exterior does not
depend on us, so in a certain sense, our inner being is also
given us. There are powers in us which do not easily
obey us, and neither does God say: Go and command !
but He rather tells us : Steer carefully and make for what
is right !

If we have divined this threefold "*justitia*" we have
comprehended the design of God and with it the "*pax
et gaudium.*" How good it is there ; how good and warm ;
the soul blossoms : "*justus ut palma florebit.*" There
there is strength, "*sicut cedrus Libani multiplicabitur,*"
the righteous grow like the palm and become strong
like the cedar. We get rid of innumerable disappointments, much trouble and despair !

FASTING AND TEMPTATION OF JESUS

" *Then Jesus was led by the spirit into the desert. . . . And the tempter coming said to him : If thou be the Son of God, command that these stones be made bread. Who answered and said : It is written, Not in bread alone doth man live, but in every word that proceedeth out of the mouth of God.*" (*Matt.* iv. 1-4.)

(*a*) Eat ; occupy the world ; live. Let there be bread, let this be our chief concern, every stone and each grain of dust should serve this endeavour. Make bread and live strongly in the knowledge of thy power ! . . . Jesus protests against the tempter : bread is needed, but man not only lives from bread, from breaking of the soil and stones, from occupying oceans and worlds ; more necessary than all is the godly inspiration, the beautiful, pure, noble life, joy and peace of mind ! The world of culture is a great temptation to man ; the beautiful earth makes him forget the inner-world, and productive work makes him forget heaven, and when creating anything he forgets the building up of his soul-world. And besides this he goes on in a wrong direction and sees in soul-and-body-breaking work his aim of life. O Lord, we inhale Thy breath, with this we realize ourselves and recognize the most important work ; this will be the bread and joy of our soul. We work, but the work is not our goal ; it is our tool. How far from this is that culture which drove man under the yoke of "*improbus labor*" ! At best this can only be transition. This is how we have to feel towards the great world and arrange our own one.

(*b*) Jesus leads us between material and spiritual necessities. We have to develop our talents and we have to work, but we must not expect happiness from work and culture. Such mentality cleaves to the earth ; the child of God becomes a worldling, the inner world dries up because of the exterior. But Jesus wishes to help to success just this kingly God-child, this Sublimity born to immortality. He awakens it to consciousness and superiority, saying : " For what shall it profit a man if he gain the whole world, and lose his soul ? " Therefore with the consciousness of our great task we have to require of ourselves to value our soul highly and take good care of it.

(*c*) Elsewhere also Christ has but little trust in the earth, culture, and riches, for He says : " a rich man shall hardly enter into the kingdom of heaven." (*Matt.* xix. 23.) Not as if these would be bad in themselves, but because they often induce us to become materialists and full of worldliness ; they imprison the soul, capture and strangle it. The world, riches, and power are good, but only if they serve great aims. O Lord, do not let our souls dry up and shrivel, neither from riches nor from poverty ! We will not let ourselves dry up from any kind of earthly cares.

THE SECOND TEMPTATION

" *Then the devil took him up into the holy city, and set him upon the pinnacle of the temple and said to him : If thou be the Son of God, cast thyself down, for it is written : That he hath given his angels charge over thee, and in their hands shall they bear thee up, lest perhaps thou dash thy foot against a stone. Jesus said to him : It is written again : Thou shalt not tempt the Lord thy God.*" (*Matt.* iv. 5, 6.)

(*a*) The second temptation is the world. " Let it look upon us as prophets, as saints ! Let it honour you and pay homage to you ! Step upon its neck ; it needs a master." . . . Yes, we also wish to be masters. Our reign is a true, not only seeming, power, which consists of the beautiful shaping of our soul ; this is where we are masters and do not crave for honour. The world should not distract our attention from the great mission of our soul, neither should semblances or appearances ; those also deceive. The kingdom of God is the inner reality ; this is the real sovereignty and sublimity. We should stand above the world ! Not stoically, for that is also a lie ; but in the spirit of St. Francis, who loves all and is pleased with all.

(*b*) Let us bravely go forward with head held high and eyes open. No temptation should distract us, neither sweet nor bitter. In whatever shape it may come to us we should follow our sovereign soul. It is Jesus who places us upon this way and here sometimes He even appears hard. As a boy of twelve He questions His complaining mother : What do you seek ? Have you not known that I walk in the will of My Father ? When He was preaching in Capharnaum in the first spring of His activity " his friends went out to lay hold on him " and later " there came his brethren and his mother, and standing without, sent unto him, calling him." (*Mark* iii. 21, 31.) But He is firm against their demands, He does not yield to the body and its wishes, and goes onward upon the way of His great mission. This is how we have to gain victory and to lift the soul beyond the various influences. The more great-minded and generous we are, the clearer and stronger we will be. The perfect man should not be a scarecrow but a true, noble, brave, whole man, who loves children, parents, and wife, but never at the expense of divine love.

(*c*) On account of this He also exacts sacrifices from us, which we can only value rightly in this light; He sometimes requires us to go against such feelings which He otherwise orders. " If any man come to me and hate not his father, and mother, and wife and children, . . . and his own life also, he cannot be my disciple." (*Luke* xiv. 26.) You might have a vocation for complete devotion. If these are up in arms against your mission, be strong ; do not offend the Lord God from misunderstood love. Break off everywhere all that is against God. The kingdom of God deserves this from its children. Therefore we have to be more attached to God than to parents, brothers, wives, and husbands, for we do not verily love them if, by this love, we cheat and degrade ourselves.

THE THIRD TEMPTATION

" *Again the devil took him up into a very high mountain, and shewed him all the kingdoms of the world, and the glory of them ; and said to him : All these will I give thee, if falling down thou wilt adore me. Then Jesus saith to him : Begone, Satan ! For it is written : The Lord thy God shalt thou adore, and him only shalt thou serve.*" (*Matt.* iv. 8, 10.)

(*a*) All this I give thee if thou wilt kneel to idols. The idol is not God, therefore neither truth nor life. Or if idols mean life, then only so far as illusions live in our head, the end of which is bitter deception. Do not let us go towards the idols. We seek for the world, a greater, better world by honouring such idols as power and enjoyment, beauty and our own passions, and when we wish to possess all we degrade ourselves. What use is the world to us if we do not possess a heart which is capable of living and rejoicing ? What use is a garden to us if we have no eyes to see. This lovely, glorious world will be pain and suffering to us without a beautiful and glorious soul. Its pleasures will not satisfy us but embitter us with illusions and disappointments. We will endeavour to guard well our freedom that it should not conquer us with its mirage. " *In libertate labor*," this liberty demands work and strife.

(*b*) Just the opposite is the truth ; it is then that we possess all, if we do not bow to these idols—that is if we are noble of soul. Jesus also shows us on the occasion of another temptation how determined we have to be, not to leave the ways of the Lord for the mirage of glory and ambition. On one of his journeys to Jerusalem He told his disciples that He would suffer and die and then " Peter taking him, began to rebuke him " (*Mark* viii. 32) "saying, Lord, be it far from thee, this shall not be unto thee. Who turning, said to Peter : get behind me, Satan, thou art a scandal unto me." (*Matt.* xvi. 22.) How determined the Lord is in putting off the " human ideas." We are not allowed to spare ourselves ; who spares himself here will be his own destruction. Therefore in every temptation we have immediately to say : get thee behind me, Satan, we walk the ways of the Lord ; we strongly and decidedly will it. Against all mirages of the world and of philosophy immediately lift the flag of the reign of God and assert the consciousness of the children of God !

THE CALLING OF THE FIRST DISCIPLES

" *And (John the Baptist) beholding Jesus walking, he saith : Behold the Lamb of God. And the two disciples heard him speak : and they followed Jesus."* (John i. 36.)

(*a*) Vocation in us is the sense for the Sublime, for the soul and what concerns it. God appears to us and draws us to Him. Let us accompany Jesus in our thoughts and address questions to Him, forgetting our personal self ; for instance : " Master, where dost Thou live ? " and let us go and see and stay with Him " that dáy." Let us speak of Him to others, let us tell them that He has become the subject of our interest, that we have found the Messias —Jesus, the Son of Joseph of Nazareth. If others would object : can anything good come out of Nazareth ? then we defend Him and show our enthusiasm. Behold this is life-devotion, this is the dawn of Apostleship ; we have to unite it with purity of heart, with prayer and with a goodwill for work. Jesus casts His glance upon us and into us !

(*b*) " *Rabbi, thou art the Son of God, thou art the king of Israel."* (John i. 49.) The supernatural values become detached from the crust and shell of human views and worldly feelings ; Christ is supernatural force, His influences are supernatural effects. These effects possess also bearers : individuals, the Church, the Sacraments ; this tendency is like a flowing stream ; it carries kingly barges, but it also carries away rubbish with it. Therefore to comprehend grace as the vocation of strength in the world and to offer one's services for its cause—to trust in its strength and make use of it in holy reaction in opposition to the worldly spirit—this indeed is Christ-like, apostolic vocation. " Grace, that is Christ-like strength of soul," should be our thought ; we will not repel this thought, but merit it in humility and highly value it . . . this is the sense for Apostolic vocation. We will take care not to stand in its way ; we will be humble, love the poor, and value the soul that is in everyone.

(c) From God's part vocation is a calling, drawing, animating force—love. " No one can come to Me, if My Father does not draw him," says Jesus. Nobility of soul and supernatural sense prove the connection of God with the soul ; such a soul has sense and fire, therefore it possesses the Holy Spirit. It is God who gives such grace. He it is who picks out souls for the tasks of Jesus, for the services of the Holy Ghost, and for distributing His Sacraments. This is no mission to world-fame, but to ardour and zeal in the interests of Christ. Let us highly value every such call, let us answer immediately : behold my Lord, we are ready for Thy command. Speak, and we hear.

THE FIRST MIRACLE OF JESUS AT CANA

" *And the third day there was a marriage in Cana of Galilee . . . and the wine failing the mother of Jesus saith to him : They have no wine.*" (*John* ii. 1.)

(a) Accustomed to the modest circumstances of Nazareth, the Mother of Jesus soon noticed their embarrassment and her good heart instigated her to intercede. She approaches her Holy Son with deep, reverential homage, approaches Him who equally feels the embarrassment of the wedding guests and understands her wish to state her demand. Whatever the answer may be, it cannot hurt her; she knows the heart of her Son and she knows that she will be heard. The loving hearts who cling to God know that they will be heard, if not this way, then another. Jesus also says: "I knew that Thou hearest me always" (*John* xi. 42), for whatever I ask for, I always beg for the accomplishment of Thy holy will. This is what the Holy Virgin was like. This is how we also intend to pray; the chief motive of all our demands should be . . . Thy Holy Will.

(*b*) "*Vinum non habent*"—"They have no wine." The feast of our life is often very sad. There is much food, heavy food, which science and politics provide, but our wine is missing, which should refresh the soul and fill it with pure, noble joy of life. Oh, our Mother, intercede on our behalf with Thy divine Son! Show Him our need; tell Him with trust: "They have no wine." He will provide for us.

(*c*) "*This beginning of miracles did Jesus.*" (*John* ii. 11.) It is indeed a modest beginning; a friendly gift in intimate surroundings. Others brought various wedding gifts. Jesus also brought a gift; "his chalice." He gave them; "*calix inebrians*," "*præclarus*." Sweet wine, fiery wine, the Lord Jesus gives to our bridal soul; He warms and heats our heart. Oh, sweet is the wine of the first, fiery love, of the first elating zeal; it makes us forget the world. This is the precious chalice we thirst for!

(*d*) "*Every man at first setteth forth good wine . . . then that which is worse.*" (*John* ii. 10.) Here it is different. At the start of the spiritual soul-life, God gives much consolation, which pleases the faint-hearted, wavering souls; the Lord bears their weakness in mind, He fondles and encourages them; later He holds them more firmly and wishes them to serve Him even without a consolation which is felt. Oh, this is more, this is better; this already is strong life. We will not make our service depend in any way on the consolations we are able to feel. Duty and the love of God prescribe to us what we have to do, and this we will do unconditionally, for it is not our consolation we seek but the will of God.

NICODEMUS COMES TO JESUS BY NIGHT

" *And there was a man of the Pharisees, named Nicodemus, a ruler of the Jews. This man came to Jesus by night, and said to him: Rabbi, we know that thou art come a teacher from God. . . . Jesus answered: Amen, amen, I say to thee, unless a man be born again he cannot see the kingdom of God.*" (*John* iii. 1.)

(*a*) The inner man has to be reborn, he has to take upon himself the Christ-type . . . essentially, otherwise he misses his aim. The new man becomes so by grace. In the beginning this shape is imperfect, it is more a germ, a beginning. The traits of God such as faith, hope and charity are as yet undeveloped. Our supernatural psychology is like the child's vague notions and impressions; they are slow to penetrate our consciousness, and becoming like Christ is a long, slow proceeding. This is what St. Paul speaks of when he says: "My little children, of whom I am in labour again until Christ be formed in you." (*Gal.* iv. 19.) In this state there is much unconsciousness and imperfection. Small is the circle of our supernatural vision. We suffer much, we are full of indignation and restlessness. God and religion frighten rather than draw us. Our inclinations are directed towards sensual things. Weak and unreliable is our virtue. Behold the infirmities of childhood. Let us be obedient and allow ourselves to be guided.

·(b) So as not to become dwarfs we have to develop. We have to conceive the truths of faith consciously and these must supply us with motives for our feelings and activity. We have to understand ourselves, our physiology, psychology, inclinations and desires of the body as well as those of the soul; we are not to take for sin the natural desires, especially those concerning sensual life; but we have to know the moods and colours of our feelings, we have to enlarge the rays of our conscious world and to force them under the protectorate of the will. In this orderly, sensible, rational inner world we can approach God, approach eternity, Christ, the animating Holy Ghost, and we will not seek virtue in who knows what kind of holy " *excessus* " but we will live it in every condition of life, day for day. The Lord did not live in the desert of the hermits nor in the cave of the penitents, but He lived in the house of Nazareth !

(c) *Spiritus et vita* . . . peace and independence of the soul achieved in the long strife for liberty ! We have to go through much struggle, till we acquire solidity of the soul, and allow our faith to reign in our view of the world, and the grace of Christ in our feelings. We go through much sentimentality, but we will not allow ourselves to melt with it; we will overcome the onesidedness of the soul's pubescence and confident, presumptuous desires; we will give up the illusion that identifies holiness with raptures, scourgings, and visions. In the life of the saints we should regard, not so much the miraculous, but the deep inner life. We are convinced that Christian perfection consists of a life which acquiesces in the holy will of God, is disciplined, unpretentious, and simple, and is inspired by eternal hope. We wish to have little *materia* and much soul, little of the world and much of Christ! Let us give ourselves over to this spirit. Let us start. " *Post Alpes Italia*, over the Alps to beautiful Italy," said Hannibal to his troops. And he succeeded in crossing the Alps along with his elephants. Cortez burnt his boats when he arrived at the land of his hopes. We also will break with our low, rough, stubborn, petty self.

THAT WHICH IS BORN OF THE SPIRIT, IS SPIRIT

" *That which is born of the flesh, is flesh; and that which is born of the Spirit, is spirit.*" (*John* iii. 6.)

(*a*) Beautiful morals are the most beautiful masterpieces. There are different lovely products in stone and colour; but this beauty all flows from the soul. That in itself is more beautiful than all these. A beautiful soul, pure morals and harmonious life; this is the real masterpiece. Therefore the Lord God leaves the statues and pictures below, but takes the beautiful souls over to the museum of Heaven. For the marble masterpiece can be burnt to lime and the picture turn to rags, but the soul which is formed after the likeness of God will be an everlasting remembrance; this masterpiece the Lord God also finds pleasure in. Whereas the immoral man is ruin and decay; he is not a shape but shapelessness; not rhythm and not proportion. There the body is in excess over the soul;

the idea is killed by passion, and one passion kills the other ; the immoral man is a chaotic world where forces struggle and cannot develop . . . let us endeavour to be Christlike, to be the sons of God, to be more valuable men . . . this is what our inspirations urge us to ; let us pray for this, that we be able to accomplish it.

(*b*) And where do beautiful souls grow ? Everything has its native soil. In the olden world the shrubs grew to mighty forests ; since then they have shrivelled, for the earth cooled. The lion in the menagerie is a shabby king and is not in his own country but in a cage. What he needs is the endless desert. And where is the native soil of holy love ? Nowhere so profoundly as in the Gospel, and if we view the life of zeal, it is nowhere to be found so intensely as in the atmosphere of the Holy Eucharist. The pure, harmonious, beautiful souls, the air, water, and sunshine they need, and the rich energy, we find in the Holy Eucharist. There it is we find broad, open views and liberty which give happiness. God is with thee, thou art free. Christ is with thee, in thee. Thou art greater than Cæsar, greater than Napoleon, not looking at power and not at genius, but taking the sovereignty of life. Thou art the temple of God. God values more highly the prayer whispering in thee than the church of St. Peter and the catacombs. And where do we feel more that such values are in us than in Holy Communion ? There man awakes to the knowledge of his own dignity, his richness, and the fact of his being indeed the son of God. Oh, how good this is for him !

(*c*) Holy love further needs sources which give pure water ; wells void of fever and typhoid bacillus. With this I allude to holy purity, for holy purity is the freshest and most beautiful morality. Man becomes blinded by passions, especially by those sins which violate the sixth commandment; his blood thickens and his brain dries up. What is able to freshen this dry waste? The grace of the Holy Eucharist; it is that which educates noble generations. Those souls which the Pontificale Romanum calls " *sublimiores animæ*," sublime souls, those are all favourers of holy purity. The Holy Eucharist creates the immaculate intactness and transparency of the soul. Where this is missing, there the strength, beauty, and harmony of morality is also absent.

(*d*) Finally, a beautiful soul needs warm impulse. Warmth is full of energy and impulse is full of force. Without these there is no freedom, no start, no enthusiasm, and no courage. The Eucharist gives us the spirit of sacrifice. The comfort of our struggling, suffering soul is the Heart of Jesus. Endurance is the lower grade of sacrifice; the higher grade is voluntary sacrifice—to tread upon the body, sensuality, and the world, inasmuch as these can be stepping-stones for the soul, whereby it may rise. This self-sacrifice was the magnificent dower of the Church. "*O beatam Ecclesiam*," exclaims St. Cyprian, "*fuit quondam in operibus fratrum candida, nunc facta est in sanguine martyrum purpurea !*" The robe of the Ecclesia was shining silver and gold brocade, *fuit quondam candida*, in the glory of Pentecost fires; then the Lord Jesus wove into this gold and silver brocade the fiery roses, the blood-red threads, and *facta est purpurea !* Every soul which loves the Lord Jesus wears the sacrificial characteristics on its brow, which come to the surface in Holy Communion; it renders it willing for self-sacrifice. This is where, according to the words of the poet, the

" *magna anima prodigæ* " grow, who lavish their soul and life, but in such manner that they are repaid a hundredfold.

THE MOVEMENT OF THE SPIRIT

" *Wonder not that I said to thee, You must be born again. The spirit breatheth where he will, and thou hearest his voice; but thou knowest not whence he cometh and whither he goeth. So is every one that is born of the Spirit.*" (*John* iii. 7.)

(*a*) The Spirit comes when it wishes. A word here and there in a book, a feeling in prayer, a thought, an idea in meditation warms, encourages, and reassures us. The ideas of God sparkle in us as the grains of sand in the sunshine. When they come to us like this, let us accept them aright and act accordingly.

(*b*) The spirit comes as it wishes, sometimes solemnly and sometimes joyously ; it humbles or elevates ; at times it animates, at others it shames us, it sometimes frightens us, but also stimulates ; we sometimes crouch at its feet and at others embrace its heart. Sometimes it is far from us, so that we should long for it, and again it is near, so that we should not despair. At times it covers our soul in the shape of mist or cloud . . . and at others as a glorious intuition ; and in this also it acts according to its will. Sometimes it incites to joy and consolation or to patience and sacrifice ; sometimes it humiliates and at other times arouses us with the incentive for great deeds. We have to make use of it all ! No one should say, What does one live for ? and be bored. No one should say it, for can one not give a glass of water to the thirsty, or a good word, advice, feeling, and service to a fellow-man ? Live and do not grumble; for you can just as well live and make your life a heaven upon earth.

(c) Nothing can replace its gifts, the names of which are : life, joy of living, self-esteem, trust, joy, animation, peace, bravery, happiness. . . . Divine gifts are these : Jesus also gave such : light to the blind, health to the sick, life to the dead ; this is the divine way. Oh, come, Holy Ghost, and give us much of Thy life, give more and more.

FOR GOD SO LOVED THE WORLD

" For God so loved the world as to give his only begotten Son. . . ." (*John* iii. 16.)

(a) God loved us in His Son. Until He loved us this way, we did not fully understand Him. Infinite is He and has no human feelings, the variations of emotion do not live in Him ; He neither breathes nor faints, He has no blood ; pure, eternal Spirit is He. In nature He showed us that He loves us. He created the glorious sun, but also the Arctic Ocean and the snow-fields, flowers full of scent, but also volcanoes ; splashing waves, but also storms. He spoke graciously, but also crashed in his lightnings. O Lord, we do not wholly comprehend Thee ! Concerning morals moreover ; the beauty of virtue filled our heart, but the flood of wickedness also rushed over us ; the warmth of holy love and the flush of shame alternated upon our countenance, and the knowledge of Thy love became darkened. Does He love us, we question, with that absolute goodwill which our nature demands, with almightiness ? And is our human feeling satisfied with this ? Oh, this is a deluding idea. For we know that God loves us with the heart of Jesus : " God so loved the world," He loved it so. This we comprehend and are reassured.

(b) This is the way He loves, with such a divine heart. Amongst men there also are blessed hearts; they open the fairy world of betrothed, parental, filial love, and the love of friendship ; they strew life with sweet, perfumed feelings. Further, the heart inspires the world of art. Then comes faith with a new world of feelings. Into what world does the heart of Jesus lead us, the heart with which God wished to love us, in order to lead us into a divine world of love ? Thus did " God love the world."

(c) This love excelled in every respect. It was conceived by the Holy Ghost and born of the Virgin without sin, therefore it became " *speciosus*," beautiful. Charm was seen in its face, love spoke from out of its words ; as a symbol it chose the lamb, the " Lamb of God." In His child-soul His lovableness dimmed the glory of all arts, and from His eyes only the innocence and charm of the infant shone. His manhood was spent in the magic of the soul's power : " Follow me," He said, and they followed Him, sinners and crowds alike. Without Him the home was bare and with Him in the desert they forgot their home. Apostolic souls are His shadows; St. Dominic in his white, woollen garb and the special personality of St. Francis of Sales both remind us of Him. He loves mankind and it is drawn to Him; He went early to pray, and before the rays of the sun fell on the Mount of the Olives He was praying beneath its trees. He speaks and talks, teaches, and exchanges ideas and feelings ; He is not cold, not mechanical. He has not a permanent home ; Nicodemus comes to Him at night

and when no one comes, He prays—sometimes the whole
night through. His garments and His hair are damp from
the dew of night, but He feels it not, so deep-hearted is
He. Once or twice the Holy Scripture talks of His eyes ;
He looked upon the rich youth with ravishing love, upon
Peter with deep sorrow ! What an effect He had upon
Matthew, Zachaeus, and Magdalen ! " Thus did God
love the world."

(*d*) With such love has He loved " all along," and so He
equally demands love. Let us also love Him with warm,
human, ardent love. Cecilia and Agnes love Him as their
betrothed ; the heart of St. Philip Neri was so enlarged
by love that two of his ribs were displaced thereby ;
St. Catherine loves, and the Lord Jesus places a ring upon
her finger. He wishes us to love Him feelingly. " Look
at this heart," He says, " which so dearly loved ! " O
dear Lord, we love Thee in return with all our might.
We so dearly love Jesus that we offer ourselves to Him
and do so joyously !

JESUS AT JACOB'S WELL

" *He cometh therefore to a city of Samaria, which is called
Sichar . . . now Jacob's well was there. Jesus therefore,
being wearied with his journey, sat thus on the well. . . . There
cometh a woman of Samaria, to draw water. Jesus saith to
her : Give me to drink.*" (*John* iv. 5.)

(*a*) Give me to drink. I am an exhausted pilgrim, I
seek after souls ; in reality they are my drink and the will
of God is my food ; but thee I also ask, give me to drink.
" *Sitio.*" Jesus seeks souls and thirsts for their salvation ;
He approaches them, asks for their love . . . therefore He

it is who starts to speak; in the guise of a Prophet but with the humble directness of Apostolic love, He approaches the soul of the woman. " Give me to drink " means as much as " Give me thy soul." This is how we also have to go after souls, to speak to them; we must not be shy; and as St. Ignatius of Loyola says : I wish to go to them through their gate, that I might lead them out by mine.

(b) " *Then the Samaritan woman saith to him : How dost thou, being a Jew, ask of me to drink, who am a Samaritan woman ? for the Jews do not communicate with the Samaritans.*" The prepossessed soul stands rigidly and coldly in the way of the Master, rejecting Him; it does not feel in His voice the accent of love, and reads not from out of His eyes the wish of the Apostle : it lives in other ideas. This is how we also behave with God ; we are not fine, sensitive souls; so do others behave with us, who have other views of the world, a different education and life. This should not make us recoil. Zeal is patient and persevering. Without patience it would be fanaticism, as patience without zeal is indifference ; the former is lava, the latter ice ; neither of them is fertile soil.

(c) " *Jesus answered and said to her : If thou didst know the gift of God, and who he is that saith to thee : Give me to drink ; thou perhaps wouldst have asked of him.*" If we would know these two worlds, the one which comes towards us and the one which is hidden in us ; if we would know what kind of soul speaks to us now, oh, how our frame of mind would change ! Thou art night, I am sunshine—thou art eager for pleasure, I am joyous— thou art degraded and I am full of glory—thou art shedding thy blossoms and I am intact ! If thou wouldst know how strong I am and how weak thou art and what grace is capable of and what it creates! But this is the gift of God. He it is who creates soul, life, beauty, strength, joy, happiness; these are the gifts of God. These we have to wait and beg for. Let us go to meet them, beg for them; He will give effective, creating, delivering strength.

(d) " He would have given thee living water." Living water, water of life. It refreshens, renders strong and healthy, gives good blood; it is pure water, not weedy and foul, there are no bacilli in it. Those journeying in the desert have greatest need of water to refresh them. We become tired; we are in need of living waters. Other wells dry up, they dwindle into weak, thinly dripping streamlets; this living water, on the other hand, is a torrential stream. Youthful enthusiasm and idealism, little by little, also fail; whilst the grace of God is inexhaustible—" fluminis impetus." Other water loses its strength, it becomes stale and decomposed; whilst the waters of the soul are continually stirred up by the angels of prayer and those who are immersed in them will be healed—" a well of water springing up into everlasting life."

(e) " The woman saith to him : Sir, give me this water, that I may not thirst, nor come hither to draw. Jesus saith to her : Go call thy husband." The waters of life I cannot give thee; thou art unchaste, faithless, fickle; thou art a perjurer, a forsworn one, an adulteress. So also is the sinful soul; the Holy Scripture speaks with great reverence of the souls who love God, but it attacks the unfaithful ones with burning words. They do not receive living water. How shall the Lord let the crystal-clear streamlet into the swamp? are we temples, that God might reside

in us ? In small things there can also be much faithless-
ness ; are we perhaps undisciplined in our prayers, and
are our thoughts also moody ? Are we perhaps reckless
in our way of seeing, feeling, and in being touchy and
over-sensitive ?

Oh, how delicate is the Lord Jesus, He only just touches
the wound. This is how it should be done ! This
educates the reprobate to a sense of honour. The doctor
shall keep to his intransigent standpoint where decay is
concerned. The Apostle shall breathe morality and rebirth.
This is how the wounds of the soul shall be handled in
confession ; for the humiliated sufferer feels the slightest
touch !

(f) " *The woman saith to him : Sir, I perceive that thou art
a prophet. Our fathers adored on this mountain ; and you say
that at Jerusalem is the place where men must adore. Jesus
saith to her : Woman, believe me that the hour cometh, when you
shall neither on this mountain, nor in Jerusalem, adore the
Father. . . . God is a Spirit ; and they that adore him must
adore him in spirit and in truth.*" Woman, do not look to
the mountains and burning altars, but endeavour to
approach God with soul and prayer, that is with pure heart
and devotion. This is the first and chief thing, then follows
the ritual of the outward service of God. More necessary
than altar and sacrifice is the feeling of penitence, ardour,
and real emotion ; only hereafter shall we care about altar
and penitence. God is Spirit, therefore shall we be firstly
spiritual ; spirituality and what comes from the soul
inspires our outward religiousness. This is the meaning
of the words. But divine service has also to have fine
ways in which to be expressed, ways which capture the
frame of mind. Why should divine service be puritan

when God has created disposition, beauty, and feeling ? Surely those pray " in spirit and in truth " who adore God with their whole nature. Therefore God shall be praised in church also by art, music, song, flowers, and incense ; these shall aid our human nature to ardent devotion and adoration.

(*g*) " *The woman saith to him : I know that the Messias cometh. . . . Jesus saith to her : I am he, who am speaking with thee.*" He presents Himself and lifts her up to Him. Elsewhere He hints at His identity, in parables here He openly discloses it. The woman is already all fire and glow ; she only has one thought—Him. Forgotten are her jug, the well, and the water ; she has already caught fire, she hurries, runs and announces what has happened to her ! Well does the Lord shape, He educates to receptiveness and devotion and at the same time lets us remain in the state of our humility and modesty. Oh, come, hurry, that you also should know the Messias. He told me my sins and opened my eyes ; I see already, you all shall also do likewise, says the woman. Supernatural life begins with the recognition of our sins and with penitence.

JESUS AND THE RULER

" *And there was a certain noble, whose son was sick at Capharnaum . . . went to him and prayed him to come down and heal his son : for he was at the point of death.*" (*John* iv. 46.)

(*a*) It was the faith of the nobleman which led him to Jesus ; it showed him to whom to go and what to think when nature failed ; what to hope for when human

strength was no more at his service. Behold faith, the
shining light of our overclouded soul ; it is a good strong
knowledge. Let us educate it. Jesus also alludes to faith,
He sends us towards it ; to faith which shall seek life
eternal, which shall be reassured, even at the grave of our
beloved ones. The " noble " man does not as yet comprehend this ; he has not yet experienced faith, not really
felt it ; for he only views it as an implement against
earthly evils. For faith is an answer to all the questions
of existence, time, and eternity. We have a longing for
eternal life, and our faith tells us that we already live
eternal life, of which death is merely the transition to
happiness or unhappiness. We live in this knowledge
and feel accordingly. There can be a great difference
between faith and feeling. For instance, we believe that
God is present, that He has counted every hair of our
head, and that our soul is an infinite treasure ; but we may
be very far from feeling these intensely. Our faith is like
the perennial root at the time of frost, there is strength in
it but it is undeveloped. God implanted the divine roots
of faith into us in baptism. Our duty is (1) to realize
that faith is not the sum total of the questions of the
Catechism, which we have merely to learn by heart.
We have to experience its truth. We have to experience
God and His secret influence on the soul. (2) We have
to practise faith ; Carlyle also says : " He who doubts
should act ; action banishes doubt." (3) We should
support our endeavours by prayer : " *unctio ejus docet.*"
By our prayers our faith becomes adorned and attractive.

(*b*) The nobleman is led by his love. He wishes to heal
the one he loves and who suffers. He takes part himself
in the saving work ; he hurries hither and thither, begs,

endures, and humiliates himself. This care accompanies him and shows him the way. He is confident that Jesus will understand and help him. Do we also love ? Do we love our soul ? Do we care about it when it is ailing ? And how do we act when others are ill, when their body or soul is ailing ? Do we help them ? Have we mercy ? Do we notice if the servants of our house do not care about their soul and do not go to confession ? Merciful love is able to convert ; it not only endeavours to give bodily healing but also spiritual healing to the poor invalid, for it sees beyond the ailing of the body that of the soul. Let us beg for and hasten the healing of both ailments, let us carry it into effect even by means of sacrifice.

(c) " For he is at the point of death," his vital force diminished ; the limbs are growing cold, the beating of the heart is weakening, head and breast ache, the eyesight fades. The vital force of the soul is faith, devotion, love, ardour, enthusiasm, and joy ; this is the real throb of the heart and blood, from which there come strength and substance into the soul. Oh, how good this is ! There is also a cooling of the soul ; this is when we are neglectful and become slack, when our prayers and Communions are cold ; when we feel far away from the Lord. We have to despise this state of dying, and must not suffer it. We must examine the cause of our coldness and awaken faithful love. When the soul is whole, healthy and strong and goes with enthusiasm towards its ideals, then such states of mind do not present themselves ; but in case of slackness they grow to weeds. This is how we feel even when we have committed no particular sin ; our whole spiritual life is weak and joyless. We should shake ourselves out of such lethargy and take to heart the exhortation : " *esto fidelis.*" We are unfaithful, therefore we make no progress. We should have faithfulness even in the simplest things, such as disciplining our eyes, tongue, and thoughts, and in being willing and joyous.

(*d*) The way of decay is marked by many venial sins, by many unconsidered stumbles, faults, and insults, with which we offend God and which we look upon as trivialities. This does not coincide with love at all. He who lies, calumniates, hates, offends, he who is touchy, impatient, and nervous, who takes his duty too lightly and does not honour man, is like an unwashed, unkempt, ugly visage and not at all like the child of God. Such a heart is not vigilant, and the spirit of God does not dominate it. What we need is vigilant moral beauty !

THE NECESSITY OF FAITH

"*Jesus therefore said to him : Unless you see signs and wonders, you believe not. The ruler saith to him : Lord, come down before that my son die.*" (*John* iv. 48.)

Man will go to any length when need and misery make their appearance. If he is ailing, he wants to be cured ; if danger threatens, he runs to Christ ; but the Lord would wish us to acquire in the first place deep, zealous faith for relieving our troubles and suffering. To believe, to cling to God, and live in Him—this is what the soul needs.

(*a*) *My faith* is a strong force ; that draws the soul to God. And Jesus says that the spirit of the Father attracts, and powerfully too, not violently, but with trust, love, and feeling. Violence is a weak attraction ; love, joy and goodwill are the greatest. And so that our faith should be more attractive, we have our dear Jesus, the Holy

Virgin's beloved Son ; that is why we possess a mother in the beauty of virginity and in the sweetness of mother-hood. Mount Sinai is different from Bethlehem . . . in the place of flashing clouds an Infant and His mother ! The mount of Elijah, where fire consumes the people, is different from Golgotha ; there we find glowing fire, here the pallor of the Man of pain and of the suffering Mother ! O dear Jesus, who art so sweetly human, Thou who impartest charm, grace, and unction to our faith, we beg Thee to attract and soften us. We make more progress by practising our faith than by arguing. We wish to live according to Thee, for then mental difficulties will not overwhelm us.

(b) Our faith should be an ardent, warm emotion. There are many different kinds of faith : cold, distrusting, dry, tasteless faith and incredulity. Some do not think, but believe ; others think but do not believe ; others again think, believe, but do not live. These are all dead or dead-alive. We must put heart into the lifelessness, then there will be faith. Faith is devotion to the leadership of God ; we trust His words and guiding hand ; we surrender ourselves completely, as is due to the centre, aim, and hope of all. If thou believest with thy whole heart, then will I baptize thee, said Philip to the Ethiopian. This is what we also need ; we have to believe with our whole heart. We complain that our faith is wanting ; but have we worked for it with a whole heart, have we searched for it with goodwill, and have we endeavoured to pursue it with a child-like mind ? Have we understood the innermost impulse of our heart ? Have we listened to its plaintive longings, its longings for the noble, pure, sunny heights ?

(*c*) Our faith is a strong persevering disposition. The word of the Apostle denotes the nature of it : " *Credidi et certus sum,*" I believe and do not waver. We also have our difficult moments, our mental darkness and our suffering of the heart, but we oppose this darkness and suffering with our will. My Lord, we wish to be reassured in Thee ! With Thee we also go to death ; at Thy word we cast our net and know that we will catch a treasure in it. With this strong, comforting will we free ourselves from doubts, waverings, and uncertainties. Dear is the faith of the child which has no doubts, but lovelier is the faith of the Apostle who freed his faith from doubt. " I knew whom I believed and I was reassured." Such faith has indeed Easter—Whitsuntide—peace. This faith overcomes the world.

THE CALLING OF SIMON AND ANDREW

" *And passing by the sea of Galilee, he saw Simon and Andrew his brother, casting nets into the sea . . . and Jesus said to them : Come after me, and I will make you to become fishers of men.*" (*Mark* i. 16.)

(*a*) We do not know God directly, only indirectly ; and unspeakably better than forest, ocean and sky, God leads the way to Himself, firstly by way of history and finally through Christ. But where is Christ Himself ? Behold He spreads His hands over Peter, Andrew, and John, and makes them His Apostles. These in their turn lay their hands on Paul and Barnabas, Paul on Timothy, and they hand down the power by the laying-on of hands, by the anointing of the priests from generation to generation. The power of the clergy presents to us the Gospel of Christ, the Sacraments of Christ, and ensures

His grace. We have to see Christ in our priests; " Let a man so account of us as of the ministers of Christ and dispensers of the mysteries of God." (1 *Corinth*. iv. 1.) This is our faith and joy. Therefore if we say of our priest-acquaintance : I know him, he was my playmate ; then let us also believe that he is sent from God when he says : " This is my flesh . . ." " I absolve thee " ; and let us honour him thus.

(*b*) " I will make you to become fishers of men," but you also have to take part in this work with heart and soul, with your whole life. I give power ; in exchange, you must give your life. I give mission ; in this mission you have to walk continually. I lift you to Myself ; you must experience this proximity to God ; you are not My mechanical tools but Apostles. I entrust you with the Eucharist ; your life shall be the commentary of its hidden force ; the Gospel I give you, you have to live in its depths. In one word : I make you Mine, but you stake your whole life for Me.

(*c*) This indeed is a great thing ! But if it is God's wish, and Jesus accomplishes it, then it is sure to succeed ! The Sacrament is the well of strength ; the heart of Jesus is the brazier ; the blessing is the love of Christ. And if He sent Gideon from the barn, David from the field, and Saul from the mount of Ephraim to become hero, prophet, king, and ordained fishers to be Apostles, then He now also ordains and sends priests from families where deep faith lives—from the side of mothers who are like the mother of Samuel—sends and ordains them in seminaries above which glows the burning torch of purity, prayer, meditation, and zeal, indicating God's most favoured abode and the garden of the Holy Ghost.

JESUS TAUGHT AS ONE HAVING POWER

" For he was teaching them as one having power, and not as the scribes." (*Mark* i. 22.)

(*a*) Jesus as man is the point of contact of the world with God, full of force and strength. His human soul is the soul of the Son of God, which sees God, and though being finite, does not quite comprehend Him, and still by His seeing God He is infinitely more wise than the geniuses walking the earth and working with induction and syllogism. He sees God and the world, the infinite stream of life and its flood, and from this it is that His soul becomes beautiful, tender, deep, strong, and magical, and this is what flows from Him in the freshness of His personality and unflagging vigour; this radiates from His eyes; this unfading disposition mysteriously touches souls. This freshness and strength of life goes hand-in-hand with the divine, supernatural influences, about which He says: " No one can come to Me, if he is not drawn by My Father." Influence us, dear Lord, that we may revive, that in our inner world we may come in contact with Thee. We place our soul, our heart, and our disposition under Thy influence. Our Jesus, our Master!

(*b*) The strength of Jesus is the mind filled with reality, truth, intuition, and conviction—the heat and crystal purity of feeling—the beauty of disposition pervaded by God. In His ideas God is mirrored; truth became sweet milk upon His lips; all that He did and said referred to life: " *panis vitæ*," " *fons vitæ*," " *lignum vitæ*," and this beautiful, strong life was placed in us by God through Christ, it was shaped upon us by His grace and touch. His heart is the power and His blood the price for which He bought us. Blood unites us with Him, and what blood it is! And all this continually instigates and encourages us to take into ourselves this Christ-like strength. If we carve in stone the lovely shape, let us submit to the Christ-type being formed in us. Let us often rise to the heights of His thoughts, feelings, and longings, and let us dive into the depths of His soul which clings to God, and thus we shall feel that He lifts us, as well as shaping and attracting us. Do not let us look on this as merely words but as vital strength. Let us try to live it.

(*c*) The effect of Jesus was not only the radiation of the soul but grace was also in His words and example. God touched souls, and from His touch they changed. Many speak from the heart and yet without effect ; grace, that is the divine touch, is needed for speech to have effect. Souls united with God and filled with God, as Apostles, saints, and prophets, are really able to have effect. We also have to be filled with Him ; by Him we become strong !

JESUS HEALS SIMON'S WIFE'S MOTHER

" *And Jesus rising up out of the synagogue, went into Simon's house. And Simon's wife's mother was taken with a great fever ; and they besought him for her.*" (*Luke* iv. 38.)

(*a*) The soul also is taken with fever, even the course of purification is fever, which does not happen without pain. We shall have anguish which burns like fire, and in its heat our sinful inclinations and wishes will change into energies which please God. The restless, flurried soul is also feverish. The nervously interested, ambitious soul likewise; and also the soft, impressionable, sentimental, loving soul. The correction and purification of the soul should always have a liberating, not an embittering effect, so that it may have inclination as well as energy to dive into the wasp's nest of the heart. As we have to dive into it, let us do so with an iron determination.

(*b*) Jesus approaches the bed of the invalid; takes hold of her hand; influences her by His strength. His sure, calm look sinks into the soul of the sick one, it reassures and draws her to Him. His sublime, beautiful soul satisfies the greatest need of sinful, feverish, ailing hearts, and their longing for beautiful, strong, joyous life. For is it not this that the feverish souls need? And the Healer says: Why do you gasp, why are you flurried, why do you tremble? Be calm; here am I! And the soul which lost its balance in the desire for knowledge and pleasure feels that *health* approaches it in the shape of moral order, and *cheerful beauty* in the shape of divine life's harmony. This attracts it, it comes to love it, makes an effort, and is healed.

(*c*) And rises and serves Jesus. It becomes strong; it is able to rejoice, therefore it is willing. The strength of her body and soul she places at His service, for she loves the sources of her joy and health. And the more willingly she serves, the stronger she will be. How good it is to be strong. "If ye do not believe, ye do not comprehend." In deeds have you to experience it. Here and now we have to rejoice that we are the children of God, that we wish good and do good, and that our soul accordingly is sunshine which cannot be darkened by any night, only if we forget what we are and what divine life can stream forth from us.

ALL SEEK FOR THEE!

"And rising very early, going out, he went into a desert place : and there he prayed. . . . And when they had found him, they said to him : All seek for thee." (*Mark* i. 35.)

(*a*) We all seek Him, for firstly He gives us assurance that our sins will be pardoned, and secondly that we will partake of the glorious, divine, eternal life. Above all, our soul urges the remission of sins; for in the sublimity of the moral system it perceives and adores the bliss-giving or condemning will of God. Let us comprehend the human heart, it does not wish to know, to beg, to trust, but *to exist ;* it wishes not to be ruined. It has many sins—and the cry of the heart for purity, stainlessness, that is, remission of sins, this is the most ancient and most thrilling psalm. A pure heart give us, O Lord, otherwise we perish . . . and Jesus comes and encourages : I will give ! This is the great fact which is not affected by the world, this is the all-important tidings which is not brought by science, art, and culture. An English philosopher relates that in the poor quarter of Dublin he came upon a dying woman, who lay on straw upon the floor and beside her lay her dead child, as if it had been of wax. Its small hands were linked and its finger-tips pink. All around on the floor there was water ; for according to the instructions of the dying mother the father had baptized his child. The woman looking up at the philosopher, asked weakly : "Are you the doctor?" "No, but he will soon be here ! " " Pray," she whispered, " that God may not take my soul away in sin."

The philosopher knelt down and prayed with the woman's rosary, until the priest and the doctor arrived. " God reward you ! " murmured the invalid, " now I am at rest."

Supposing, continued the philosopher, that I had told her all I know of the Greek sages and writers and what I had found in the mazes of philosophy : What use would this have been to me and still more to her ? You will answer that it would have been of no use in this case, for the poor woman was uneducated. But let us suppose that she belonged to the upper-classes, would this have altered matters ? Philosophy and education are good things, but they are only *ornamental*. They are good for those who live peacefully in the world and are in good health, but the knowledge that elevates and makes man happy, this knowledge it does not give. What is more, education dealing only with the outer world mostly makes us superficial towards inner values, it expects more good, more life from externals ; and the inner moral world becomes flat and weak against demoniacal powers and darkness. Culture has no consciousness of being able to help mankind. It is incapable of lifting man out of the darkness surrounding him, or of rescuing him from the ruin that is threatening him ! It is Christ who does this ; therefore the hope of man relies on God, life rises upon Him, and through Him science and art possess their true value.

(*b*) It gives us consciousness and reassurance about our partaking in the glorious, divine, eternal life. Life is reality . . . eternal life is the greatest reality, and all that

gives us this eternal life has real, bliss-giving strength.
Jesus gives strength for shaping eternal life within our
souls. Every rising and progressing age adores strength.
The ideal of modern culture is also great strength. The
present age moved and brought into motion the whole of
nature, awoke its forces, and from them it expected happiness and better men. An immense longing for life and
an unquenchable thirst for happiness characterized it.
But great complications arose : strength somehow got
lifted away from life, it became an independent power
which rather makes of man a servant than a lord through
the tremendous work it requires of him. And in this work
man withers away ; he has no time to become more noble
and to develop the spiritual contents of life. The joy
which goes with the production of strength is also spent,
for only strength which elevates causes joy, not strength
which enslaves. What is the good of awaking strength if
slavery comes out of it ? Lord Jesus, Thy strength also
demands work, but this work always raises us ; it demands
co-operation, but this always liberates and never enslaves.
This force and work cultivates the soul, consciousness,
life ; it gives more life, stronger life, more beautiful life.
Let us walk among ironworks, sledge-hammers, forges,
earth-shaking machines, smoking factory chimneys, always
with the knowledge : Jesus ! Thy work is superior, Thy
strength is more sublime, Thy work is more ideal, Thou
developest eternal life, Thou educatest ruling souls !
Thy forces are forces which rise from the depths to the
heights where the soul flourishes. O Master, teach us
what we must do to possess eternal life !

(c) He does not only give eternal life, for the soul to
live in, but He renews our life and places it in the state of

innocence and immortality; He assures unfailing re-assurance not only for the soul but for the whole of man. And this is indeed what we are in need of; we need to find a creating, restoring arm which shall re-create man on the point of death; we await resurrection, restoration, regeneration! When we die, we do not need a biographer who buries a past life in lifeless paper with dead letters; nor a sculptor who copies our figure, now crumbled to dust, in numb stone or cold iron, and places it in the market-place or by the wayside, so that we may stand there blind and dumb. What we need is *regeneration*; so that He who created us should in the same way recall us to exist-ence, but to more beautiful, immortal, and yet human existence. This is what Our Lord promises us, this is what He will bring to us some time, resurrection, life—He who showed his plans in His own person and sowed them in our soul upon the glowing dawn of His Easter morn. Oh, come life, sweet, risen life, Thee I await, for Thee I glow with ardour!

JESUS TEACHES THE MULTITUDE OUT OF THE SHIP

"*And it came to pass, that when the multitudes pressed upon him to hear the word of God, he stood by the lake of Genesa-reth, and saw two ships standing by the lake . . . and going into one of the ships that was Simon's, he desired him to draw back a little from the land. And sitting, he taught the multi-tudes out of the ship.*" (*Luke* v. 1.)

(*a*) What an enchanting sight! The streaming crowd and Jesus who separates Himself from them, but only a few steps, "a little from the land." The crowd throngs on the shore; in the low water-reeds, straw and rotting leaves float about; the earthy people of the coast, stand there, looking to the sea . . . from this surrounding Jesus longs for the pure element. . . . He does not say " *odi profanum vulgus* "; not in the least, He loves it; but at the same time He also knows that life is terribly poor, swampy, dirty, and foul; but He and His truth and pulpit are pure and holy. The Lord Jesus lets us see this holy difference between Gospel and life, truth and the world; He does not tear Himself away from the people, but He is superior to them, more sublime; it is from another element, from another world, that He speaks to us. Even while standing on the shore, and even if we are in shallow waters, let us only look towards the ship and hear the words of the Lord! . . .

(*b*) " *He desired him to draw back a little from the land* . . ." How good and kind the Lord is; He was quite close to us, He became quite human. The Lord wishes for something, but He asks for it. He can express Himself in every conceivable way, from the absolute assertion of the Sublime to the soft breath of grace; the voice of the Lord now roars, now whispers, now crushes, now caresses, now tears us away, now draws us on, now commands, now entreats—in one word it is strong and fine; it has soft, sweet, tender tones and suggestions. We too are drawn towards the Lord, He draws, encourages, and calls us; His grace is like to the waves continually touching the shore. Oh, let us obey its slightest touch!

(*c*) This is Peter's ship. What would he not give to and do for his Lord! He starts well, that he might not only serve the Lord with a fragile little ship, but that he might become the unshaken, fundamental rock of the Church.

The little ship is a symbol, so is the rock and the miraculous draught of fish. The first indicates the fate of the Gospel upon the ocean of human will and caprice, the other two indicate the absolute victory of the Divine word. From all three points of view let us attach ourselves to Peter and the Church; his little boat leads us across agitation and bewilderment and his rock offers safety and attachment amidst doubt and strife. The blessing of God is upon the hand of the fisher of men, for he casts his net at the word of Jesus and by His grace. I also am His captive.

"LAUNCH OUT INTO THE DEEP"

" Now when he had ceased to speak, he said to Simon: Launch out into the deep. . . ." (*Luke* v. 4.)

(*a*) These depths open in our own souls. We stand at the precincts of the eternal; these entrances are sublime; this is where science makes its appearance and speaks of what is true and real; this is where art spreads before us the play of harmony; here it is that life ebbs and flows, life full of deep instinct and yet unspeakably shallow. This is whence we view the star-world and realize that it sails through the universe like a glorious fleet; our flagship is the sun. Mars, Venus, and our earth reel around it like tiny galleys, and this whole fleet of stars upon the deep ocean of the sky dashes forward and goes—whither? Wherever it may go, it will not emerge from the precincts of eternity, it remains " *dans le vestibule de l'infini.*" Behold the worlds of heaven and the heavens of the world. He who stands in these precincts, and looks into eternity, on him the mysterious presentiment of infinite existence descends! here must be eternity, he murmurs; the feeling of humility and dependence takes possession of him; he feels as Job felt " *in terra Hus* " three thousand years ago. Our souls have not changed since then; we are all the brothers of Job and the Prophets. Man kneels on the shore of the infinite and says with Descartes : " I feel that I am a finite being, which continually longs for the better, the greater, the more perfect." Oh, let it long freely; let it long and not be afraid! It shall look up to the sky, or into the calix of the flowers and say : I acknowledge Thee, my Lord, for Thou art so near to me that I feel Thy breath. I feel Thee, my beloved, mighty source of existence! I feel Thee and rejoice in Thee!

(*b*) Eternity offers entirely different perspectives to the soul from those time can offer. Time looks backwards into the past and forwards into the future. Backwards on to the trodden paths of history, then on to the faint traces of prehistory, then it creeps among the thread of tales and myths into an uncertain world, and finally its way comes to a standstill; but when history is struck dumb, when the light of myth goes out and science opens the layers of the rocks of the earth and stones speak of the ancient worlds, then what follows? What then? Oh eternity! We are from out of time and yet we are thy children. Without thee we cannot exist, though with this tiny brain we break down under thy infinite weight. We break down but this is the shudder of the sublime in us, which makes its entrance into our soul and fills its sanctuary with mist and incense. This accordingly is God; this is the necessary, eternal truth that fills my mind; this is the infinite power which created me and lovingly draws my will towards it. He is the original cause. All and everything is from Him and out of Him ; the world is His design, the creation of His love.

(c) In this creation, in this world, we find that wonderfully unfinished, and yet infinitely valuable work : man. And man reasons and doubts, and thereby and still more by his love and enthusiasm he points to those eternal attractions, which are the centres of the spiritual world as the sun is the centre of the planets, all of which concentrate in God. What a great trouble it is, when man cannot turn towards this sun with trust and joy, when he knows that without it he cannot exist and that elemental forces drive him towards it. What great trouble if he thinks dwarfishly and pettily of the infinite and asks whether it loves him or hates him ! What perversities of the human soul are these ! This is caused by the philosophy which completely encloses the spiritual life within the " I " and looks upon it as independent from divine influences. This is not right at all, life, the soul, and the world are all filled with God !

Therefore, let us seek God with a loving and longing spirit ! Let us humble ourselves before Him in humble faith, for

> Matto è, chi spera che nostra ragione
> Possa percorrere la infinita via,
> Che tiene una sostanza in tre persone.
> State contenti, umana gente, al quia.
>
> (*Dante.*)

(2) *Let us receive with willing joy* God as He comes to us in His revelations ; He is the moral world's greatest and most exalted fact, our Lord Jesus Christ. We can

say with Amadé Thierry: "We do not understand philosophy but we can see and admire the great facts of history."

(3) Let us be *attached to Him*, even if we do not fully comprehend Him. Leibnitz made the following remark about the attempts of philosophers to explain the riddle of life: "We may say about these explanations what Queen Christina of Sweden said about her crown: 'I have no need of it, and it does not satisfy me.'"

(4) And let us *love the Lord and live for Him*, let us say with Claude Janet: "*Je parle à Dieu, je l'aime, je l'adore, je l'attends.*"

THE MIRACULOUS DRAUGHT

"*Let down your nets for a draught. And Simon answering said to him: Master, we have laboured all the night and have taken nothing; but at thy word I will let down the net.*" (*Luke* v. 4.)

(*a*) If it is true at all, it is true concerning souls, that having toiled a great deal we have taken nothing; the tremendous work has little effect. But we must not be discouraged; a great sense of duty and deep feeling accompanies us through all our life. It is God who gave both. Though seeing no result is a great trial, still with the aid of these two gifts we conquer it. At the repeated warning of zeal we also answer: "At Thy word I will let down the net," and we will do so where and when and as often as Thou wishest it. We also know that much toil has success only after many years. Jesus and His Apostles saw little result of their labour, but they knew that their work would bring forth fruit. Working for God and with God we too know this; therefore, onward! An excellent frame of mind is that which does not become maimed by failure, for " deep feeling " leads towards God.

(b) "*And when they had done this, they enclosed a very great multitude of fishes : and their net broke.*" Jesus wished to recompense and encourage His followers in this way. But this success did not touch the merit of their obedience. It might have happened, that having cast their nets according to the words of Jesus, they caught nothing; Peter might not have been inspired, he might not have become enthusiastic, but his virtue would have been irreproachable. But Jesus helped in the way He did, and Peter was able to experience this help directly and with deep conviction. The hand of God had appeared in his life, and shaken by it he cries : " Depart from me, for I am a sinful man, O Lord ! " Thou art so near to me, O Lord, Thou stretchest into my soul, Thou helpest and encouragest . . . lovest and helpest, and at the same time awakenest me to the knowledge of my worthlessness. I am not worthy of Thy helping hand, Thy faithful love. God is near us. What a powerful motive this is for all good.

(c) *And Jesus saith to Simon : Fear not : from henceforth thou shalt catch men.* Jesus makes us feel the power of His love and mercy, and he who has once experienced this becomes His follower, disciple and Apostle. Jesus draws us . . . this is His power ! St. John the Baptist encouraged men by saying : Repent, for the judgment of God is at hand ; and Jesus gave encouragement that the kingdom of God is near, and St. John sums up the Gospel in the following manner : Let us love the Lord, for He first loved us ! Only those can be the Apostles of Christ, who have comprehended and return His love !

HEALING OF A LEPER

" *And there came a leper to him, beseeching him, and kneeling down, said to him : If thou wilt, thou canst make me clean.*" (*Mark* i. 40.)

(*a*) Two men face each other : the leper and Christ. The leprous wound sucks up the blood and as rotting life it spreads over the body ; the human being withers and becomes disfigured. Contrasted with this, what a sublime image of God is the Son of God ! This image of God we can spoil in ourselves ; it is sin which spoils it ; it beclouds our eyes, beclouds the recognition of sin ; it furrows our brows and we become beastlike types ; it makes us deaf, it numbs our sense of God ; we become tired and sad. How much leprosy there is upon souls ; but even if the sores do not corrupt it, where is and what has become of its beauty, strength and nobility ? Let us jealously guard and work upon the image of God in us and take care where it is reduced in us, and what causes it to be disfigured in us. If we would come upon a buried Greek statue, or a painting by Raphael in the lumber-room, we would clean and wash it and rejoice at its beautiful lines. This is how we have to act concerning the soul !

(*b*) The leper approaches ; like his, the steps of the soul are longing, endeavour, work, sacrifice . . . and it kneels down ; this is the greatest step ; we reach eternity with it if we do it in faith and humility. Then it beseeches. If we could understand this ! If only we could ! Let us kneel down and beseech, and beg, only for a few minutes, but with the soul, with the right mind, as the beggar begs for bread.

(*c*) "*If thou wilt thou canst make me clean.*" Loathsome thing to be consumed in dirt, to waste away in the dirt of the soul. Yet this is the dreadful fate of souls . . . to wither in dirt for forty, fifty, sixty years! "If Thou wilt," this is what the saints and the sinner likewise say, "Thou canst make me clean," that is, Thou canst give us a forcible awakening, reactive soul. And to one He gives a soul that does not suffer the slightest dirt upon itself; it is all-luminous; such is the soul of the saints. In others the soul achieves a continual, but slow purification; these are the weaker but endeavouring souls. Others have not valued the soul; the hardened sinners, those who relapse and stumble with a weak, shaken will; these are the ones who have to say with deep faith: If Thou wilt, if Thou wilt . . . Thy will is strength. But on the other hand the Lord urges them: but thou also hast to "will" He says; grace I give, but I also say: If thou wilt, thou canst become clean!

HEALING OF ONE SICK OF THE PALSY

"*And they came to him, bringing one sick of the palsy. . . . And when they could not offer him unto him for the multitude, they uncovered the roof . . . and let down the bed.*" (*Mark* ii. 3.)

(*a*) Jesus entered a house and there the people thronged in. They came because of Christ. He is the centre of the House, of the Church. It is a sublime house; its history is grand, but finally every age seeks only Christ in this House; soul, bliss, sin and grace form the basis and content of every theology, whether we pray in cathedrals or in a tent. The poor swineherd steps into the Gothic cathedral, though he does not understand art and culture; the master-builder also enters as well as the artist, and all three kneel down. And this is the only thing that matters; they seek Christ who takes away their sins, and they wish to be at home in His House. This is what we also have been seeking since the time of Honour: it is for God that men long.

(b) "*And there were some of the scribes sitting there and thinking in their hearts . . .*" Who are those who surround Jesus? Critical Pharisees, and ordinary, well-disposed or indolent people, that is the crowd; and finally men of strong faith, who bring the sick one through the roof to Christ; they not only come to Jesus, they also bring others. Their faith and love carry the one sick with the palsy. Christ is the first who carries: He is the "*aquila provocans,*" He lifts on His shoulders; the Apostles and Saints carry generations upon their shoulders and in their heart; teachers, parents, and those who give good example equally carry tired, weak, cowardly souls.

Let us carry the weaker ones; it is a great joy to bring souls to Christ. Let us carry forward the ignorant, the sinners, the unfeeling; let us lead them to confession and to the Holy Sacrament!

(c) "*Which is easier, to say to the sick of the palsy: Thy sins are forgiven thee; or to say: Arise, take up thy bed and walk?*" "Thy sins be forgiven," says Jesus. A powerful, creative, redeeming summons. For the soul this is the greatest good. If we should do wonders and make the sick rise with a word, we should not accomplish as much as if we pardoned sins in the name of God. Souls with depth in them experience this, though it is the former deed the world values whilst it clings to what is provisional and finite and does not comprehend the graces of the soul. Jesus blames this superficial opinion which looks upon sin, remission, the Gospel, and grace as mere words, but looks upon healing as a deed. Very well, He says, I will enact a deed, a divine deed; I heal the sick, but I do it that ye may look upon the grace of penitence which I brought ye as upon a divine grace. Believe in penitence and acquire it for yourselves. We believe that if we confess with deep contrition, we receive greater grace than if we were miraculously healed.

THE CALLING OF MATTHEW

"*And when he was passing by, he saw Levi, the son of Alphæus, sitting at the receipt of custom: and he saith to him: Follow me.*" (*Mark* ii. 14.)

(*a*) Levi, that is St. Matthew, saw the Lord, and knew who He was; he felt how far he was from Him; he saw the Lord in sublime heights and himself in the depths upon the custom-bench. This is where he cheated and extorted money from the people, and they despised and hated him, but Jesus they loved and followed. Jesus did not collect anything from anyone, and still how rich He was; so rich, that He gave to everybody from His riches. How can this mighty, rich Lord look upon him, is what Levi thought. Yes, the Lord looked upon him, with the look of understanding, and calls him to the highest. Others He has rejected, of him he makes an apostle, for He sees his interest, his longing and dissatisfaction. The Lord also calls us by means of duty, recognition, sight, and finally enthusiasm.

(*b*) " Follow me." What summons, what revelation ; the sight of Christ shines into his soul and fills it with light and strength. Though this happens in " passing by," it happens victoriously. In the face of this mighty revelation, every other voice is silenced, the heart becomes light, it moves and starts : " I run upon the way of thy commands, if Thou enlargest my heart." This equally is a creative summons ; it creates a new man. Do not let us doubt strength ; it can do much if it comes upon a soul.

(*c*) " *And rising up, he followed him.*" He arises ; this already is another man than the one who formerly sat here. He arises and departs, tears himself away ; his heart aches and longs ; but his great decision conquers. Such words as " went away," " died," " he arose," are short words ; but what worlds they hide ; worlds full of ravaging, painful feelings, decisions, and dismay ! From these the Lord does not spare us, but He gives us His help, that we may follow Him with steps which take us from world to world. If we come to a purer, more beautiful world, we go willingly indeed !

JESUS EATS WITH PUBLICANS AND SINNERS

" *And it came to pass that as he sat at meat in his house many publicans and sinners sat also together with Jesus and his disciples.*" (*Mark* ii. 15.)

(*a*) Jesus obtained deep, sweet grace for Levi—who is our St. Matthew—it conquered him and induced him to follow joyously. Therefore he prepares a feast for the Lord ; he rejoices and shows the Lord his gratitude. The Holy Scripture often likens the relation of the soul to

God, to a feast. The soul which loves God is joyous; it feels well even in mist and frost for the Lord. Near to us and with us is the Lord; we rest on His warm heart. Flowers, the scent of the grape, the flavour of the wine, and song, draw out the joy of our soul. Much more than scent and flavour is the Lord to us. Therefore, why should our soul be sad? Pure, transparent, and deep is our joy as the wells of Hellbrunn; soft and sweet is its music as the calix of the flowers!

(b) "*And the scribes and the Pharisees, seeing that he ate with publicans and sinners, said to his disciples : Why doth your master eat and drink with publicans and sinners?*" Outside, dark, joyless figures loiter, the partisans of conceited truth and self-righteousness, which drives away and does not draw; does not feel intensely and judge correctly. It raises objection against the Saviour out of envy and against the sinners out of haughtiness, and consequently shows its poverty of soul and the desolate barrenness of the conceited frame of mind; it does not ennoble itself and does not better others. Oh, prejudice, thou art also fed from the soul, but only as the mould and mushroom feeds from the sap of the tree! Let us take care of our judgments, that prejudice, narrow-mindedness, unsociability, and bad will should not filter into them.

(c) "*Jesus hearing this, saith to them : They that are well have no need of a physician, but they that are sick.*" Here it is that Jesus is in His place amongst the misled, seduced people; He did not come to enjoy Himself, but to show men the way. Fasting, prayers, paying tithes for caraway-seed and mint are no good without love of humanity; Jesus teaches them to love. He walks amongst them as the betrothed and wishes to awake bridal joy in them. They shall feel that God is good and that He is the physician of sick souls. Let them feel that He draws them as a loving Father or a betrothed, and that with Him they can settle all the troubles and sorrows of their souls. If they learn this, then they will also fast and keep the law. It is with love that we have to accomplish every religious task.

THE PHARISEES REBUKE OUR LORD

" *Many publicans and sinners sat down together with Jesus and his disciples. And the scribes and the Pharisees, seeing that he ate with publicans and sinners, said to his disciples : Why doth your master eat and drink with publicans and sinners ? "* (*Mark* ii. 15.)

(*a*) Jesus loves life ; He does not turn away from it ; The soul whose bliss is in the flowers and in the children stands within life and elevates it. He loved men and sat down with them, that He might conquer in them what had turned away from God, and had fallen away. And as the Prophet Elijah lay upon the body of the dead boy and the boy began to revive, so Jesus also spread His warm strong soul upon them, so that they might also feel, and better hopes might awake in them ; He knew that they could only be cured by a life more beautiful than their own and by joys more glorious than theirs ; they felt the greatness of His soul and were healed by it. In the background of a glorious sunrise bats still squeak and are annoyed at the miracles of light. Oh, Jesus, our Master, Thou camest to us ; and now we respond and follow Thee . . . !

(*b*) *And the disciples of John and the Pharisees used to fast. And they come and say to him : Why do the disciples of John*

and of the Pharisees fast, but thy disciples do not fast? And
Jesus saith to them : Can the children of the marriage fast, as
long as the bridegroom is with them ? . . . when the bridegroom
shall be taken away from them . . . they shall fast in those
days. (*Mark* ii. 18.) Jesus means bridal-feast, joy, and
song to us ; at the bridal feast we have not to worry about
fasting ; He did not come to teach us in the first place
to fast, but He came to teach us joy, to teach us divine
feelings. The faded world has not to be revived primarily
by fasting. Fasting and self-abnegation are not aims in
themselves, but only means ; our aim is to develop in
ourselves a mind that clings to God ; this shall be our
strength and joy and we will be able to subordinate to this
the flesh, enjoyment, and the world. Empty formality
and joyless, soulless fasts are Pharisaic waste of time ; all
this is not perfection. It can be scandalized by John, who
fasts, or by Jesus, who did not come to us in severity,
but in the beauty of divine feeling. We will submit
all to this point of view ; we will also fast with an obedient
soul, but only for acquiring a better soul, a purer and more
divine disposition.

(*c*) " *No man seweth a piece of raw cloth to an old garment :*
otherwise the new piecing taketh away from the old, and there is
made a greater rent. And no man putteth new wine into old
bottles ; otherwise the wine will burst the bottles and both the
wine will be spilled and the bottles will be lost. But new wine
must be put into new bottles." (*Mark* ii. 21.) Oh, ye cobblers
and patchers, that is, men without conceptions, without
great, warm ideas ; our troubles and ideas are continually
concerned with holes, rents, rags, and patches ; ye sin
and confess, and confess and sin again ; ye dawdle over
faults and relapses ; ye go to doctors of the soul and the

flesh; and there is one thing ye need, and that is that the spring of the great soul of Jesus should live in you, the " *novitas vitae*," the novelty of life, the great, trusting, rejoicing disposition. We do not fear, Jesus is with us; we look into His face in the Gospel; we accept His redeeming grace in our willing and devoted faith; we partake of His soul and life in our filial love, which is always cheerful, and even when it weeps, sheds but the tears of the child. To create afresh and anew, to clothe ourselves in new life—that will be no affair of rags and patches.

(d) " *And it came to pass again, as the Lord walked through the corn fields on the sabbath, that his disciples began to go forward and to pluck the ears of corn. And the Pharisees said to him: Behold, why do they on the sabbath day that which is not lawful? . . . And he said to them: The sabbath was made for man, and not man for the sabbath. Therefore the Son of Man is Lord of the sabbath also.*" (*Mark* ii. 23.) The sabbath is for man, that his soul should revive; but man can satisfy his wants also on the sabbath. The spirit never crushes the man, and his institutions serve its development and happiness. The sabbath should also be a spirit and not a letter, and in this case man who has acquired noble liberty by the love of God will dispose the day and do what life according to the ideas of God and its necessities demands.—We also celebrate Sundays and feast-days and we would indeed feel guilty were we to miss the obligatory divine service because of laziness, or because of some other petty reason; but if occasionally we are unable to go to Holy Mass on account of some just cause we need not worry; following the footsteps of Jesus on such occasions we are masters of the sabbath. Thus,

Jesus teaches us to comprehend the law more perfectly, and to interpret it more correctly.

THE HEALING OF THE MAN WHO HAD BEEN INFIRM FOR THIRTY-EIGHT YEARS

" *Now there is at Jerusalem a pond, called Probatica, which in Hebrew is named Bethsaida. . . . And there was a certain man there that had been eight and thirty years under his infirmity.*" (*John* v. 2.)

(*a*) To be ill for thirty-eight years with a Christlike soul is a heavenward-aspiring greatness of soul indeed. To say great things is easy; to live in strife and hard labour is easier than to lie ill. Here I lie, says the sick man, my life is useless; I am a burden to others! But what a great life it is, if it possesses the soul which says: It shall not be according to my will, but according to Thine. Therefore we have to esteem and make good use of such a time of trial. All does not depend on health, illness, great deeds, but all depends on whether we accomplish the holy will of God. And is there a greater deed than that of bearing witness to God and His unconquerable grace with patience and goodness, and to give souls the good example of suffering well borne? Many sick-beds are mission colonies. The face of one suffering with patience ranks among our most profound memories; it shines into our soul with encouragement and peace.

(*b*) " *Him when Jesus had seen lying . . . he saith to him: Wilt thou be made whole?* " Wilt thou, really? Dost thou wish for all the conditions and consequences of health and for all its duties? Dost thou wish for it with all the work, self-discipline and self-abnegation? Dost thou wish to become healed and to work for a more beautiful, stronger life ? This will exists in few people, for just this indolent, weak, lazy, undisciplined frame of mind is the illness of their soul. But how are we to wish for it ? In small, in simple, concrete things we have to educate it in ourselves ; we must wish to do this and that and we must carry out our purpose. Let us hate irresolution and indecision. Let us rejoice that we are able to wish with pure, straightforward, healthy mind and soul.

(c) " *The infirm man answered him : Sir, I have no man, when the water is troubled, to put me into the pond.*" Sir, I have no man. . . . No man who would strongly, bravely and magnanimously take up my cause. Indeed, this is the complaint of the Church, the people, and the public cause ! How many ailing would be healed, if they had a man, a help. How many would rise from out of the depths of misery and darkness, if they had men in whom there is soul, fire, and strength. " *Homo sum,*" says the weak man to excuse himself ; so let the strong and efficient man also say, " *Homo sum,*" who is not of flesh and blood, nor of blind, hardhearted nature, but of God. We love and help. Jesus can also complain, pointing to many families, institutions, congregations : I have no men, He might say, who ought to be parents, teachers, shepherds, Apostles ! That is why there is so much trouble for few are the men !

(d) " *Jesus saith to him : Arise, take up thy bed and walk.*" Behold man ! We cannot complain that we have no man ; Jesus is our man. He it is who helps us to rise, who heals us, who gives us creative words, soul, and strength. Who wishes to rise shall not wait for future energies, for the welling of mysterious waters ; shall not wait for new ideas of culture : neither for moments of emotion and enthusiasm, nor for the pathos of sentiment and inspiration. . . . Jesus is here, and He it is who says : Rise. It would be folly indeed to wait further and to think : I cannot rise ! This is mere moral hypochondria, which amounts to blasphemy. We are able to and we will rise.

JESUS SPENDS THE NIGHT IN PRAYER. I

" And it came to pass in those days, that he went out into a mountain to pray : and he passed the whole night in the prayer of God." (*Luke* vi. 12.)

(*a*) We have to pray, so that we may be deeply convinced of God and His grace, that we may reach Him, get closer to Him, be more deeply united with Him, so that we should revive in our soul, become purer and develop.

This is the sublime work we enact in our prayers ! In them we experience what an immense and inextinguishable great good the Lord is to us ; He is the warmth of our heart, its warmth and joy. We do not see the visage of the Lord, and though we know Him to be incomprehensible, yet we feel Him to be real. If we were asked why we cling to Him, our answer would be : brain, heart, sentiment, disposition, will, in one word our soul, our soul binds us to Him. The deepest reflections of philosophy lead eventually to the realm of supposition, from which hang the chains of conclusions which form a connecting link with faith and its mysteries. From the depths of the soul come knowledge and its law, which is logic ; thence, too, come the moral law and idealism. The great, starry, flowery world points us to God ; but likewise does our inner self point to Him, the clear, moral consciousness, the individual's world filled with inspirations, longings, and inclinations. Let us become absorbed in the necessities of our heart; our heart is one of the most powerful sources of religion; if we start from our heart, from our inner soul-world, we will find the Lord. Thou art here, O Lord, Thou art in us. If we look into ourselves, our consciousness seems as the entrance of the cave through which and out of which we look into a sublimely beautiful, ethereal, glorious world. It is into Thee we look, O Lord, it is Thee we see !

(b) Let us seek God in these our soul's intellectual, sentimental, moral ways, and let us be convinced when we are absorbed in ourselves. The wonderful world of the soul is the mirror of God ; let us look into it and blaze up with love for Him. Do not let us disdain it, for consciousness is to us the first and chief reality. The outer world also we see only by this inner, mysterious energy. Therefore all that this inner world requires becomes reality. Our life of the flesh requires food, warmth, sunshine, peace, so that it should not perish; this is reality and nature. In like manner, our soul-life, our soul-world, requires God, morals, ideals, eternal aim, and happiness ; this also is reality and religion and life. O Lord, give us childlike eyes ! With childlike eyes do we look into our soul and into Thee ; we continually question Thee and believe in Thy answers, which we hear in ourselves. The world sometimes confuses and nearly alienates us from Thee. A wonderful, heavy curtain is the world, which hides Thee ; it is woven from wondrously rich threads of events, which divert attention from Thee and keep it caught in itself ; it often opposes our feelings also, for its law is the necessary, mechanical chain of events, and it is this heavy chain which makes all of us groan, but if we turn to our inner self with the sense of strong life, there

we will come upon spirit, soul, upon God. These are
the sources of life ; here we discover strong life's bright
warm, sunny atmosphere ; here it is that we get rid
of the nightmares of pessimism or agnosticism, and
rise to glorious heights ; it is from here that we see the
unbelieving, discordant world's unspeakable misery.
From here we view the mutilated fancies of positivism,
which would identify the soul, the mind, and the will with
motion and impulse ; it is here that we can have pity for the
moderns raging in the unconsciousness of megalomania ;
and it is from here that we view humanity whether it
be revelling in the sunny garden of life, or sprawling
in the darkness of life's misery. We see this hell and
turn from it with loathing ! How intensely therefore
we love thee, our pure, sweet, divine world.

"*Signatum est super me lumen vultus tui.*" Thy visage
shineth upon us, that is the infinite, spiritual reality,
beauty and goodness, strength and happiness . . . the
" all " expressed by infinite, happy life ; this is what shines
upon us ; we are made out of it and we strive towards it,
and if we live according to it we are sure to come near it
and to live in it. And this means that that wonderful life,
that life of ours which presents itself in us and stretches
and develops in our longings, will at one time be completely absorbed in it—in that light which is infinitely
more beautiful and richer in colour than the sunshine ;
in that taste which is sweeter and more enjoyable than
any flavour or sweetness ; in that life which is more full
of enthusiasm than any other joy. It calls us to divine life ;
it gives us strength and grace, so that we should be capable
of it ! "*Justificabit ipse justus servus meus multos.*" (*Isaiah*
liii. 11.) By his knowledge shall my righteous servant
justify many.

JESUS SPENDS THE NIGHT IN PRAYER. II

" And it came to pass in those days, that he went out . . . to pray : and he passed the whole night in the prayer of God." (*Luke* vi. 12.)

(*a*) The Saviour was a contemplative soul. Prayer is actual observation. God promises "that I will pour out my spirit upon all flesh ; and your sons and daughters shall prophesy, your old men shall dream dreams, your young men shall see visions." (*Joel* ii. 28.) The ardent, enthusiastic souls see these things. Our vision is the contemplation of great realities. God comes down to us ; He comes near us. He is condescending. (1) *In nature*. Creation in itself is a great condescension of the infinite. It descends upon the ladder of its works, to touch and awake us, so that the soul may realize that everything is filled with God's spirit, that God is dwelling in our midst. (2) God is condescending in *history*, above all in the history of divine contact and revelation. We have understood from the soft voice, from the sweet word, from " the word which became flesh," how near the Lord came down to us ; down to the unity of blood, to brotherhood. As the Lord bent down to us from the heights, so He also lifted us to Him and *magnified* us. He could merely have given happiness. . . . My God, for this alone we ought to give infinite thanks, but God also gave us the sonship of God, He gave us divine life and the prospect of our contemplation changing into the vision of Him face to face ! It is the God who calls us and draws us whom we have to view in our prayers, and we have to contemplate His traces with ecstasy and fill our soul with them.

(b) A praying soul. When ye pray, your hearts shall speak. " Be filled with the Spirit . . . singing and making melody in your heart, to the Lord." (*Ephes*. v. 19.) The heart shall speak because of God who is in it and who fills it with His warmth; let it swim in its feelings; let its wings beat; the soul then speaks, when it is moved; when it is moved by the feeling of depth or the dread of the Sublime, or by the flood of its own incomprehensible instincts. In such souls a psalm awakes from the breath of the infinite. *Hymns* arise from the motives of praise and adoration, *songs* arise because of the feelings of joy, for great is the Lord and He is Holy and also ours, whom we can and must love! Such praying men is what the Apostle wishes for, men who sing " in psalms and hymns and spiritual canticles " (*Ephes*. v. 19), and who are able so to beseech that by their humility they bend the divine will. O Lord, Thou gavest us soul, Thou wishest that we should desire; Thou hast caught us in the chains of necessity and the iron clamps of natural law, but Thou hast given us will towering above necessity and natural law; therefore Thou wishest that we should beg, that we should groan and tell Thee what troubles our heart. Thou, O Lord, fillest our soul to overflowing, behold we pour our feelings at Thy feet! Oh, help; help and make us strong! Our soul is as yet undeveloped, lift us to Thyself and give us strength that we may walk the paths of insight and duty with a full heart, and not merely walk but fly along them. Into the meaningless, dry world of social position and official duties we place our heart warmed by Thy touch; we wish to be filled with Thy spirit, that the wayside of our life's dusty roads should also be bright with the flowers of divine feelings.

JESUS CHOOSES TWELVE APOSTLES

" *And it came to pass in those days, that he went out . . . to pray : and he passed the whole night in the prayer of God. And when day was come, he called unto him his disciples : and he chose twelve of them whom also he named apostles.*" (*Luke* vi. 12.)

(*a*) *Jesus* prays on the mountain all night with His soul looking to heaven and filled with God! This is His direction, hither He turns humanity. He prays hard, for He feels what great thing is before Him : He wishes to choose Apostles, who should be His "caliphs," His governors; who should go and act for Him, who should possess His soul. Deep soul is wanted for executing the commission of following the Lord ; an absorbed soul is what is wanted, which rises above semblance, surface, and narrow views. Asceticism is wanted for the strong man to be able to rise from out of the crowd ! For such souls Jesus prays !

(*b*) The Lord calls them to Himself . . . up to Himself ! He seeks for the higher man ; the Church also wishes to lift its priests out of the crowd, out of the bonds of sexual life, out of business life, it calls them up to the mountain. It educates them to a nobler, higher mind. Jesus prays the whole night ; how intensely has the Church to beg and pray ! Those who educate should pray a great deal for souls, that the Lord should give their pupils receptive, great souls. We have to strive up the hill, to Jesus, to His truths and His example.

(*c*) And what sort of men are these the Lord chose ? Fishers ? How are they clothed ? Where do they sleep ?

What is their food? How would they enter Roman
drawing-rooms? There is no perfume of verbena upon
them. How do even the Pharisees look upon them?
They are forceful, simple people—*infirma mundi* in the
strictest sense of the word, that is, there is little of the world
upon them. It is God who made all here; that is His
passion; to do all. "It is I who choose you." I rejoice
in this absolute, commanding will, as the cloud of insects
in the evening sunshine. And what has the Lord pro-
duced from them? Fishers of souls, martyrs, saints;
the cathedrals of Rome are their mausoleums! And what
would have become of them, if they had remained on the
sea of Genezareth? Christ, dear Lord, it is Thou who
really liftest souls to eternal glory!

THE EIGHT BEATITUDES

*" And seeing the multitudes, he went up into a mountain.
And when he was set down, his disciples came unto him. And
opening his mouth, he taught them."* (Matt. v. 1.)

(*a*) Jesus talks to the repressed, discouraged people at
the time of the merciless, foreign rule. Into the suffering
peoples' cloudy world of feelings, at the time of violent
Roman politics and Pharisaic formalities, He brings His
own great soul. He gives them a direction, which is
necessary in the first place, but it is not all. He goes
up the mountain. His mountain rises above the mounts
of culture. The sun of His divine, unparalleled mentality,
the sun of the eight beatitudes rises above this hill.
It is from there that the *" invictus sol "* shines towards
us. It is a high mountain, it is the height of the new law,
of the noble, superior, perfect will. We are on the way

towards this mountain; the way leads by steep paths, over rocks and whirlpools; we see how His followers strive towards this mountain; some exhausted and full of burdens, some hesitating and fainthearted; it is upon Christ that we will look; for in spite of His height we feel Him to be near, and we go bravely forward; He it is who will help us.

(b) " Blessed are the poor in spirit : for theirs is the kingdom of heaven." Every man's treasure is his soul, and his duty in the first place concerns his soul, not his rights, position, career, and riches. Those are in command of the situation who work with a simple heart and magnanimously for the salvation of their soul, and verily those can be called blessed who are not captivated by economic interest and earthly longing, who are superior to historical and cultural claims. Blessed are these free, emancipated souls ! Such are rich in themselves, and from their riches they give to many poor-wealthy ones. Poor in spirit are those who do not know the captivating riches which kill the soul and harden the heart. This poverty of spirit is not beggarliness but nobility.

(c) " Blessed are the meek : for they shall inherit the earth." Blessed are the meek who do not work with violence, hardness, and conceit; whose spirit is not arrogant and who do not know self-conceit, which leads to haughtiness. What profit accrues to the wielders of force if they suffer from the unhappiness of their subjects ? The Gospel aims at the happiness of the individual; it measures perfection according to devotion. Strength and power ought to be imbued with the spirit of the Gospel, so that there should be as much morality and as little violence as possible on earth. This does not mean that we should be weaklings and that we should only wish to solve the problems of the world by love ; the world has to have a strong hand, there has to be administration of justice and severity ; but that is merely the subordinate characteristic of the order of things and not happiness of the soul.

(*d*) "*Blessed are they that mourn: for they shall be comforted.*" God is the comforter of mankind, tormented with poverty and misery ; mankind should expect and seek for its consolation in Him ; it will find it. To mourn is no blessing, no happiness, and we need not mourn for the sake of being comforted ; but when trouble pours down upon us, let us believe that we have a comforter ; the sinner has a comforter as well as the fallen ones, the harassed and the ailing. "That you be not sorrowful, even as others who have no hope." (1 *Thess.* iv. 12.)

(*e*) "*Blessed are they that hunger and thirst after justice : for they shall have their fill.*" The Lord does not like those who are satisfied with themselves and their perfection, who have no wish for more, for what is better ; these are corpses. Who, after hearing these words of Christ, can be satisfied with the spirituality already achieved, with the present state of his soul ? Who can exist without longings and endeavours ? What mountains rise up before us ? The mountains of reality, sublimity, knowledge, and magnanimity ! The hunger for these is the sign of the health of the soul, the symptom of strength, which stretches, works, and refills itself ; this is our road. We believe in our ability to become better and better.

(*f*) "*Blessed are the merciful : for they shall obtain mercy.*" We always find opportunity. We have to lift broken hearts, shipwrecked beings, men who suffer from the consciousness of their sins. " The mercy of the Lord is boundless." In the Lord we find a home, we who in spite of good intentions know what consciousness of guilt and misery mean ; it is by the Lord that we learn mercy towards the sufferers in body and soul. In this way we will recognize in the beggar the child of God ; it will be our mission to pour the balm of mercy into the heart of others, and the wisdom of life and patience will follow our steps.

(g) " *Blessed are the clean of heart : for they shall see God.*" There are many different kinds of eyes ; some see little, others see more ; in the eyes of some the shrub, mountain, forest, turn to masterpieces of colour, wonder, and depth ; they have a soul for it. The eyes of the pure in heart are such deep-looking eyes ; they see God ; recognize Him ; world, flowers, thorns, stars, seem different to them ; where others see mist and fog, the pure in heart see the sun through the fog, and where others see only darkness they see also stars ; they see the Lord : *Dominus est !* . . . Do not let us dull the eyes of our soul with dust, mud, and earth ; the brutal man does not see the divine features ! What joy it is to see what is divine and one day to see God.

(h) " *Blessed are the peacemakers : for they shall be called the children of God.*" Jesus always appraises superior spirituality and not stupid passivity ; He magnifies peace which is the fruit of goodwill, of strong, patient, prudent, moderate goodwill, not the fruit of aggressive, violent despotism. For this peace we have to struggle much, this peace also holds a sword in one hand and a palm-branch in the other. Let us be at peace firstly with God, that is we should have a pure heart ; and we should be at peace with our fellow-men. Irritability is an evil; after every quarrel we own that it would have been better not to have entered it.

(i) "*Blessed are they that suffer persecution for justice' sake for theirs is the kingdom of heaven.*" Blessed are they who so love righteousness that they suffer for it, who do not yield an iota of their conviction, faith, or virtue, and rather lose all than give way to violence, rather lose favour, promotion, homage, friendship, riches, life. These are the aristocratic souls, in whose eyes the world has lost its value compared to the eternal value which opposes it. Let us not hesitate for a second in the sacrifices small and great that we make for the sake of truth, virtue, and God. We need not be martyrs and still can suffer neglect and resentment for the sake of truth and virtue. This should not disturb us. But we can also suffer in such a way for the sake of righteousness that being innocent we are abused, judged, put to prison, deprived of our position and means. To suffer for the truth and to appear pure only to God, this is true sublimity. The revelation of these souls will be the zenith of the Last Judgment!

BLESSED ARE THEY THAT SUFFER PERSECUTION

"*Blessed are they that suffer persecution for justice' sake.*"

(a) This "blessedness" suffuses the works of God with wonderful light. So it is possible to suffer persecution for the truth, and divine providence permits this. God loves heroic souls and permits them to be martyrs; He allows hearts to bleed, permits saints to pine away, allows His Son to die upon the Cross. Thus providence looks firstly at the soul; it does not always assure life, wealth, and health, but through pain, loss, and suffering it takes care of the soul. The aim of providence is not worldly happiness—suffering and bitterness may be our portion—but happiness of the soul we can rightly have in spite of persecution and anguish. In good and bad fortune, health and illness, wealth and poverty, we should always look to the soul, it is the soul we should love and take care of, in co-operation with divine providence.

(b) To suffer for the sake of righteousness means to suffer unjustly and not because of one's fault. How many men have been condemned to death unjustly, how many girls seduced by violence, how many have been ruined by the fault of others, how many despair because of failure and bad judgment! And man says: Why does not God destroy the evil ones with His lightning and how can He allow these abominations? I would not allow them if I had my way! Behold the great complaint against providence and God's answer to it: Blessed are they who suffer for the truth. Our life is subject to physical laws and is under the influence of the free will of others; to demand miracles from God against physical dangers is unreasonable, and to interfere with the free will of others by means of immediate punishment or reward, would put a stop to moral order. The world would be a puppet-show. In God's scheme for the world free morality has to develop, and the avenging divine hand is not allowed to stand in the foreground. We are not to avoid wrong for fear of punishment, nor do good for the sake of reward; this would be a low standard of morality. We have to assert the moral order in spite of physical laws and brutality, and we have to believe that our losses do not deprive us of our heaven. Amidst physical misfortunes and cruelties this is the knowledge we have to be conscious of : we carry an immense treasure within ourselves ; we will not give it up, no one can take it away from us, and not for anything will we lose it.

(c) Let us adore God, when our soul groans amidst conflicts. Our feelings and sufferings are merely fragments of stone in the structure of the world. God's way is divine, so let us not be astonished that the divine is not exactly as the human ! . . . Our most important task is dauntless, devoted, perseverance ; not soft feelings shall guide us, but the words of St. Paul : Who tears us away from Christ ?

LIGHT AND SALT OF THE EARTH

" You are the salt of the earth. But if the salt lose its savour, wherewith shall it be salted? It is good for nothing any more but to be cast out and to be trodden on by men." (*Matt.* v. 13.)

(a) There is much evil in the world ; it is like the stable of Augeas and the swamp of Lerna. Swamp is corruption, and darkness the frivolous, immoral opinions of the masses ; want of character amounts to friendship with sin and malice. " Ye are the salt of the earth." . . . Be the enemies of sin, for the Lord has placed enmity twixt your soul, your grace, your spirit and those of ruin and sin ; this is your glory. Let us fight against that poverty which leads to sin ; against tyranny and selfishness which oppress whole strata of society ; against uncleanness which serves the reign of instinct and its degeneration. Let us realize that we are struggling with the devil, who is cruel, murderous, immoral, evil, and full of hate. Do not let us expect anything else from him and his followers. We should not be scandalized by the power of decay and its sad work. The salt of the Gospel is inexhaustible. It disinfects our souls and kills the bacillus of corruption if we but use it prudently and with energy. Let us all, especially the priests, struggle against every evil. Let us read the letters of St. Paul and think on the slightest good that we have succeeded in doing and rejoice in it.

(b) " *You are the light of the world.*" This is what the Lord means concerning the priests : You are placed in the darkness as columns of fire. (1) Through your lives. For Herculean work a Hercules is needed ; we must not object to this. We have to be greater, we have to be Christlike. Our personality must exemplify a programme which has a definite aim, which encourages the weak, incites, supports. (2) By your teaching. Filled with the spirit of God, let us lead mankind to Christianity ; not only that they may know the Catechism, but that we may help them to raise their inner self and to comfort them. They have to experience God and to feel His wonderful grip on the heart. Our religiousness often wavers between superstition and materialism. (3) Lead mankind to a rational, simple way of life and work, which they should live as men and not as beasts, and encourage whatever endeavours lift mankind out of sensuality and beastliness, whether it be in the name of art, science, hygiene, or social action. It is a wonderful vocation to serve the cause of enlightenment ; this is the real sunshine ; the real strength and joy of God ; the glory of Christ !

(c) And if the salt itself rots, if Apostles and priests weaken, if the light goes out and double darkness covers the paths of heaven, what deep sorrow is upon the face of Christ, what fresh shame and misunderstanding descend upon His Gospel! This is the loathsomeness of decay in the holy place! This is bringing faith, grace, and the Sacraments into disrepute. Whole nations become ailing, and humanity, misled by the power of worldly feeling, sacrifices to false gods. Be thou the salt of that company and the light of that house in which God has placed thee; do not wait for others to be good; be thou good; do not wait for others to give light and warmth, "thy light shall light." Dangerous is that frame of mind which expects every good only from others; salt and lamp is what we have to be through our healthy, strong, Christlike mind.

JESUS CAME NOT TO DESTROY THE LAW. I

"*Do not think that I am come to destroy the law or the prophets. I am not come to destroy, but to fulfil.*" (*Matt.* v. 17.)

(a) There is law, but with thee it only means letter and formality; thou dost not apply it to ideas, thoughts, feeling, and will; I have to fulfil it, that is, I have to teach thee so that thy spiritual world shall be that of goodwill, truth, straightforwardness, sincerity, and beauty. God appears to us as truth, goodness, beauty, strength; zeal for Him walks the ways of obedience; longing for the ideal life and the strength of passion demands the detailed work of discipline; with this we arrive at real liberty and individuality. To fulfil the law, that is to want according to the law, to correct the half-truths of sentimentality; we have not to suffer constraint but to persecute despotism in ourselves.

(b) " *You have heard that it was said to them of old : Thou shalt not kill. And whosoever shall kill shall be in danger of the judgment. But I say to you that whosoever is angry with his brother shall be in danger of the judgment.*" Anger is usually violent and unjust, it mostly has claws; in the pure, ethic sphere there is no place for such brute force. There is temper and passion in us, as well as uneducated inclinations; we have to curb and train them; every temperament shall pay homage to the moral order. Let us have strength to be masters also in storm. It is then that we sin, when passion runs away with our insight and moderation, and degrades us.

(c) " *And if thy right eye scandalize thee, pluck it out . . . if thy right hand scandalize thee, cut it off.*" The spirit has to fight against its own nature, against fallen nature; nobly has the spirit to break with attachment and soft feeling for the sake of salvation. If it does not do it, its life is death; if it does it, even its death will be life. Goethe said: " die and live "; we have to sacrifice for the fuller and more beautiful soul. We shall turn away our eyes for sake of the spiritual light and restrain our hands so as not to become soiled. At the time of Napoleon's Russian war the initial N of Napoleon was branded on the arm of a Russian peasant; the Russian cut his arm off; he did not want to belong to Napoleon; his heart was the Tsar's. Our heart belongs to God; we arrange everything according to this.

JESUS CAME NOT TO DESTROY THE LAW. II

"Do not think that I am come to destroy the law or the prophets. I am not come to destroy, but to fulfil." (Matt. v. 17.)

(*a*) He does not destroy the law but fulfils it, that is, in place of its chapters and symbols He places reality ; He explains the letter which kills, by the spirit. He does not evade the law, for the law is for the beautiful life ; therefore he who wishes that life has to live according to the law. Law is not something that is dictated to us as a set of formulas ; but it is the outline of life ; this is the way our mind, our heart, our ideal aim looks upon the law and identifies itself with it and willingly chooses to fulfil it. Let us love the divine will, for this is our own rightly recognized and deepest will. The righteous one has no law, in so far as he completely identifies himself with the divine will, and that is why he does not feel constrained by forms and regulations.

(*b*) *" For amen I say unto you, till heaven and earth pass, one jot or one tittle shall not pass of the law, till all be fulfilled."* We put the whole man under the law of Christ and in our moral life keep that law to the last jot. Where one has to feel, suffer, and love, we only recognize one point of view : that of Christian morals. Therefore (1) our worldly wisdom does not consist of crumbs of philosophy but of the mighty system of eternal life's principles. When we speak of life, our whole soul becomes filled with the consciousness of our *Credo*, of our faith. Our ideal is Christ ; the Gospel to us is not a doctrine, but " *Dei virtus.*" (2) Our culture is not civilization, institutions, knowledge, and art, but pure morality, the pure state of being children of God—" race "—" *tertium genus*." (3) To us morality is liberty and release ; release from beast-like, instinctive, sensual, violent, distorted existence. Morality to us means spirituality, that is rising from the blindness of matter. To us morality is strong, united will ; to will what God wills. (4) Progress to us does not mean philanthropy and altruism, which look for things to be done in others and not in oneself. The "I" begins in ourselves and ends in ourselves ; I am in the first place, neither you nor he. Therefore it is senselessly insufficient to seek progress in altruism, for this concerns our relation to other things, that is, to formality and outwardness ; whereas our morality and perfection is latent in our purified, ennobled spirituality which clings to God, and His supremacy above sensuality and selfishness. If there were no other man in the world, or if we were hermits, even then we could be deeply moral. Therefore it is in ourselves that we have first of all to shape a purified, beautiful, noble spirituality.

(c) " *He therefore that shall break one of these least commandments and shall so teach men shall be called the least in the kingdom of heaven. But he that shall do and teach, he shall be called great in the kingdom of heaven.*" To unite these two : the ideal and reality ! This costs much ; it is not easy. We know that there are many ignoble, bad inclinations in us, those we have to break and ennoble. Our soul is no garden of Eden, where saints walk ; our burden is sin, and our greatest necessity is mercy. We cannot look in the eyes of eternal life if we carry death in our soul, and from that neither knowledge, music, nor sport will release us. Our energy is not a conceited optimism which says "that we can do all, if we only want to."

We neither know enough, nor can we do all. The needs we have are the needs of depth, and these are solely satisfied by faith. What we need is redemption and divine force, we need consolation which men and the world cannot give. Facing incomprehensible life and death, we can entrust our soul only to the consoling love of God, for that alone is reasonable, and to the hope springing from it !

(*d*) Who teaches and does not act is a poor figure ; poor and sad also are those who believe and teach without the devotion of a life. Such prepare to create life and to shape the depths of existence to consciousness, and behold they snatch after small petty patterns instead of faithfully following the great ideals, and beside the grace of God they listen to nerve excitements and impressions. They would be Michael Angelos and become village potters ; they would be Beethovens and are impressed by .the chirping of the sparrows. Oh, the poor, bungling souls ! Oh, my God, we unconditionally go after Thee and live what we believe. Thou sufficest us ! Jesus is our pattern ; we shape our life according to Him ; so we escape the accusation made against us, that upon torn garments—mantles of Socrates, togas of Plato and palliums of 'Zeno—we put Christian patches and are after all only mending tailors. No, no, we are " the seed of God," we are of the school of Christ. His words and His example are spirit and life in us.

ANGER

" *But I say to you that whosoever is angry with his brother shall be in danger of the judgment. And whosoever shall say to his brother, Raca, shall be in danger of the council. And*

whosoever shall say, Thou fool, shall be in danger of hell fire."
(*Matt*. v. 22.)

(*a*) Not to be angry, not to quarrel and offend but to bear goodwill towards our fellows is what we have to do. We have to feel that love streams from our heart and that we attract. What can bring this to be ? Not beauty which attracts but only superficially ; not knowledge which when it goes hand-in-hand with pedantry is unbearable ; nor a superior, strict, exacting virtue ; but a disposition and frame of mind, which wants the good, which elevates— which does not make its own superiority and others' smallness felt, but forms and guides. This is the really superior and moral disposition. This disposition can adapt itself ; it does not command and dispute, but makes the unstable ones understand what they are to do, and imperceptibly makes good what the other spoils, neglects, or forgets. It is to its surroundings as spring is to nature ; its scent, beauty, and warmth are felt without violence ! To practise this is bliss indeed !

(*b*) Quarrelsomeness is the disharmony of our own soul ; the dirty stream of our irritability pours from it, and it is we who suffer by it mostly, whether it originates from our roughness and rudeness, or our faintheartedness and repugnance. Others may also be guilty and circumstances unbearable, but however it may be, we must not allow ourselves to become embittered and infuriated. Therefore we endeavour to be of service to others and to be their consolation and help. If others want something that is not sinful, we willingly help. We look upon repugnance as a mere weakness of our nature, which is of no importance and should not affect our decisions. Concerning it we willingly make the sacrifice of resignation, self-abnegation and willing advance. God is our example, we look to Him.

(*c*) Economic strife and the war of principles estrange men from each other, for there is love in neither. Let us sometimes declare a truce and approach our fellow beings with love ; let us forget the strife, hurt, and sorrow, and endeavour only to understand and forgive. By so doing we correct the onesidedness of our minds and prevent an increase of repugnance and estrangement. Let us sometimes say to ourselves : to-day we forgive, to-day we forget all ; to-day we wish to love in all straightforwardness and sincerity. We wish to be good, to be of use to everyone. " All things whatsoever you would that man should do to you, do you also to them." (*Matt.* vii. 12.)

THE LAW OF CHASTITY. I

" *You have heard that it was said to them of old : Thou shalt not commit adultery.*" (*Matt.* v. 27.)

(*a*) Against this old law the world is weak. In a barbarous way it breaks the fine sense of purity. In its bloom it withers and consumes the strength of youth, dries up the sources of ideal attachments and true poetry. With the pure blood, the energy of life is also spent and we can reproach youth with the most bitter elegy : *cinis est cor ejus*, its heart is ashes, its blood spittle. Impurity dulls ideals. Everything ought to be directed towards serving ideal aims ; nature, teaching, art, the training of the body should work with religion to help the pure, moral life to develop, so that every child of God should become disciplined in body, consciously pure in soul, should develop to an individuality capable of ruling its instincts. This will be our endeavour, and at all costs we will strive to show in deeds and in the assertion of a victorious will the commands and the grace of God.

(*b*) There is no commandment without its corresponding grace. When God commands, He also gives strength for it. We have *first* to be deeply convinced that just as we would rather die than consciously acquiesce in a sinful thought, so God will give us grace at all times for conquering temptation. This conviction becomes elevated to a prayer each time we think of the great duty of purity and its fiery ordeal; and every time we are involved in these battles let us pray so that we may be filled with the awe of God and the loathing of sin. Let us pray that we may have strength to conquer temptation. Let us cast our eyes down and say with contrition: Lord, Lord, help us ! *Secondly*, we have to educate ourselves to valuing purity, so that we see the holy will of God in it, which commits purity to our soul as the correlative of the development of nature and strength: so that in the battles fought for purity we see the assertion of strength of will and of character, which is the condition of noble feeling and of the development of a beautiful, sublime, happy, inner world. For impurity only develops ignoble feelings, which in the higher cultures amount to outward propriety meant only for the eye. According to Holy Scripture, "*reprobus sensus*," base, perverse feelings, grow in impure souls, which equally show themselves in modern sexual over-excitement. *Thirdly*, let us recognize and rightly estimate our natural instincts and all that can awake impurity in us, and let us take up a right point of view concerning these. The lower life has two focuses : selfishness and longing for pleasure.

Selfishness can spoil our judgment, pleasure can poison our flesh. These natural forces have to be moulded and the harmony of virtue has to be spread over them with the aid of the law. It is not possible to set the instincts free; they have to be conquered. The modern age wants to succeed with sexualism without violence and moral battles; it raves of free love, of new sexual relations, and through these it hopes to pour satisfaction on unbridled longings. In opposition to this, let us believe the words of Christ which say: I bring not peace but a sword. Here a sword is needed, here we have to cut and conquer; only then will there be peace.

(c) Let us ennoble our senses, especially our eyes, so that we shall not look at or read anything that incites us to sin. Let us always seek for God's ideas, and for the soul. Real beauty not only brings forth feelings, but also ideas. How many see only the lovely body and are the victims of it; the cult of the beautiful weakens when it only vibrates on the surface; in the shape of sensual beauty we always have to look for the element which is significant for the soul, the element which affects and touches the heart. Let us further remember that impurity destroys true love; it profanes the soul and drags it down to the shame of blind passion; it degrades itself and the object of its love, and deprives itself of the bliss-giving consciousness of self-esteem and reasonableness. Brothers, let us mould the instinctive animal elements into the shape of virtue and discipline. Let us fight and strive, and let us have ardour for the strife; the love of God and the awe of God should inspire us. Let us pray in our temptations and approach Jesus in the Sacraments. The Sacraments of Penance and Holy

Communion are capable of educating a pure race, if we partake of these Sacraments with great consciousness and true faith. Behold the food of the Angels, the bread of wayfarers ! Through it the travellers through life become angelic !

THE LAW OF CHASTITY. II

" But I say to you that whosoever shall look on a woman to lust after her hath already committed adultery with her in his heart." (*Matt.* v. 28.)

(*a*) Jesus wished to educate divine men and to clothe them in superior beauty. And just as art breaks shapelessness with shape and conquers material with beauty, so the Lord Jesus had to break the instinctive man by morality and to create in the first place holiness, inspiration, beauty, and strength, that the " *tertium genus*," the divine man, might arise. He creates this by assuring a pure, healthy atmosphere. This is given to the soul by truth, by idealism, by strength of will, and martial spirit. It is necessary that our ideas be not dark, impotent, or wild ; it is necessary that our feelings be not sickly and hysterical. Concerning sexual life the sons and daughters of the modern age grow up in an unhealthy atmosphere, which is filled with weakening allurements. Their outlook is tainted, they are the victims of exaggerated sexuality. Their art is the slave of this problem ; their life resembles more and more that inferior animal-world, the chief function of which is to conceive. This one-sidedness guides feeling and disposition in a wrong, unhealthy direction, more and more in the direction which the Apostle characterizes : " *in ignominiam . . . in reprobum sensum . . . stulti facti sunt . . . digni morte,*" decadent, perverse people. Contrary to this, the pure, moral man's ideas are filled with common sense and the light of faith. In the woman, he sees a companion and only expects so much pleasure from sexual relations, as he can win by way of virtue. He is not intoxicated, not neurasthenic and does not tear the flowers of love, but tends and enjoys them according to the will of God! Oh, ye who love humanity, ye sweet Utopians, who demand sunshine, forest-breeze, and blue sky for the town-folk, demand in the first place sunshine and fresh air for their souls, that they should not fade in the unhealthy atmosphere of immorality! Oh, ye who teach mankind that their houses should not be low haunts, teach men that their heart and soul should not be the low haunt of disgusting ideas, rotting feelings and desires. Oh, ye who wish to reform life with art, bring men to their senses that they carry the shape of virtue into their inner life, their feelings and ideas, and that they assert in this ugly chaos the power of discipline and self-negation; then they will also better understand the Lord Jesus, whose first demand is the pure heart, the pure spiritual world, which informs the whole man and his whole life. My Lord, a pure heart create in me; pure, noble ideas, and feelings full of strength we ask of Thee for our soul, that it should not fade. We will fight with all our strength against impure ideas and desires.

(*b*) The Lord gives us strong, blossoming, spring-like force of life. If in place of beauty and virtue we have beast-like instincts, then every tie is loosened and the root of the strength of the nations' life rots. Impurity is fire which consumes life in its blossom; not only the marrow, but with it the joy of life, energy, and the creative genius. This is nowhere to be experienced so much as in case of self-pollution; self-pollution truly draws the forces of life, the vital forces, into a swamp, and such a generation justifies the words of Dr. Bouffon, who says that the great part of humanity dies by self-murder. So nature, which has been profaned in its forces and defamed in its life-giving vocation, will rise up in arms against us and instead of being the source of life, will become that of decay and death. Nature full of vital strength, which lives inside the borders and boundaries of virtue, begets life; violated, defamed nature spreads misery in its children, unfit for life. Impurity poisons the source of the life of nations; at the door of the brothels Satan and death are sitting. All ye doctors who wish to secure for humanity pure blood and fresh soul and joy of life, struggle against the bacillus and against prostitution, but also keep in mind that the soul and strength of human life is moral, and that without moral strength, without self-denial, penance, discipline, and prayer, ye only support drunkards with all your science; they are not men, but sacks; these ye can never teach to struggle and to conquer; if they wake from their trance, and if they will and struggle and make sacrifices, then they will prosper. Let them approach Jesus; His heart is life, strength, and burning love. He burns so as to ignite. His cross is the sign of life, let us crucify upon it the death living in us, sin and the devastating, murderous agonies of passion, and then we will live. Let us be united with Jesus in the Holy Eucharist; this Holy Feast imparts to us the pure, shining, blossoming world of His divine soul which is full of vital strength; thus death perishes and life lives.

SIMPLICITY OF SPEECH

"*Again you have heard . . . Thou shalt not forswear thyself . . . but I say to you not to swear at all . . . But let your speech be : Yea, yea : No, no. And that which is over and above these is of evil.*" (*Matt.* v. 33.)

(*a*) Jesus wishes sincerity and straightforwardness. Telling the truth is the service of truth that we do for our companions. The Christlike soul does not lie, neither when it talks, nor when it is silent. Secrets have to be kept ; to be clumsy and indiscreet is not Christianity ; we have always to act as those who serve the truth. When there will be more of us who feel like this, then there will be no need amongst us for oaths. Let us love the truth bravely ; let us have faith in it and persevere in our convictions. It is easy to live with convictions in a hidden place or amongst men who agree, but very difficult in an inimical and disunited world. Who argues much and looks in many directions becomes cowardly and easily lies. What we want and strive after is a Christ-like soul.

(*b*) "*You have heard that it hath been said : An eye for an eye, and a tooth for a tooth. But I say to you not to resist evil ; but if one strike thee on thy right cheek, turn to him also the other.*" There is a law for revenge and reprisals, we have a right to this and that, we have a right towards others, which it is forbidden to offend. True, the law and right are necessary ; they are the corner-stones of life, but at the same time a one-sided and not very elevating fact. Do not let us trust too much that they will enrich our life and make it happier. Of law there is sufficient ; but let us give more good-will, noble feelings, brotherliness, willingness, and readiness for service. For law is after all an impersonal strength; and we long and wish for a loving, noble personality. Let us be generous, noble sons of our Father, who makes His sun to shine on the just and the unjust; let us love our fellow-men, even if they do not love us much, and let us influence them and value them so as to raise them.

(c) " *Judge not, that you may not be judged.*" (*Matt.* vii. 1.) Do not judge with inimical feelings, neither from subjective points of view; this will be a guard against many mistakes and injustices. If our feelings and our personality creep into our judgments, how can we then be just? Therefore, when we judge we have first to acquire a noble, emancipated, unprejudiced disposition; we shall will the good and will it well. Do not let us judge harshly; let us remember our own instability, and how much was needed till we achieved something worth mentioning, if in fact we are better than others! "With what judgment ye judge, ye shall be judged." Strict, harsh judgments are mostly the outcome of a lack of self-knowledge; let us be conscious of our feebleness and our faults.

DO NOT YOUR JUSTICE BEFORE MEN

" *Take heed that you do not your justice before men, to be seen. . . . And when you pray, you shall not . . . pray in the . . . corners of the streets.*" (*Matt.* vi.)

(a) Do not let us care in the first place for the exterior, the colour and semblance; for the outward is the flower of the inward; the outward is the scent and warmth of the heart. It is this inwardness we have to tend, then its strength and light will break through. What is the use of the exterior if it is not the radiation of the beautiful inner world ? What is the use of a lovely tombstone ? Between zeal and hypocrisy there is the same difference as between a lovely face and a painted mask. Poor, empty mask ! What we need is strength, joy, life, and ardour. This fills us and enables us to reform the outer world.

(*b*) Accordingly, we shall shut ourselves up in our inner self. In this holy seclusion the Lord is present. " *In indepicto fundo cordis*," in the transparent depths of the soul, there where we have parted with appearance and illusion, there where with pure child-eyes we have seen and recognized ourselves, there it is that God and we meet, where the soul and the Father meet. " Enter into thy closet, and when thou hast shut the door, pray to thy father which is in secret." Who has entered this closet is less liable to distraction. The deeper we sink into ourselves, the better we pray.

(*c*) Educated people as a rule do not willingly take part in public profession of their faith, such as processions, etc. This disinclination ought to be corrected. We have to take part in the exterior worship of God. It is the will of Jesus, as we have also to adore God in company and brotherly union ; but otherwise, let us only penetrate into the depth. At the public service of God, humility and acknowledgment of our faith also form part of the real inner values.

FAST NOT AS THE HYPOCRITES

" *And when you fast, be not as the hypocrites, sad. But thou, when thou fastest, anoint thy head.*" (*Matt.* vi. 16, 17.)

(*a*) Not for the eye, for what good is that ? Let us do all for the soul. Fasting is the help of the soul against the flesh. The body is heavy, lazy, instinctive, given to excess, and with its weight it crushes the soul. Soul we need in this body, soul which is light, ordered, willing, disciplined agile, strong, quick, and tenacious ; which does not lie inert but reaches outward and upward. If we verily fast then we pray more willingly ; our spiritual world is purified, there is not so much dusk and fog upon our souls ; our instincts are not so fiery and violent but more godly. And fasting is also our penance ; for we punish ourselves.

(*b*) " *Therefore when thou dost an almsdeed, sound not a trumpet before thee.*" (*Matt.* vi. 2.) In the service of the eyes, the heart and soul become lost. The left hand steals the good from the right one. Human glances are all thieves. They are like exhibition wine-flasks ; the flask and the label are there, but only water is in them . . . water, only water, stale, tasteless water. The moral value has fallen out ; the heart is empty. Goodwill and nobility of heart give value to alms ; if we lack these we are simply throwing our money into the streets.

(*c*) We are full of formality ; the husks of good actions exist but their seeds have fallen out. Our heart is an empty vessel and our soul a shadow. Therefore, we have to fill it with feeling and life. Whether we eat meat to-day or not, in this we follow the letter of the law ; but let us go deeper by experiencing our sins and the sufferings of Christ ; we can weave all and everything into soul and feeling ; fasting also can become expiation, homage, humility ; in a word, it can become divine life. It is this warm life that man forgets ; there is little of religion in him, little of it in the form of an experienced idea ; man has emotions but he cannot create a " godly kingdom " out of them ; he is incapable of finding pleasure in them. He can neither believe, nor be reassured, he cannot be animated nor pleased. Let man find pleasure in humble homage, and joy in the purification of the soul by which it achieves love of the betrothed. Oh, yes, let us experience our soul, let us rise and rejoice ; otherwise what Eckhardt said in the Middle Ages may be applicable to us : " What is the use of my being a king if I am not aware of it ? " We have to experience our soul.

PRAY IN SECRET

" But thou when thou shalt pray, enter into thy chamber and, having shut the door, pray to thy Father in secret." (*Matt.* vi. 6.)

(*a*) To pray . . . to spread and stretch our soul towards God as the butterfly stretches its wings in the sunshine, to absorb the divine impressions, light, and energy, and then to experience them ; this is what we have to do. This is continuous, silent prayer and.life. God imparts Himself and we experience Him. Albeit we have work to accomplish and a vocation upon earth, let us not forget to shape and form our consciousness and inner soul-world. Much energy is spent on earning our daily bread, on obtaining power, culture, and pleasure ; let us put much energy into prayer also. Nature wants strong lions, strong eagles, strong lilies. Our own feelings also urge this, therefore let us develop our consciousness beautifully, nobly, virtuously ; let us build it up according to Christ-like motives. There have been silent artists who have spent their whole lives carving one portal, painting the initials of one book ; we also are such silent artists, we work upon our life during our whole life. This is true art, which has no mercenary motive.

(b) Let us do everything for the higher life. The essence of life is not gain, success, and effect; not the work one accomplishes outside oneself, but that which one shapes in oneself. If we cannot create masterpieces in marble, colour, wood, word, and sound, no matter; the important thing is to do so in our own feelings. We work out existence so that it becomes feeling, trust, hope, peace, love, joy, harmony, beauty, music; we shape instinctive nature into liberty and liberty into Christlike personality. To achieve this we devote time and energy. We will not look upon the time spent in meditation and in putting our souls in order as lost. Our object is that we should not act according to the impulses of our instincts but that we should drive these instincts into our service. We honour the mystical souls, for they breathe life as the forests and are peaceful as the valleys; these are the souls who experience and write *The Imitation of Christ*.

THE OUR FATHER

"*Thus therefore shall you pray: Our Father who art in heaven.*" (*Matt*. vi. 9.)

(a) Our Father . . . Thou sweet, strong, personal spirit . . . filled with bounty. It is when we call Thee Father that we approach Thee most. The inspiration of our heart is needed; our mind walking on wooden legs stumbles upon the way of seeking God. Therefore our " conceptions of God " are anæmic or even distorted ideas. God is life and spirit, and our ideas about Him are weak and our imagination deceiving. With this word " Father," our " Father," Jesus showed us the way upon which we can go towards God. Do not let us torment ourselves with other ideas, let us love and be children. Let us hand ourselves over to our Father and to Christ, whom He sent, as the Gospel teaches us. Let us approach Him with loving faith, with humble, atoning, longing will, which is full of homage. In these feelings the soul shows a fine sensitiveness; without them it becomes dark, fades, and dries up. Therefore let us strive to draw near to God, to His sheltering, encouraging, reassuring presence. He is our Father and our strength; we draw strength from Him; only thus can we progress; He makes up our insufficiency; we revive from His touch. One drop of His sweet love is worth more than an ocean of knowledge. Oh, our dear Father, speak to Thy children; fill us with consolation and reassurance. *Pater mi, pater mi !*

(b) " *Hallowed be thy name.*" We need inspired reverence towards the eternal, infinite Sublimity; we have to adore Him. We are small and finite: Thou, our Father, art infinite; we live in time and space, Thou art eternal. Thou art the great Lord, we are Thy servants, and in us Thy greatness and the dependence of the world on Thee develop to consciousness. We honour Thee, and look upon Thee and up to Thee with deep reverence, to Thee who holdest us above the depths, not in order to throw us down into them, but for our salvation. Therefore our reverence turns into love and joyously we say: Holy, Holy, Holy is the Lord God of hosts. Heaven and earth are filled with His glory. Yes, filled it is to those whom the Lord fills; filled with strength and beauty to those who know Thee; but to those who do not know Thee, the earth is full of incomprehensibility, suffering, and darkness. Oh, Lord, draw us on, so that we may feel Thee, lift us so that we may praise and glorify Thee for ever. We will endeavour to exalt Thee in ourselves. . . . What grace and happiness that we can do so !

(c) "*Thy kingdom come.*" Yes, Thine. Others also have kingdoms ; nations have kingdoms as well as science and culture. These kingdoms do not satisfy ; they spread and become larger in time and space, but do not approach the heights and depths of the heart. Thy kingdom, O Lord, fills these depths and guides us to these heights ! Thy kingdom is strength, life, and joy in the heart and soul ; Thy kingdom further is the more just, more noble, and more human earthly existence ; Thy kingdom is the great unity of souls, the Holy Mother-Church, and, at last, eternity. Something of this, Thy kingdom, already exists in us and around us ; we beg Thee to see that it ever grows in us. Let our souls develop, let the world develop according to Thy ideas ; let everything prosper. Let there be less darkness, suffering, ruin, and death around us ; let us recognize Thy infinite bounty in Thy works ! It is in this Advent that we live, we live in the hope that the kingdom of God will spread, and we work for this . . . Thy kingdom come, this is what every prayer of ours, all work and strife, breathes !

(d) "*Thy will be done on earth as it is in heaven.*" Thou art unconditional in existence, holy and perfect in will ! But Thy will is not human, and Thou infinitely surpassest the measure of human conceptions, ideas, and feelings. Thou arrangest all the good and evil. Evil also, from that we cannot flee, for we are being ground in the mechanism of the world, but Thou orderest the evil also for moral good. Therefore we must not grow faint because of troubles and strife; even when the wave of bitterness overflows us, let us ask immediately: What are we to do to obey the will of God? Dull, flat suffering is not His will; trusting, striving, patient suffering is what God wishes. In all else also we will do what mind and faith, nature and grace propose. This is the will of the Lord. The will of the Lord will always be done if we do justice to the believing, trusting soul and lift it above the world, bitterness, toil, and strife.

(e) "*Give us this day our super-substantial daily bread.*" We have necessities and claims; we need bread, clothes, and a house to live in; we need a little portion of the world, so that our soul can develop in it. The world should not overcloud the soul, but neither should the soul waste away for want of the world. Give us as much as a simple, unpretentious, noble life demands. Many souls waste away not from want, but from abundance or a too ardent chase after what is necessary. What good are nervous excitement and pleasure which ruin healthy life? The words of Bouffon are true: men do not die, they kill themselves . . . by a senseless way of living. "Make the stones become bread," says modern soul-and-body-killing work; but what is the good if we die from all this bread? The bread also becomes stone to us. Let us value simple food, good water, air, and our night's rest. O Lord, teach us to live!

(f) "*And forgive us our debts, as we also forgive our debtors.*" As we wish to live corporally so we have to wish to live all the more spiritually. This wish is the deepest and most glowing longing of the heart, it is the cry of the soul: "Hear my prayer, O Lord, and do not despise my supplication, hearken to me and hear my cry." Forgive our sins, this is what we ask of Thee. This we can merely beg for, because, as for us, this can neither be the subject of merit or striving, only of grace. Only Thou canst give it. If Thou givest this to us, then we live; if Thou dost not give it, then we die for ever. Willingly will we fulfil all on which this grace depends; I repent, confess, atone, and still more: I will do as Thou wilt, I hope, do to me. I will also forgive, forgive from my heart and forgive truly, for I hope Thou wilt do likewise with me. We will speak to those we are angry with. Thou hast said elsewhere that church, sacrifice, and altar will be no help to us if we are angry with our brother. And verily, why do we ask for forgiveness, that is for merciful love, if we do not show love, goodwill, and the soul of unity towards others? " I wish for mercy and not for sacrifice."

(g) " *And lead us not into temptation.*" In life there is much darkness, difficulty, strife and incomprehensibility. These are the temptations of our soul. We pray, and the Lord does not hear us; we suffer unjustly; what we need is patience towards nature and mankind; the balance of our soul becomes disturbed; we do not understand ourselves and the world. Our God, lead us not into temptation; do not cover us with darkness; do not let us feel the cruelty of existence and of strife. Temptations we will have, our instincts will contradict our conscience; the flesh, the world, and the devil are not dumb; grant that we may hold our ground; give us a persevering, brave soul, ready for sacrifice in our temptations. Give us the necessary bravery to do good and do our duty! But, for our part, let us also do all so as not to enter into temptation; let us beware of the paths of evil in our thoughts, feelings, and imagination. Let us mistrust everything that disturbs the peace of the soul. The disturbance of the soul's balance is easily followed by shipwreck.

(*b*) " *But deliver us from evil.*" The personal evil is the devil. The Holy Scripture points to him and there is no psychology which is able to explain the obscuration of our soul life and its bitter disturbances; doubt and distrust often originate from him; dark, cold ideas concerning God and His grace can also be ascribed to the nearness of the devil. Deliver us from the evil which walks the earth and which is already so cold and dark and kills life, and deliver us still more from the evil beyond; guard us so that we may not be at its mercy! This is what casts body and soul upon the fire of Gehenna. Save us, Our Lord, from eternal death. Here the curse of " evil " is sin and death, and beyond it is eternal damnation.

THE EYE THE LIGHT OF THE BODY

" *The light of thy body is thy eye. If thy eye be single, thy whole body shall be lightsome. But if thy eye be evil, thy whole body shall be darksome.*" (*Matt.* 6. 22.)

(*a*) Our eye is our soul; its light is poured out on us. Verily our soul is poured over our body; it can plunge us into fever and infect us. Sin, which is in the will, disturbs the body also. Anger, envy, grief, jealousy, and anxiety poison us; discord and bad temper are worse than infected atmosphere. The sweat and spittle of the infuriated, agitated man is poisonous, the soul has poisoned it with its own ideas, imaginations, and desires. Whereas love, joy, and animation give fresh strength and youth; they also build and shape the body. Therefore we have to wash out from our soul every distracted, miry, languid, angry, mean feeling; we have to secure and allow the crystal-streams of the soul to go unhindered. No one shall say, I cannot; no one shall believe in evil, but he shall believe in good and its strength; he shall think and love with the ideas and love of God.

(*b*) Let such a luminous soul radiate from us; the world takes upon itself the colour in which we clothe it. " The soul is all; what we believe, we will become." " Make your soul the home of beautiful ideas. No one knows, for no one has tried it from early youth, what fairy castles of happiness we could build from noble, good ideas, in which we could securely find refuge amidst our struggles." (*Ruskin.*) It is true indeed that the soul creates a world; from the height of its feelings it is able to bid defiance to lowly vicissitudes. Therefore, let our soul be a source of light and heat; for there is more of God in our soul than in the whole material world!

"BE NOT SOLICITOUS"

" *Be not solicitous for your life, what you shall eat, nor for your body, what you shall put on. . . . Behold the birds of the air, for they neither sow, nor do they reap. . . . Consider the lilies of the field . . . they labour not, neither do they spin.*" (*Matt.* vi. 25.)

(*a*) To work, this is the first Gospel the Creator preached. This is the way of our greatness and masterliness, it is the correction of our mistakes, the dispersion of our doubts. Christ does not oppose this, but condemns that feverish, selfish, egoistical cruelty with which man pushes on and ruins others; condemns that anxious thrusting, over-excited economic fight; that senseless desire for riches which wants more and more, and by so doing picks to pieces the beauty of one's own soul and the harmony of the world. Why increase pretensions and claims in food and clothing? Is there a more beautiful life than simple, blossoming nature, full of song? If we live in a grand style and snatch everything away from others, a world crisis must result. This chase after riches is not according to the Gospel, but to work and be spiritual.

(b) The Lord demands this chiefly of His Apostles. They should be able to live on crumbs! What becomes of the Gospel if the Apostles earn money? The simple life and unpretentiousness is the "*pondus Evangelii*," the moral seriousness. There will always be men who will give up everything for the Gospel. Just as the warrior when he hears the trumpet, tears himself from the fond embrace of his wife and child and leaves his house and home, so souls, apostolically inspired, are able to renounce all and start without scrip and staff into the world. This is the will of Christ!

(c) "*But I say to you that not even Solomon in all his glory was arrayed as one of these.*" With delight the Lord Jesus looks upon the divine pomp in which the flowers of the meadows are clothed. He loves, enjoys, and praises beauty; He possesses the soul which makes Him see it divine. "Wherefore if God so clothe the grass of the field, which to-day is, and to-morrow is cast in the oven, shall He not much more clothe you, O ye of little faith!"

So God clothes us more beautifully; He gives us beautiful nature, divine traits in grace and shapes, and forms us with the fine touch of grace and mercy. He weaves sublime feelings into our soul; why do we not trust His loving art? Do our surroundings and the many different failures frighten us? Oh, yes, the beautiful can be spoiled and beauty made void, but this should not disturb us; in spite of dry stalk and leaf the flowers of the meadow open in the sunshine! Let us carry our treasure, which is God, in our heart and experience His grace; we will have dew, blossom, oil, scent, upon our soul; but we will also guard this flower and cherish it more than Solomon and all the pomp of history, for behold, we are more than these!

(d) " *Behold the birds of the air, for they neither sow, nor do they reap.*" Behold the soaring bird, the favoured one of nature dressed in festive garb; it makes use of earth and existence to be able to rise and soar. To rise . . . to become filled with grace . . . to pray. But soaring and flight demand much energy. What a magnificent sight the eagle is, swimming in the heights of the sky! What is it therefore we need? (1) We have to emancipate the soul by the glowing love of the spiritual. To love, so that we should not be depressed even if worries torment us. (2) To educate ourselves and others so that we should have but small needs. This is how Jesus educated His Apostles and yet He asked them: Have ye suffered need in anything? Ye have not, have ye? (3) We need great trust and reassurance in God; we must frequently rejoice in the words of the Psalm: " Who lives in the help of the Sublime, remains in the protection of the God of Heaven."

THE COMMAND TO LOVE OUR ENEMIES

" Pray for them that calumniate you. And to him that striketh thee on the one cheek, offer also the other. . . . And if you love them that love you, what thanks are to you? For sinners also love those that love them." (*Luke* vi. 28.)

(*a*) In the physical world there are sources of strength ; let there be also in the moral one; such a source of strength is the will, which wishes the good and the noble, which endeavours to achieve an aim, creates order and balance, vanquishes obstacles and smooths differences away, in a word a spring of strength, light and heat, a healing spring. We should carry about with us this tranquillising order and balance and creative force. Let us leave ourselves behind and practise good ; let us love, raise, and inspire. If ye love only those who love you, ye are not men of morality, but are merely subject to the law of action and reaction ; this is what sinners, non-spiritual men, also do ; ye shall love where ye are not loved ; then will ye become suns, healing springs, healing herbs ; this is when ye give something from out of yourselves. Behold, what nobility : to give and do something that is not barely reaction and mechanism.

(*b*) *" And if you do good to them who do good to you, what thanks are to you ? "* Then ye are mere material, weight, quantity ; there is no soul in you. Therefore we have not barely to react, but to be souls, that is to take the initiative. To do such to those who are repugnant, so as to lift them ; let us seek them and win them. Let us want to be of use to others to-day with all our heart ; let us want to do them some service and find pleasure in it.

(c) " *Judge not : and you shall not be judged. Condemn not : and you shall not be condemned. Forgive : and you shall be forgiven.*" This command should be obeyed from the point of view of positive spiritual strength and creative goodwill. It is not the advice of foolish simplicity, which says " Amen " to everything. We see the faults of others, but do not make them a stumbling block for ourselves ; their clumsiness and offence should not be a dead-weight upon our soul from which our inner world becomes rough and obstinate. Oh no, we are filled with positive electricity, we rise and are capable of enduring man and of promoting his good. Otherwise we should have to suffer for our own unwilling, pessimistic and therefore suffering soul. Give us liberty, O Lord, from inner deformations.

(d) " *Give : and it shall be given to you : good measure and pressed down and shaken together and running over shall they give into your bosom.*" He whose soul is active and energetic and is educated for positive effects, he who does not only wish to suffer, groan, and complain in the world, but wishes to be sunshine and forest, brook, meadow, and healing wayside grass, he is the one to whom shall be given good and overflowing measure of life, cordiality, consolation, and joy.

THE BLIND CANNOT LEAD THE BLIND

" *And he spoke also to them a similitude : Can the blind lead the blind ? Do they not both fall into the ditch ?* " (*Luke* vi. 39.)

(a) The blind are those who do not believe and hope, who have no sunshine, those who cannot lead, educate and raise. Likewise those who are dazzled by their immediate surroundings and are prevented by custom, tradition, and human considerations from looking into infinity—these, too, cannot lead. Just as those who are bewitched by the lovely body and beautiful earth, and who overcloud and cover the inner light by these things and forget the soul, these, too, cannot lead. They shall lead who see, who do not look into a fog, who are free, who are spirit and life ; not the pessimist, the Pharisee, not the epicure, but " one is your master," the seeing, glorious Son-of-God, and if we also wish to lead, we have to become like Him.

(b) " The disciple is not above his master : but every one shall be perfect, if he be as his master." If you choose lowly masters and take their actions for standards, then in the tracks of bunglers you will be awkward and clumsy. If we are to mould life and soul, then let us take the most Sublime for example ; that is why God became man. Jesus is not a Jew-type, not a classic, not of the first century ; Jesus is eternal, " yesterday and to-day." The contemplating, thinking man somehow always rises from out of the time ; the Saints all stand above their times and live eternal life. Therefore our master is not Kant, not Goethe, not Wagner, not Nietzsche ; " excelsior " is our motto. The soul needs an infinite horizon ; Christ gives this.

(c) " And why seest thou the mote in thy brother's eye : but the beam that is in thine own eye thou considerest not ? " Behold the picture of the instinctive man who is made for outward show and is as yet unconscious of himself. Because of his instincts he attends to the exterior, and he has not yet got an emancipated consciousness which contemplates himself. He is not yet an individual that can view himself as an object ; he does not see inwardly, only outwardly, therefore this is not real consciousness. He sees always others and the mote that is in others ; he does not see himself, even when there are beams, that is great faults, in his soul. What pitiful clowns and, if they mean it seriously, what clumsy hair-splitters. Jesus sees the crippled soul-world, these dwarf-people, and wakens them ; He wants to raise these shrivelled figures and to smoothe the creased, wrinkled souls. We do not seek to be hair-splitting, petty judges, but beautiful, noble, upright souls and to i.·fluence others with the weight of our own worth and virtue.

THE NARROW GATE AND THE BROAD WAY

" *Enter ye in at the narrow gate : for wide is the gate and broad is the way that leadeth to destruction : and many there are who go in thereat.*" (*Matt.* vii. 13.)

(*a*) There are many who walk the broad way ; they are those who do not discipline themselves and who follow instinctive nature. For this no strength, struggle, or endeavour is needed. Who wishes to be unclean, untidy, lazy, unwilling, unfriendly, sour, bitter, malignant, has only to let himself go . . . broad is the way. He who follows his instincts and dulls his conscience, who does not control his coarseness, also walks the broad way. What a beast-track this is ! The tracks of the Lord Jesus are not to be found here ; neither does smiling beauty walk these ways ; the way leads among swamps and burnt walls of rock, by the wayside there is nowhere a flower, nowhere a cross. In our mind we see and hear, as if the devil were

driving herds of chained men in front of him; prisoners
walk the broad way. What a disgusting, loathsome way
it is; dark and muddy, it leads to the grave and to hell.

(b) " *How narrow is the gate and strait is the way that leadeth
to life : and few there are that find it!* " This is what is written
upon the signpost: I am the way. This way is narrow,
but magnificent; it mounts continually, and if we start
upon it sunshine and fresh breeze is found there; its
borders are full of healing herbs; pine forests, dewy
flowers, and springs are by the wayside. One cannot
walk upon it with a quantity of baggage and comforts,
but if we free ourselves of these, it is easy going. Sin does
not walk upon this way, neither that dark, sad shadow of
worries which does not know the Father. The sufferers,
the sick, and those who are dying, are taken care of by
God's glorious angels on this way. But how few find this
sublime way! Why? Resolution and determination are
needed if we are to make for " the mounts of God "; but
if we have done so we are no more afraid, and the higher
we mount the more our heart is filled with joy.

(c) " *Strive to enter by the narrow gate.*" (*Luke* xiii. 24.)
In Greek it says: " ἀγωνίζεσθε "; struggle for this
entrance as if in your death-agony. We have to keep
ourselves strictly in hand. We must make every effort
to compel ourselves to enter the narrow way, to keep
strictly to the law, to force ourselves to discipline our
passions and inclinations, to cultivate self-denial and
readiness for sacrifice, " *corde magno et animo volenti,*" with
a willing soul. Let us ask ourselves if we are not lazy in
the mornings when rising, or slow and slack in accomplishing our duties?

WARNING AGAINST FALSE PROPHETS

" *Beware of false prophets, who come to you in the clothing of sheep, but inwardly they are ravening wolves.*" (*Matt.* vii. 15.)

(*a*) Many prophets walk amongst us. Let us beware lest externals mislead us; lest the sheep's clothing cover a wolf-like soul. There are some who wear the nimbus of art, philosophy, education, fame, and literary excellence; some ignore God with philosophical tranquillity; or laugh at believers with audacious bravado of language and dazzling ideas; others seek with great love of humanity the new type of success and happiness, and overflood the world with half-truths. There are some who while preaching dark resignation, offer the "real" Gospel to the world. Knowledge, art, refinement, elegance, nobility, position recommend them; but beware, who denies Christ tears your souls to pieces. They tear and pick to pieces—they want the world without God, Christ without miracles, Gospel without Church, Church without Pope, men without souls, souls without immortality . . . behold the vultures! How much refinement we find in society, and what indifference towards the Church and the Sacrament of the Altar. There we find much wit and attention to every branch of knowledge, but dark, shameful ignorance concerning faith and soul-life. Chivalry and nobility at every step, but an apparently diabolical hatred of faith and grace. There is little good and much evil; what we want is the wholly good.

(*b*) "*By their fruits you shall know them. Do men gather grapes of thorns, or figs of thistles? Even so every good tree bringeth forth good fruit.*" We judge the doctrine by its fruit. The fruit of the true soul is a warm, shining consciousness, peace and confidence, joy and love, trust and courage towards all that is good. " God with me " and " God in me." The grace of Christ gives us the internal, beautiful world which externally also is strong, just, and self-sacrificing. Do not let us follow doctrines by which our eyes, meant for the infinite, become over-clouded—or by which our strength becomes crippled in the dark and we feel no vocation to fight against every evil—or our disposition becomes soft and passive, or hard and cruel. And we have to judge our various tendencies likewise, for sometimes a worldly and reckless, or a sensual and dark, untrusting spirit gains the upper hand in our soul. We have to be strong, brave, trusting children of God; all that darkens and disturbs, and robs the peace of our soul we will strictly scrutinize.

(c) " *Every tree that bringeth not forth good fruit shall be cut down and shall be cast into the fire.*" We must cut out the evil root. With the same interest with which we clip the trees of our garden, we must break off the evil tendencies of the soul. It cannot be done by any axe and shears method, but our darkened, suffering, em-bittered, groping soul must be brought to see the spirit of the one real Prophet, the Spirit of Christ. Let us oppose glory, joy, sweet strength, and confidence to darkness, suffering, and depression. Brooding souls must be shown the joy of holiness. This we have to show in our own selves to our brothers who listen to strange prophets. In ourselves also we must cut out the evil roots; the sensual, hard, selfish, dark tendencies; we wish to be good trees; Christ has planted us; we wish to develop and flourish according to Him and bring forth fruit accordingly; therefore we will not spare the bad, predominating nature in us.

WE MUST DO THE WILL OF OUR FATHER

" *Not every one that saith to me, Lord, Lord, shall enter into the kingdom of heaven : but he that doth the will of my Father who is in heaven."* (*Matt.* vii. 21.)

(*a*) We love Jesus if we live in His grace. Grace is the " *semen Dei*," the germ of God ; divine life given as latent force. This force becomes released ; this germ germinates, and from the God-germ the supernatural man develops. This actual, supernatural store of strength is the treasure of Jesus in us, He gives it to us ; where this is lacking He has neither place nor home. These supernatural forces come to our consciousness in the inspirations of faith, in the strength of conviction, in the magnanimity of feeling, in attachments, longings, and devotion. The divine feeling full of grace comes from the grace of God. This is why Jesus lays so much stress on grace. What can we do therefore without grace ? How are we to develop if the germ of God, the strength of Jesus, is not in us ? Love of grace and horror of sin are the heart-beat of Jesus in us !

Let us not say that we comprehend Jesus, if there is no germ of God in us, if we do not value grace. The chief care of the deep, serious, Christian consciousness is that it should be in the state of sanctifying grace.

(*b*) We love Jesus if we develop the life of grace to conscious, sincere friendship. Jesus is our friend, and we not only do not tear ourselves away from Him, we do not even wish to sadden Him, so near He is to us. In our eyes, no one is more lovely than He, no one warmer, more glorious, and intimate ; His personality possesses us and keeps us prisoner. Is it therefore a wonder that the world does not cool our ardour and lead us astray ? Is it surprising that we do not forget Him, and that in this unity of the soul we do not purposely commit even venial sins ? Such developed, intimate love walks in the way of humility, for it is a devoted, clinging, tender feeling. The lamb clings to the good shepherd, longing for his gentleness ; it crouches beside him and expectantly waits for the touch and caress of his hand ; it shows its gratitude by its happiness. How could it offend the good shepherd ? Offend him ? Why ? This would be unhappiness, the violation of our most tender feelings ! It does not wish to offend, but to love ! *Diliges dominum Deum tuum !* With the feeling of this faithful friendship it is easy to accomplish our duties punctually, to be of goodwill, not to lie, to be lenient, prudent, and indulgent. Let us endeavour to form our whole life from morning till night according to Christ ; to lift our family and business duties to a divine standard by way of our feelings, and to answer life's small demands with an ardent, lofty soul.

(c) Bishop, prophet, miracle-worker—anyone can be lost if he relies solely on the grace attaching to his vocation ; everyone has to heighten and augment perfection and saintliness in himself. What a great trouble and scandal it is when the " chosen ones " are not holy ; of no avail are the " Lord, Lord," upon their lips and the symbol of God upon their robes ; the sublime Lord looks for divine value below the brilliant robes. It concerns us all, therefore, that we should not trust the enthusiasm of zeal, when we do not serve the Lord by our actions. Let us do the will of God and measure our perfection accordingly ; in this way will we be accurate judges of ourselves. If we seek for perfection in tears, emotion, and sentimentality, and ignore deeds, that is pure self-delusion.

THE CENTURION OF CAPHARNAUM

" *And when he had entered into Capharnaum, there came to him a centurion, beseeching him, Lord, my servant lieth at home sick of the palsy and is grievously tormented. And Jesus saith to him : I will come and heal him. And the centurion making answer, said : Lord, I am not worthy that thou shouldst enter under my roof.*" (*Matt.* viii. 5.)

(*a*) The feeling of the presence of Sublimity penetrates the soul of the centurion ; he feels that he stands before a supernatural power which creates, heals, enriches, and makes happy. Before this power he becomes so small ; therefore he pays homage. It is a great happiness to be able to pay homage, that is, to recognize the Sublime. This is what we are meant for, to turn our soul towards this Sublimity, to seek its traces and to recognize it with reverence. Our soul feels God as our eyes feel sunshine. In many ways this soul of ours becomes coarse and dumb ; let us awaken it and render it nobler. Let it realize that every form of existence is a revelation of God, and that God is manifested in Nature, in the flowers and in the sunset. All this is a veil from under which beauty and spirituality peep forth. We are indeed His relations, for we feel, recognize, and embrace him. In us the Lord is present, He hides Himself in the foliage of our ideas and feelings, as formerly in the shades of Paradise, and we

call the Lord : My God where are Thou ? Thou art
near to me, art Thou not ? Thou art in me !

(*b*) I am not worthy that Thou shouldst enter, but if
Thou deignest to enter, my heart is filled with homage,
joy and happiness. Jesus enters willingly. God is poured
into our soul, as the sunshine into the forest ; He wishes
to enter every heart. This is what the Scripture indicates :
Behold I stand at the door and knock. He came. He
was not called for ; He came as a beggar who begs for
bread ; as a lover asking for a loving heart ; as a servant
wishing to serve ; as a child sitting at the doorstep of the
parental house ; or as a wanderer. No, no, He is the
great Lord, who walks in disguise ; who came to
strengthen, heal, and render souls happy. He does not
come burgling, but asking for admittance ; if we wish it,
He enters. God does not force us ; He does not thrust
Himself and His graces upon us ; but let us realize that
He longs for us, knocks at the door of our heart ; He
waits and stands before our gate. And He perseveres and
does not depart ! Oh, what sweet, strong love !

(*c*) To realize this must mean the opening of door, gate,
and window. In opening door and window we are to have
humble faith, warm longing and fine sense. The noble soul
cultivates the nearness of God, His presence, and union
with Him ; it wishes to be divine in feeling, and in the
acquiescence in His holy will ; it applies itself seriously to
making an abode for the Lord, and preparing a lovely
home in itself. Therefore it begins by bringing its
inner soul world into order. The more man is diligent
in this, the more he feels that God is with him. And
whatever happens—whether he mingles with other men,
or his hands become rough from labour—the divine

intuition, the sweet secrecy of love will not forsake him. Let us faithfully make use of God's graces, and we will find that God willingly makes His abode in us.

HEALING OF A LEPER

" *And when he was come down from the mountain, great multitudes followed him. And behold ! a leper came and adored him, saying : Lord, if thou wilt, thou canst make me clean.*" (*Matt.* viii. 1.)

(*a*) Before Jesus stands the symbol of sin, the leper, with that dreadful malady, that living death that sucks out the vital fluid from the body of the sick one, eats away his joy of life, and renders him horrible and loathsome. Facing this stands the " *speciosus inter filios hominum,*" the loveliest of men. Strong, beautiful, sublime is the Lord, but He does not disdain the wretched one, He is compassionate towards him ; He sees misery and is merciful ; world-sorrow does not descend upon His soul, but strength of action with which He gives life and beauty. This is Christ ! One must needs be an iconoclast like Nietzsche, to regard this sublime figure of Christ as a slave-type.

(*b*) " *And Jesus stretching forth his hand, touched him.*" He has touches with which He purifies and shapes ; each touch of His is grace. He shapes His image in us. Sometimes He touches us in such a way that our heart becomes contracted, at other times He makes our heart quicken, at times He raises, at others humiliates. These are the works of God's hands and arms. He fears not the leper, His hand will not be harmed. We also live in hospital ;

we breathe the air of plague; unbelief, irresolution, cowardice, selfishness, and cruelty surround us. We also are in contact with sin; we have to deal with sinful, distorted souls. The hand of Jesus is wanted for this, a pure hand; a strong spirit is wanted, which abhors sin. We have to descend from the heights of pure, noble feelings, or rather we have to remain in that pure region and bend down to raise and heal. Only those help in this world who bend down to it from the height, so as to raise it.

(c) "*I will. Be thou made clean.*" This is the absolute, imposing will; to that there is no obstacle, no hindrance. This will creates and heals. This is miraculous. In the physical world He gives orders with this lordly, divine will; but in the moral world God stops with respect at the threshold of free-will and demands: Dost thou wish to become cleansed in thy soul, to become better, to resemble Divinity? If thou willest, then I also will it. Thou art sovereign, but thou art subject to one law; thou hast to will.

(d) "*And forthwith his leprosy was cleansed. And Jesus saith to him : See thou tell no man.*" Jesus teaches us selflessness and pure, clean intentions. Let us work for God, not for fame. Do not let us lead men to ourselves, but to God. As soon as we seek our own interests, grace forsakes us. For we have secret interests and personal vanities. The clear, pure intention is a great perfection, therefore do not let us presume too soon that our intentions are pure. Those who are soon " clear " with themselves, have no idea about the depths of the soul out of which our feelings, moods, and inclinations arise. Discipline and purification must touch these depths.

(e) "*But go, shew thyself to the priest and offer the gift which Moses commanded.*" Jesus does not injure the framework of positive religion and does not place us in the realm of subjective thought. He keeps in view the just demands of authority and wishes that we should respect them. Jesus did not reject religious forms, but He did not wish soulless, empty forms. We also respect the law, and keep to the rules; but we fill them with spiritual content and cherish the freedom of the soul.

JESUS RAISES THE YOUNG MAN OF NAIM

"*And it came to pass afterwards, that he went into a city that is called Naim . . . and when he came nigh to the gate of the city, behold a dead man was carried out, the only son of his mother : and she was a widow . . .*" (*Luke* vii. 11.)

(a) "Naim" means "pleasant." What a contrast between the name of the town and this sad procession ! The world and life are each a "Naim," we have pleasant places in it but there are also sad processions; we meet not only brides but sorrowful widows also. By the light of faith we see even sadder sights; we meet dead souls whose grave is eternal damnation. We must not allow these shadows to darken our spiritual life; we must not lose spiritual confidence and strength. Disuniting forces must not be permitted to tear asunder the symmetry of our soul. Our centre is God; we trust Him and know that He is good; we also know that our soul is a source of light, a burning lamp. We too believe the words of Dostoievski, who wrote from his prison in Siberia : "Here too one can live an ideal life." All and everything is good for us that is good for Thee, O Lord ; nothing is too late, nothing too early. The youth who died early can die in an ideal way, and his widowed mother can likewise live ideally even in her veil of mourning, if she lives in Thee and from Thee, my Lord.

(*b*) " *Being moved with mercy towards her, he said to her : Weep not.*" We have to feel the suffering and pain of souls, then mercy and deep compassion will awake in us also. We do not feel and experience the misery of souls, we do not weep for our brothers, though their soul be dead and is being carried to the grave. . . . St. Peter walked among us with such deep compassion and animated us to have mercy and assume the feelings of Jesus. Weep for thy brothers, pray for them, draw them on gently, and lead them to the Lord. Let us say with Esdra : " I sat down weeping and complaining, many days I fasted and prayed ; I beseech Thee, Lord, hearken to the prayer of thy servant with which I have prayed to-day for the sins of thy servants with which they sinned against thee. . . ."

(*c*) " *And he came near and touched the bier.*" We have to go to the dead, we have to take part in the world's commotion. We must not follow in the footsteps of Cain, who did not want to be the keeper of his brother, but in those of Paul, who preached to the " world." We never approach the Lord Jesus so much as when we throw the sun-rays of faith into darkened souls. Let great love inspire us towards mankind, great faith in the natural goodness of the soul, energy and manliness, and let us always endeavour to raise humanity.

(*d*) " *And he that was dead sat up and began to speak.*" His bandages fell off, his eyes opened, the soul of life pervaded him and breathed upon his face the warmth of love and joy ; he who was a corpse sat up and showed that he lived. We also live . . . live in spite of coffins, funerals, and graves ; we live and do not decay ! The youth looked around him ; how much love and gratitude there was in his glance towards Jesus ! He had experienced the terrible struggle between life and death ; on the brink of death the sun of life had shone in his eyes : *lux orta est illi.* He saw Christ, as no one of those who surrounded them. Oh, how he watched this " *dominus*," how fresh, strong and divine the Lord of life and death was to his eyes ! *Vita, dulcedo, vis et fortitudo !* Strong was this Lord, by His strength the youth now lives and sits up ; death is weak compared to this strength, and the encouraging glance of the Lord penetrates into his soul ; it says : **Live !** Why shouldst thou die ? Be not afraid, it is I !

(*e*) This is how we often are. Our mind languishes ; darkness and death surround us. The more we " learn," the darker our world becomes, for we do not find a way out. The way out is the strong life which streams into us from God ; from the field of " great deeds " where Christ beckons to us !

(*f*) " *And began to speak.*" " Lord, open my lips, and my mouth will sing Thy glory." The lips of one who is awakened by Jesus open to glory, worship, and confession of faith. And how sweetly prayer flowed from this frozen heart, from these awakening lips, as perfume from the blossoming flowers. What was said by the dumb lips was death, bitterness, anxiety ; what these opened lips say is joy and song. How many there are who are not capable of speaking, for they are dark, dumb, and bitter. Oh, if the Lord would only open these lips ! From a bitter heart cruel words flow, but from a loving soul, sweet song.

(g) " *And he gave him to his mother.*" To her who bore
and fed him, but could not save him from death ; for this
motherly love does not suffice ; it would need divine
strength. Now Jesus returns the raised youth to his
mother, who took him in the same way as of old, for she
bore him with pain then, and now also she received him
with pain, that he might all the more belong to her and
that she might rejoice all the more. What a thankful
glance she must have cast upon the Lord. " Oh, great
Lord, sweet Lord," she must have said, " Thou who giveth
life in death ; thanks be to Thee ! " Divine strength
awakens and gives back souls to the Church. The good
mother, the Church, knows this well and is thankful to the
apostolic souls who help to awaken her dead ones to life.
" *Nunc in isto cognovi, quoniam vir Dei es tu.*" This is how
she recognizes the apostolic soul in her sons. (3 *Kings*
xvii. 24.) Let us work so as to give the Mother-Church
joy. She bore us ; let not her heart be embittered by so
many dead souls.

JOHN SENDS TWO OF HIS DISCIPLES TO JESUS

" *Now when John had heard in the prison the works of Christ,
sending two of his disciples, he said to him : Art thou he that
art to come, or look we for another ?* " (*Matt.* ii. 2, 3.)

(a) St. John sends his disciples to Jesus, that they should
believe in Him and not be averse to Him. For himself he
asks no deliverance. He serves Christ in his fetters and
carries the weight of the kingdom of God upon his soul.
Full of conviction, he endeavours to fulfil his task to the
end. Let everyone do the will of God in the position

and state where the strife of life has placed him and let him not expect miracles, even if he forfeit his head. To us God also may send bitter experiences whilst to others perhaps a better lot falls. No matter. We go our ways and say : Thy will be done, and be Thou glorified in me !

(b) St. John sends his disciples to Christ. Every master has to send his disciples to Christ. We also strive towards Him and send others to Him. Inasmuch as His spirit is in me, I will be a light to others. To us the teaching of Jesus is absolute law ; as soon as we take part in accomplishing it, we immediately feel that strength pours into us and by this strength we are the successful teachers of others. We long for as much as possible of the spirit of Jesus, so that in this way we can also do good to others.

(c) "*Art thou he that art to come, or look we for another ?*" Those who have not viewed Christ in the light of eternal life and saving love, continually ask : Art thou He, art Thou He, whom we expect ? They do not seize the divine in its most beautiful and best form, but fall weakly under their doubts. We have already questioned sufficiently, and all say that it is He whom we await. Therefore let us wait no longer, but experience Him. We also say : Thou art He whom we expect, Thou " the loveliest amongst the sons of men." What else could we want ? Now let us live and act according to Him.

ANSWER OF JESUS TO JOHN'S DISCIPLES

" *And Jesus making answer said to them : Go and relate to John what you have heard and seen. The blind see, the lame walk, the lepers are cleansed, the deaf hear, the dead rise again, the poor have the gospel preached to them.*" (*Matt.* ii. 4, 5.)

(*a*) The Lord Jesus proves Himself by actions ; as if He would say : I heal people, I do good for them, for I love them ; I brought good and with it persecute evil, which strangles life ; but my mission is not to heal the blind, the deaf, and lame. I am no doctor ; with these miracles I only prove that God sent me, so that I might lead the people in the way of God. Not in healing, but in the faith placed in Me, is the real good, says Jesus, and by this faith it is that heaven comes to ye all. Ye have not to learn from me to heal the blind and the deaf, but ye have to learn to enclose the kingdom of God in your hearts. All this is for the comfort of your souls, which comfort ye find in Me. Be therefore attached to Me with the gratitude of the healed soul and with the freshness and strength of the healthy.

(*b*) Jesus is the great Benefactor ; He Himself is the greatest good, and His actions are the outpourings of His bountiful heart. His doctrine is goodness. It makes barbarism cease and renders men nobler. He lifts marriage to the height of divine union and makes the bond of hearts unbreakable. He educates the children of God in the school, and inspires men to honour ideal motives. He keeps men to the accomplishment of the duties of their position and crowns all this with the blessing of holy love. Oh, how good all this is ! We have to have great trust in the doctrines of the Lord Jesus, and to endeavour that we, as well as others, should have for all our actions the supernatural motives of the Gospel.

(*c*) What a great good is the example of Christ, this incarnate Gospel, in which depth, sublimity, necessity, longing, and suffering is all shaped in one sweet life, and comes towards us and looks into our eyes and says :

Brother, here I am, be thou also like Me ; then thou wilt
also do wonders. It is a beggarly behaviour to say great
things and live small ones. " *Magna vivere, non magna dicere
christianum est.*" Christ-like feeling and action are great
life indeed. Let us read and meditate upon the Gospel ;
let us go to the Sacraments. In our worthily partaking of
the Sacraments, light is poured into darkened souls, and
a sense for the fineness of spiritual life will be awakened.
Let us avoid every wilful sin ; let us cleanse our intentions
and let us endeavour to start all our actions from as
conscious and as noble motives as possible.

JESUS PRAISES JOHN THE BAPTIST. I

" *And when they went their way, Jesus began to say to the
multitudes concerning John : What went ye out into the desert
to see ? A reed shaken with the wind ? . . . A man clothed in
soft garments ? . . . But what went you out to see ? A
prophet ? Yea, I tell you, and more than a prophet.*"
(*Matt.* xi. 7, 8, 9.)

We read of this sublime praise with great emotion.
The heart of Jesus burns with fire when it sees such a
glorious soul, it loves and honours it with the heat of its
enthusiasm. See the one who praises, and what a praise !
The man of the wilderness is no weed but an oak, and the
pomp of kings is pale beside the dignity of his soul. This
oak, this man, is more than a king even if he wears a girdle
of camel-hair !

(*a*) Oak, not weed ! The world, human considerations,
fashion, moods—these swaying reeds whisper not in his
soul ; in him reign principles, character, consistency, and

force of will. His faith, disposition, ardour, and actions do not change according to impressions. He seems hard and cruel, but this hardness and cruelty is the consistency of his principles, and the sweet and sublime character of his soul. Principles are cruel in so far as they must have their way in everything ; they are sublime and at the same time they penetrate into the smallest details of life and feelings ; they urge the right, that is they exact that life should be worked out to its smallest particulars with unity and harmony. These principles are like the sunshine which shines from the heavens down to us, but then weaves itself into every leaf and blade of grass, and burns into the gleaming back of the lizard. Oh, do not let us spare the capriciousness of our changing, wavering temper, the tyranny of our moods, and the heaviness of our soul lost in clouds and apathy. This is what makes our inner world become ugly, inconsistent, and unreliable ; let us strive upwards to the sunshine, to lofty aims and principles ; up to the consciousness of the value of our souls, and to God who surrounds us, reveals Himself in us, up to the sublimity of the Gospel and the faith of the Eucharist ! Down below, the reed-bed of the heart's feelings waves ; we know that the reeds are not forests of oak, and whilst they are reeds they will sway to and fro, but we will not sway to and fro with them, we will form our soul and character according to resolute principles. Even if we have no mood for it, we will and act ; even if we have no sweet ardour, we do homage ; even if our soul becomes darkened, we keep on in the direction we have set ourselves. In such souls principles develop to such a power that they also touch the feelings, and principles, feelings, and will co-operate uniformly. Of such a soul the words of Scripture truly say : " The Lord called

thy name, a plentiful olive tree, fair, fruitful and beautiful."
(*Jer.* xi. 16.) " I will make Him a pillar in the temple of
my God " ; " because thou hast kept the word of my
patience, I will also keep thee from the hour of temptation."
(*Apo.* iii. 12, 10.)

(*b*) St. John the Baptist is an independent, mighty soul.
Kingly palaces, soft, lace garments, carpets and sofas do
not impress him.   Nay, more, he has an aversion for
them ; he sees few souls in that soft life.   In the roughness
of his camel-hair garb he depicts the soul's struggle for
liberty.   This is the garb of his king ; it is the smock of
the strong labourer working in the vineyard of the Lord.
Do penance ; let the soul expand in thee, for the kingdom
of heaven suffers violence !   Let us raise our soul by
penance and self-denial.   In self-denial let us insist on the
spirit taking the flesh !   Let us do everything for our
personality that makes it more beautiful and stronger.
Pro libertate !   Let us find pleasure in the discipline of our
eyes, our imaginations, and our instincts !   Oh, let our
eyes open, that we may see, see in the noble, sinless, pure
conscience our God, our treasure, our all.   Let us work
upon it so that this conscience should be a purified,
crystallized, deep, shining, magical lake, surrounded by
blossoming shores, mystical forests, and mountains of
eternity in which heaven should not only be mirrored
but submerged !   In the beauty of the believing and loving
soul and in its strength, the nearness of God becomes
manifest.

(*c*) Such a soul is necessarily filled with God, inspired
by Him ; it is the soul of a prophet.   The heights of
eternity are his home, and when he descends from there,
one can feel that he belongs to the heights, that he is the

angel of God. "This is he, of whom it is written:
"Behold, I send my angel before thy face, who shall
prepare thy way before thee." (*Luke* vii. 27.) The grace
of God accompanies him and he renders innumerable
souls happy. God walks in his footsteps and he becomes
the precursor of Christ, "he prepares the way of the Lord."
He encourages, teaches, and raises men, so that they should
approach God; his whole personality, ardour, and spirit
are enrolled in this great service that in our consciousness
there may be more of God, that is, more of the ideas of
God, more of His light, more of trust, of the strength of
life, of beauty of the soul, more of the agility of the soul
and more of youth; so that we may rejoice more and
more deeply, rest more securely, be more directly in
contact with God, and come upon Him in ourselves.
Souls, these are the touches of God—our sweetest joys.

JESUS PRAISES JOHN THE BAPTIST. II

*"But what went you out for to see? A prophet? Yea, I tell
you, and more than a prophet. For this is he of whom it is
written: Behold I send my angel before thy face, who shall
prepare thy way before thee."* (*Matt.* xi. 9.)

(*a*) The prophet is like the mountain, he is a prominent
man; the man of great ideas and enthusiasm. On him
rests the sunshine of the thoughts of God; he directs the
clouds of the spiritual world and makes the blessings of
heaven incline earthwards. Streams break forth from it . . .
he breathes cool, forest air. How does the prophet
become a prophet? Isaiah has written of it in his fourth
and fifth chapters. He has to become purified; the word
and grace of God burn him, and the soul of God fills him

with courage. We also will become purified, we will be brave, we will walk in prophet-like tracks. . . . And if the doubting, small-hearted world around us suffers, then we say : This is how apostates from God, depth, and ardour fare. All the more we wish to attach ourselves to Thee, that we may become prophets, that is, men of God. O Lord, our sweet treasure, speak to us, we beg Thee speak to us.

(b) St. John is greater than a prophet, for he is " the messenger of God." He lives for His cause and is not led by self-interest ; he is a true servant in all, he who puts his whole life into this service ; he has wings, that is, he possesses an aptness of soul for accomplishing the will of his Lord. This is how we have to experience spiritual values. We have strength, God gives it, and we do not doubt it for a second. The most beautiful thing on earth is the purified soul with confidence in God ; this beauty and harmony we have to enjoy. This feeling is necessary and it not only does not make us vain, but on the contrary it confirms us in virtue.

(c) Finally, St. John is the man of God, who loves greatly, and by his great love he takes no notice of the non-loving world, but pours out the warmth of his soul, and turns others also on to these ways. He brings the grace of dawn to generations ; of many such fiery souls we are able to say : " Who is it that comes towards us, as the dawn ? " St. Francis of Assisi, St. Elizabeth, are like the dawn ! A wonderful, new spring made its way into Italy in the tracks of St. Francis ; the forest and meadow became beautiful ; the grove was filled with the twittering of birds ; sunshine and flowers turn men to song. Why was all this ? Because they saw the world differently ;

they saw it in another light; they saw it through the exhalation of love . . . the soul of the prophet awakens souls, it opens the eyes of the soul, of the mind; he teaches souls to sing. Oh, beautiful, sweet soul; why shouldst thou be strange to us? Does not the flower blossom in spite of the soot of our factories? Does not the lark sing although our machines rattle? Why should only our heart forget its sweet depths? Men love and do not forget to live in spite of machines and factory chimneys.

MARY MAGDALEN

"*And behold a woman that was in the city, a sinner, when she knew that he sat at meat in the Pharisee's house, brought an alabaster box of ointment. And standing behind at his feet, she began to wash his feet with tears and wiped them with the hairs of her head and kissed his feet and anointed them with the ointment.*" (*Luke* vii. 37.)

(*a*) Many paid homage to Magdalen and maybe they knelt at her feet also, but her heart was not satisfied with this; for though formerly it thirsted for pleasures, now it seeks pure morality, peace; it seeks God. Magdalen was far from God when she was being adored and found pleasure in it; but now it is she who adores the Lord and therefore she feels how contemptible are the lusts of mankind. She saw in Jesus sublimity, strength, and beauty; Jesus looked at her and from this glance she awoke, she recovered and shuddered. Jesus spread His graces over her and in their light she was dirty, ugly, and loathsome, but this same grace drew her on and induced her to humble herself, and taught her to weep. Oh, pure, sublime soul of Jesus, Thy glance is like the sun, Thy approach is like the breath of the forest, Thy person is like the height of eternity, enlighten, help, and lift up the low, sensual world.

(b) Magdalen does not even glance at the world; she does not care about anyone, but throws herself at the feet of her Lord. How she despises the world! Were she pure as a lily, she would be able to forget the world on account of the divine love which burns in her heart. How much more then, when she wishes to avenge this lost purity! Oh, it is sweet for her to forget and despise, sweet to weep and mourn! Though Magdalen walks the path of humility, her steps are decided; she weeps, but her soul is strong! Now it is that she really sacrifices her heart and does it for her passionate love, for she throws herself at the feet of Jesus, bathes His feet with her tears and wipes them with her hair, and she spurns and loathes the sinful world. This is the sweetest and holiest revenge, which revenges the soul and lost grace, and which makes satisfaction to God and itself. The longing for satisfaction should fire us. Oh, let us make up for the offences against God. Holy, just penitence is this.

(c) And what does Jesus do? Lovingly He looks at the zeal of Magdalen, and rejoices in her repentance. One after the other He reviews her merits and treats them with His divine favour. "Seest thou this woman? I entered into thine house, thou gavest me no water for my feet: but she has washed my feet with tears and wiped them with the hairs of her head." Such a humble, expiating spirit is what I need. "Thou gavest me no kiss: but this woman since the time I came in hath not ceased to kiss my feet." What I need is a friendly, intimate reception. "My head with oil thou didst not anoint: but this woman hath anointed my feet with ointment," she showed how much she values me. "Wherefore I say unto thee, her sins which are many, are forgiven; for she loved much." He who loves Jesus with a true heart and with enthusiasm and ardour will win everything from Him: forgiveness, grace, and courage.

JESUS INEXORABLE IN THE FULFILMENT OF HIS MISSION

"And his mother and his brethren came, and, standing without, sent unto him, calling him. And the multitude sat about him. And they say to him: Behold thy mother and thy brethren without seek for thee. And answering them, he said: Who is my mother and my brethren?" (Mark iii. 31.)

(*a*) Jesus preaches, the force of his soul streams from Him, so that He might satisfy the hunger of His brothers. Then He was disturbed, for His mother and His relations wait outside; they came to fetch Him and wished Him to go with them. Jesus is hard; in His vocation He recognizes neither mother nor brothers who would stand in His way. These love Him, He knows that well; but another, higher, commanding love beckons to Him; the spirit opposes flesh and blood, and the spirit has to conquer. There are circumstances when our leniency and exaggerated regard is a sin against the Holy Ghost. On such occasions there must be no talk of persons, but of a principle which opposes God, and which brings us into temptation with the warmth of the flesh and blood. If the salvation of the soul is in peril, every bond has to be broken.

(b) " *And he began to teach them that the Son of man must suffer many things. . . . And Peter taking him, began to rebuke him. Who turning about and seeing his disciples, threatened Peter saying : Go behind me, Satan, because thou savourest not the things that are of God.*" (*Mark* viii. 31.) How sharply the Lord replies ; He answers with the indignation of His soul. Jesus is decided, He wishes to offer His sacrifice ; He wants to go to Jerusalem and to death. But the human feeling in Peter objects to this and he wishes to persuade the Lord to avoid the way of violence. " Get thee behind me," was the answer . . . for then the divine task would be lost and yielding to His enemies, He would not undergo the baptism of fire and blood. If He were to spare Himself all would be lost. In these hard words : " Get thee behind me," we again hear, " I am the Son of God." With us also opposition to evil and the fight with it is no harm, no misfortune, but a divine way and the task of virtue.

(c) " *He that findeth his life shall lose it : and he that shall lose his life for me shall find it.*" (*Matt.* x. 39.) Those who gratify themselves and always act according to their pleasure, those who follow the inclinations of flesh and blood as a guiding principle, think that they have lived and satisfied their pleasure ; but they are wrong ; they have not really understood the real instinct of life ; better than the world and the flesh have we to love the soul, and the soul's instinct of self-preservation has to be stronger than the love of the world, flesh and blood. Strong souls are those who assert the instinct of the self-preservation of the soul above the world and the flesh. The others are weak souls ; the instinct of life is superficial in them ; they build for themselves wretched shelters out of shifting sand. O Lord, let the instinct of strong life and the longing for the preservation of eternal life carry us away and emancipate us. Let this be our guiding star. According to this will we accommodate ourselves, take our measures, and bring our sacrifices!

PARABLE OF THE SOWER

" Behold, the sower went out to sow. And whilst he sowed, some fell by the way side : and the birds of the air came and ate it up. And other some fell upon stony ground, where it had not much earth : and it shot up immediately, because it had no depth of earth. And when the sun was risen, it was scorched. . . . And some fell among thorns : and the thorns grew up and choked it. . . . And some fell upon good ground and brought forth fruit that grew up and increased and yielded, one thirty, another some sixty, and another a hundred." (Mark iv. 3.)

(a) The sower sows ; his seed is the word of God and the impressions of grace, the ideas and feelings of faith spring from it. From out of His hand the seed does not fail ; His grace trembles upon the souls as in a quiet rain the drops upon the boughs ; it shines and trembles as the threads of the cobweb in the autumn field. In the inner world everything is saturated with soul, as nature is saturated with spores and seeds ; all germs of life ; palms, grass, firs, grow from them ; strength and weakness, or beauty and disease. It depends on the heavens, the heat, the capacity ; it depends on the readiness, the freshness, the devotion. O my God, our soul is the earth and Thou art its sower ; plough us, water us, harrow us ; pass along us with Thy prayer-inspiring thoughts, with the sunshine of Thy grace, with the dew of Thy emotion,

with the wind of Thy longing ; give all this to us and say :
soil, my sweet soil, thou wilt not deceive Me !

(*b*) " *Some fell by the way . . .*" The road is broken, but
by wheel-tracks, not furrows. It is trodden by stupid
soles, heels, hoofs ; the world comes and goes upon it.
There are also souls in which the many senseless,
muddy ideas walk in and out, ideas on which various
impressions are reflected. There are souls which are like
the inns or gipsy tents by the wayside ; there we seek in
vain for abstraction, absorption, and contrition ; there
nothing takes root. The birds which peck the seeds of
God are the rash, flighty, flitting ideas. The fitfulness of
the sun, caprice, good or evil humour, peck away the
seeds. We have to recollect ourselves and feel remorse
if we wish the grace of God to bring fruit.

(*c*) " *And other some fell upon stony ground . . .* " " *They
who, when they have heard the word, immediately receive it with
joy. And they have no root. . . .*" This is when there is
aptness for good, but no perseverance, no inner glow ;
when we are enthusiastic, but the enthusiasm has no
fire. " *Humus* " is indeed for fertility and also " *humor.*"
We have to take in the words and forces of God and annex
them ; we have to display an eager resistance against
contrary influences. Let us find pleasure in the strong
and persevering will !

(*d*) " *And he that received the seed among thorns is he that
heareth the word, and the care of this world and the deceitfulness
of riches choketh up the word : and he becometh fruitless.*"
(*Matt.* xiii. 22.) Oh, ye souls full of thorns, where riches
and the worries of pleasure become disfigured, or where
the exciting strife of life, bustling work and bitter poverty

menace . . . the rich forget to struggle ; enjoyment educates low, ignoble frames of mind ; and bitter poverty benumbs the heart. All these are barriers to the perfect development of the soul. Do not give us riches, Lord, but guard us also from poverty ; both are thorns which easily choke the blossoms and foliage of the soul.

(*e*) And what fell on good soil and sucked up the juice of the earth, and awakened in the heat of the heavens and opened its leaves and stretched its stalk and summoned energy, such a one brought forth fruit, thirty, sixty, a hundred-fold, according to the inner capability and external circumstances. And all of it was good. God expects fruit from us also ; He gave much ; we have to live in the knowledge that we would be worthless beings if we did not fructify His graces with all our strength. Let us look into our soul, could we do thirty, sixty, a hundred times as much as we do now ? It is not here a question of multiplicity, but the spirit coming from faith, the noble feeling, ardour and love. Surely we are capable of increasing these !

PARABLE OF THE COCKLE

" *Another parable he proposed to them saying : The kingdom of heaven is likened to a man that sowed good seed in his field. But while men were asleep, his enemy came and over-sowed cockle among the wheat and went his way. . . . And when the blade was sprung up and had brought forth fruit, then appeared also the cockle.*" (*Matt.* xiii. 24.)

(*a*) God " sowed good seed in his field " ; the souls are " His field " ; He loves this field over which so many clouds and shadows, so many blessings and curses have passed. It is a wonderful soil with an unspeakable amount of energy in nature and grace. Such a field are we also ; we are " the field of God " ; our life is a holy ground if we view its destiny and its graces, therefore it shall also be fertile soil ; here we have to live and die ; here it is that we will be rich or poor ; this, our soil, will be our garden of Eden or the desert of our exile. The field of God is our field, we work it, hoe it, weed it, guard and love it ; with interest we watch its fruits, for is it not our field ?

(*b*) " *But while men were asleep, his enemy came.*" Dreams generally occur at night and here they characterize the predominance of the bodily, sensual man ; amidst dream-pictures and vain shadows the spirit becomes benumbed ; it prattles, trifles, and dawdles, but is incapable of strong work, faithful endeavour, and confident strife. It does not guard its " field " and golden fruit. Others also who ought to be guarding the holy fields, such as parents, priests, tutors, teachers, may also sleep. The enemy sleeps not, he comes without being seen. We shiver when upon the holy soil of the soul we see the foot and hand prints of the enemy. The enemy also sows ; words, impressions, examples, scandals, temptations, importunities, desires, attachments, customs, and inclinations are his cockle ; and the chief trouble is that we are asleep and do not notice it ; we do not resist, we make a compromise. What madness to mix cockle among wheat ; to expose the soul to impressions which corrupt and weaken it ! If we cannot avoid receiving such impressions, let us receive them awake, but not in torpor !

(*c*) " *And the servants said to him : Wilt thou then that we go and gather it up ? And he said : No, lest perhaps gathering up the cockle, you root up the wheat also together with it. Suffer both to grow until the harvest . . ."* Cockle and wheat grow together; we feel it. We are sensual and obey with difficulty; we are not very capable of speaking and acting spiritually; our manners are proud, our soul is undisciplined. The worldly, sensual, haughty disposition grows amidst weeds. Let us kill these continually, but at the same time we must not tear out the good; do not let us become exasperated, and accuse ourselves unjustly. Energy and patience are needed. Applying this parable to the history of the Church and of humanity, we see the grandeur of the ideas and plans of God. Evil is also a factor; sweet and beautiful are the flowers of its cockle; but God does not crush and break; the wheat as well as the cockle will bring their own fruit and the Judgment will show which was wheat and which cockle and the former comes into the barn, for life, the latter into the fire. The mills of God grind slowly, but we endeavour to anticipate Him. He has time, we have not; " time is short."

PARABLE OF THE MUSTARD SEED

" *The kingdom of heaven is like to a grain of mustard seed . . . which is the least indeed of all seeds : but when it is grown up, it is greater than all herbs and becometh a tree, so that the birds of the air come and dwell in the branches thereof.*" (Matt. xiii. 31.)

(*a*) The Gospel and the grace of Christ are a straining energy, full of depth. Who looks at it from the outside does not see much; but he who experiences it finds a wonderful progress in himself and he rises out of the earth and the world. It does not depend on many words, but on their strength; and strength is spirit and soul.

Individuals experience this, and the great world also experiences it. Oh, Gospel, thou unpretentious, secret force, how we honour and love thee !

(b) What have we to do for the kingdom of God to develop in us ? (1) We have to extend our faith to our mental and moral world and have to make it rule. We look with the eyes of Jesus and not with the senses of the world, customs, traditions and human views. The world is at times imperialistic, at others cosmopolitan—at one time it is hard and classical, at other times sentimental ; our faith cannot vacillate according to fashion. If sometimes there is great opposition concerning a point, later it diminishes ! We must believe absolutely ! (2) Interest, endeavour, and exertion are necessary if we are to experience faith personally and subjectively. The same Christianity has to be experienced by us freshly and with actual originality. Narrow-mindedness and comfort, which prevent spiritual absorption, must not stand in our way. In all our affairs, in our business and social strife we continually come upon tasks which we have to solve according to the principles of faith. Let us do it ; let us think and feel strongly, but according to faith. (3) Our spiritual, soul-world develops ; because law, grace and divine will become justice, purity, patience, moderation in the spiritual world and assert themselves in the consciousness of strong, happy life. We drink these in as the forest drinks in the sunshine and the dew. Carlyle said of the time he acquired a deeper faith in God : " It was then that I became a man."

(c) " The birds of the air come and dwell in the branches thereof." The Mother-Church is our nest ; here we rest. Even if we fly about the world and look about for food, yet our heart returns; here it is at home. Each well-formed soul is a branch of the Church, and each one draws many other souls, so that we can say that on these branches the souls live and rest. What attractive power there is in St. Francis of Assisi, in St. Ignatius, in St. Vincent! More attractive and sweeter than any apologia is each beautiful, holy soul. Do not let us dispute much and criticize much, but let us live holily.

PARABLE OF THE LEAVEN

" The kingdom of heaven is like to leaven which a woman took and hid in three measures of meal, until the whole was leavened." (*Matt.* xiii. 33.)

(*a*) The kingdom of heaven makes its entry and gains a footing in man; it is like leaven which makes the soul ferment, changes and forms it. The leaven changes the rawness of the flour and gives it flavour; the same fermentation purifies the new wine and changes its sweetness to strength and spirit. Such a penetrating and re-shaping power is the Gospel, the grace of Christ, and the Eucharist. It breaks the wild strength and instinctive nature of the soul, and renders it enjoyable to God and to itself. It does this thoroughly; it picks the fibres of human feeling to pieces and penetrates into every particle. This is verily the strength of God, which penetrates soul as well as body, which ennobles our ideas, reaches right down to the smallest movements of our heart, and is felt in our speech, and rules our actions.

(*b*) The woman puts the leaven in three measures of meal; we also have to change three courses of our soul.

We carry the light and justice of Christ into our mind; we build up our soul-world upon correct philosophical and theological notions, and we see to it that we are occupied with only reasonable, true, and holy ideas. We exclude inconsistent, flashy, irrational thoughts. We carry the light and truth of Christ to the rich world of feelings, from which we cannot lock out the unconscious passions of our sensual nature, but there we sit at the threshold of our consciousness and ward off the street, the herd. . . . "*Limpidezza*," transparent intactness is what we long for. We carry the leaven of the Gospel into our will; we wish to be correct. We do not delude and deceive ourselves; our greatest longing is to wish what God wishes, even if we are not pleased with it. We are not advocates, but the sons of God; we do not misinterpret, but willingly pay homage.

(*c*) The fermentation spreads slowly in our souls. Apostolic Christianity was strong leaven, it spread quickly and brought about a magnificent transformation; in us the divine grace makes but slow progress. Maybe, there is much ailing substance, much of that other leaven about which the Lord said: "Beware of the leaven of the Pharisees." We are full of lowly, sensual, selfish feeling; we are boasters and are fastidious and do not endeavour to avoid even the venial sins. "Purge out therefore the old leaven." (1 Cor. v. 7.) Let us avoid venial sins, and our souls will become fresh, and our love for God will continually grow.

PARABLE OF THE HIDDEN TREASURE

"*The kingdom of heaven is like unto a treasure hidden in a field . . . again . . . it is like to a merchant seeking good pearls. Who, when he had found one pearl of great price, went his way and sold all that he had and bought it."* (Matt. xiii. 44.)

(*a*) The precious pearl which we have to find is the value of our soul, which is greater than everything, it is peace, confidence, and happiness. God's eye is caught by this pearl ; He loves it, " *sic dilexit* " ; He values it greatly and tends it so " that a thread of thy hair does not fall to the ground." God sent His Son to search for it, and then in His footsteps He sent Apostles and Saints ; and He gives up all for this treasure—His Son, His Blood, His Soul. Those who awake to the consciousness of this immortal value, similarly those who find peace and reassurance and mental balance in faith and love, those come upon " the kingdom of God " in themselves, and in this kingdom upon their own kingly dignity. They find precious pearls.

(*b*) The supernatural value is a precious pearl, which God places in our soul by His grace. Through grace we are like to God and after death it will be the divine life with its intensity and divinely beautifying love which will fill our consciousness. Here below we are " the seed of God," " *semen Dei* " ; there beyond we will blossom forth. What life, what flowery spring, we carry in ourselves ! O my soul, thou mysterious ploughing-field, in which the treasure of glorious eternity is hid ; thou ocean depth with thy precious pearl, indeed we value and love thee ! And the great inheritance of the children of God awaits us too, happy eternity ; for naught will we give up this right, for we wish by all means to assert it.

(*c*) The precious pearl is the strength latent in us for shaping divine life here and now. Our divine life proceeds already here below, if we possess the knowledge that by the smallest action we honour and serve God. We do not merely fight an economic battle, a battle for food, but we work upon the cathedral of God which is being built in world-history. Whether we eat or drink we do everything for God; therefore our life is rich and valuable. Mankind, though it is often in a low condition, is our fellow-brother; we always wish to lift and raise these brothers of ours. Our marriage is not the physiological union of man and woman, but a Christ-like *mysterium*. Our happiness is " health and peace "; we find pleasure in the sunshine and in the flowers of the field; and if suffering comes to us we embrace it as though it were the Cross of Christ, and always trust!

(*d*) A precious pearl also is our awakening to the consciousness of Christ-like life. Christ is with us in the Gospel, in grace, and in the Eucharist. He lives with us and teaches us the most sublime life; He lifts us above social troubles; He does not identify Himself with the age and its institutions but stands above them. Liberty of the soul is what He teaches us, lest we go under in the waves of life. He teaches us to walk upon them with an emancipated soul. We do not compromise with the variableness of either past or present; we look at the world with free spirit and soul and at the same time develop. " Have faith; I have conquered the world." There are many views and theories, but the life pleasing to God is the Christ-like one.

(*e*) For this precious pearl we have to give up everything, that is, we willingly give up all, after we have found it and possess it. In the consciousness of our dignity strong is our faith and sweet our joy! Why should we chase butterflies and trifle with vain things? Do we not willingly abandon everything for the kingdom of God we experience, and for the kingdom we expect? " Who then shall separate us from the love of Christ? Shall tribulation? Or distress? . . . or persecution?" "Nor height, nor depth, nor any other creature shall be able to separate us from the love of God, which is in Christ Jesus our Lord." (*Rom.* viii. 35.)

(*f*) Though our existence and consciousness is modest it contains treasure; the ocean of life is bitter, but although it is cruel it produces pearls. The treasure is buried; layers of dust, stone, rubble, sensual and beastly existence cover it; it has to be dug out. The pearl swims in the hardships of life, in the ocean . . . it has to be fished out. Times, customs, fashion, negligence, sin, decadence, and indiscipline make us forget the treasure and the pearl. The storms of disappointments, shipwrecks, and sufferings divert the attention; economical strife, work, workshops, worries about our daily bread change the earth to an arena of combat, no one supposes a treasure there. But Jesus says: It is there; we must not be put out by semblance, by everyday obscurity, by the earth; the treasure is in the depth; it is in you, says Jesus, if ye feel and live as I do.

LEAVE ALL TO FOLLOW CHRIST

" *And a certain scribe came and said to him: Master, I will follow thee whithersoever thou shalt go. And Jesus saith to him: The foxes have holes and the birds of the air have nests: but the son of man hath not where to lay his head.*" (*Matt.* viii. 19.)

(a) The Scribe becomes enthusiastic, the greatness and sublimity of Jesus inspire him. The soul lives on beauty and righteousness, and where it meets such it pays absolute homage. The scholar and the artist also impress us, but it is above all the Saint who draws us on. But we may not rest content with the impression and the feelings they create; we have to act. The Scribe also became enthusiastic, but Jesus pointed out His hard life: I have no house, no comfort, I am the servant of others, is what He meant, and behold thenceforth the enthusiasm of the Scribe decreased and he did not force himself to action. We will not trust such feelings as do not help us to action; we will not trust zeal, ardour, and enthusiasm which do not follow the commands of God with action; without action the feelings are misty veils. What we wish for are actions, and life according to Jesus; the feelings are only means to this.

(b) " *And another of his disciples said to him : Lord, suffer me first to go and bury my father. But Jesus said to him : Follow me, and let the dead bury their dead.*" There are dead souls who do not feel according to God, who do not accept the Gospel of Jesus, who do not take part in our faith, our hope, and our feelings. It is amazing that even Jesus met such dead ones, who asserted the sovereignty of human liberty even against Him. It is a sad independence indeed to be dead. " Let the dead bury their dead." Philosophies, tendencies, theories, fall one after the other. One could well say of them : their principle is to bury, their vocation to die. We will take care not to be infected with the poison of corpses, with the doubt of the " dead," with their indifference, their slackness ; our principle is to preserve and keep others alive and our vocation is to live eternally.

(c) "*And another said: I will follow thee, Lord; but let me first take my leave of them that are at my house. Jesus said to him: No man putting his hand to the plough and looking back is fit for the kingdom of God.*" (*Luke* ix. 61.) Who keeps looking back from beside the plough has not got his soul, his mind, there; his attention is elsewhere, therefore he does not work with the necessary energy and spirit, or he is fatigued and tired of it. For the kingdom of God also whole men are wanted, who give themselves up and put their whole soul into it and do not look elsewhere; perseverance also is wanted. The half-hearted never attain their ends; they are also inconsistent. We have to work continually, with our whole energy and perseverance upon ourselves and other souls. The stream immediately whirls away the boat as soon as it does not strive forward; we also have to be faithful every instant, we have to be persevering. Do not let us look back to see what and how much we have done already, but let us continually work and act. "What is behind me, that I forget," said St. Paul, "and what lies before me, to that I devote myself." And we must not look to see how much more work there is to do, but let us do here and now what we can. "My brothers," said St. Francis of Assisi, "let us begin to love God." Let us begin, begin continually. The psyche of beginners is joy, strength, and exertion; beginners do not look for the evening, that is what the tired ones look for, but their hands are itching for work. To do in small things here and now as much as possible, that is the secret of greatness.

THE TEMPEST AT SEA

"*And when he entered into the boat, his disciples followed him.*

*And behold a great tempest arose in the sea, so that the boat was
covered with waves : but he was asleep."* (*Matt.* viii. 23.)

(*a*) The Church is the ship of the ocean of time, it is
the carrier of great treasures above abysses and storms.
The greatest treasure of humanity is faith and education ;
these two must not be torn apart. It is not allowed to say
that the salvation of humanity is entrusted to another
ship. There are many self-willed, audacious sailors ; many
pirates ; but they neither serve the general good, nor the
happiness of their own soul. We are on the flagship ;
we are continually voyaging to new oceans with enter-
prising spirit and set sails. Our provisions do not run
short ; the waters of life do not fail ; we cannot miss
the direction.

(*b*) Jesus is on this ship ; He sleeps, that is His presence
is mysterious ; but on the ship there are oarsmen, striving
generations, who have to row with a will ; they have to
watch every change of the wind. There are storms and
they can only progress by struggling. God placed morals
in a material nature and He placed the Church in history ;
He did not even exclude schism from His plans. Let
naught disturb us. Do not let us question : why does
the Lord permit this or that ? The Lord is resting amongst
us ; He gives us strength, faith, and trust. He suffered
treachery and agony ; and we too go through storms.
There is one thing we have strongly to believe : God is in
our soul, Christ is in the Church.

(*c*) " *And they came to him and awaked him, saying : Lord,
save us, we perish.*" To cry out is permitted, the cry
voluntarily breaks from our heart ; but to doubt is not
permitted. Let us cry out and pray, but do not let us

doubt, and let us likewise cry out but let us also work.
Such sound idealism is wanted in us. The Lord Jesus
took the cry of the disciples willingly, He only reprehended
the mistrust, the doubt : " Why are ye fearful, O ye of
little faith ? Then he arose and rebuked the winds and the
sea ; and there was a great calm." If we go about in
storms, upon the ocean let us adore Jesus whose power
commands the oceans.

JESUS HEALS TWO THAT WERE POSSESSED OF DEVILS

" *And when he was come on the other side of the water* . . .
there met him two that were possessed with devils, coming out of
the sepulchres . . . *and* . . . *they cried out, saying : What*
have we to do with thee, Jesus Son of God ? Art thou come
hither to torment us before the time ? " (*Matt.* viii. 28.)

(*a*) There are enraged, dark, raving spirits and they
exert their influence on men. Hate spurs them on, and
their passion is to ruin the masterpieces of God, primarily
man ; they defame, infect, and degrade him. What a
terrible, cruel power this is ! We do not wish to be in the
same room with dead ones, neither with madmen nor
poisonous snakes : are we to dwell with the devil ? He
hates us and calls the Holy Scripture " murderous " ; he
ruins life, soul, education, marriage. Let us therefore
hate sin. We must not suffer the devil to dwell in our
heart. Our heart must not be like ruins and cursed places.
Those possessed of the devil were not clothed ; the devil
of impurity suffers no clothes. Naked pleasure stirs
up its longings, that is what it feeds on. The forceful,
disciplined soul puts up with the body, for when all is

said and done the beauty of the flesh comes from the strength of the soul. We shall find the "*corpora plus quam humana*" where the "*animæ plus quam humanæ*" are being educated. Body and soul are what are wanted, not only body and body !

(*b*) " What have we to do with thee ? " The Cain-like, cold words become a curse and rebellion on these lips ! They have naught to do with the Redeemer and His divine heart ! This is the judgment of inexpressible unhappiness ! Would any one of us dare to utter this : What have we to do with Thee, Christ ? Has not in such a one faith, hope and charity become darkened ? Has not the mental balance become shaken already, deeply shaken ? And what about our likeness to God in our daily life ? Do we show that Christ leads us and that we obey Him ? We will not break with Him in anything ! This is our aim.

(*c*) Thou camest before the time ! The sinner always maintains that grace comes to him before the time ; the time for conversion has not yet come ! This knowledge is a torture which torments, humiliates, and shames ! Then the time passes, the " *irreparabile tempus*," and he views his poverty with unspeakable sadness, for " he will have no time left." Happy is the man who has not reached the time when it shall be too late, and who makes use of this time. With what ardour can such a one look into the future, with what composure can he view the present and with what joy and gratitude will he look upon the past ! But whatever little time we have and however old we may be, let us hurry to live and make use of the time.

(*d*) " *And the devils besought him, saying : If thou cast us out hence, send us into the herd of swine. And he said to them :*

Go." Behold the wish of the mighty, but darkened, spirit. He who does not look into the sun and who has naught to do with Christ proceeds slowly but surely along the downward path; the first step is doubt, the second scepticism, the last cynicism. In spite of finery, polished floors, and perfume. Education is not morality, says Leroy-Beaulieu; at every step we experience that the beast shows through the human being in spite of titles, dignities, lace, and furs. Who does not pay homage to God in his soul becomes the slave of his body; this is our moral creed!

(*e*) "*But they going out went into the swine : and behold the whole herd ran . . . into the sea*." Two thousand swine ran into the abyss; they perished there. In many ways the world resembles this galloping herd; the instinct of fleshliness drives it on, it makes much noise, stirs up much dust, then the ignominious end overtakes it! Meanwhile the two healed men quietly sit at the feet of Jesus; their soul is freed and they give thanks to the Lord, and the owners of the swine complain about the loss. This is great loss indeed—two thousand swine for two souls! Jesus does not think it too much; He taught us that we have to suffer everything for the deliverance of the soul, and if He valued the souls highly why should we not value God highly, why should we not suffer losses for Him? Zeal often causes loss to itself or others for the sake of spiritual gains! The wisdom of the Gadarenes who wished to guard swine as well as souls is unreasonableness in the eyes of Christ.

(*f*) "*Now the man out of whom the devils were departed besought him that he might be with him. But Jesus sent him away, saying : Return to thy house and tell how great things*

God hath done thee." (*Luke* viii. 38.) " To be with Him,"
the source of strength, healing, and blossoming ; to be
with Him and to feel His protection, His refreshing, life-
giving influence, and to enjoy it, this is what the healed
soul needed, this is what every soul having come to its
senses wants. This is what Magdalene won, " out of
whom the Lord cast out seven devils " ; this was the
grace of St. Paul who was the persecutor and then the
ardent follower of Christ. But Jesus sends the exhausted
man home ; go home and serve God, leave the ways of
Apostleship to others. The Lord does not call everyone to
Apostleship, but He calls the possessed one to pure, noble,
Christ-like life. We can be full of zeal and ardour, we can
be nameless saints of the Lord, and this suffices us.

JESUS RAISES THE DAUGHTER OF JAIRUS

" *Behold a certain ruler came, and adored him, saying : My
Lord, my daughter is even now dead ; but come, lay thy hand upon
her, and she shall live. And Jesus rising up followed him, with
his disciples.*" (*Matt.* ix. 18.)

(*a*) This is the etiquette of the court of God ; those who
go to Him kneel, adore and beg. Men also may be lords,
but they are completely dependent on God. They are
created lords, created by the mouth of God, by the upholding word. Men can only be lords by the breath of
this word. If they haughtily lift up their head, they knock
it against the beam of finiteness. The depth of life, the
sublimity of power, and the mysteriousness of death
incline man towards modesty. If we are contrite, then
we comprehend the simple, noble forms of duty and
morality and we are truly sorry for the violent " superman "

and his unbelief and hollow-sounding words. God makes us become great and each time we approach Him with humility we become greater and greater.

(b) "*And adored him.*" The customary pictures of death change to touching power when they concern those we love. The feeling of our helplessness and pain becomes a cry—a cry from out of the depths. How modest the king mourning for his dead is, as is the queen feeding her infant; the power of life and death does not distinguish queen and king, it knows only yearning, longing souls, souls who pray. Oh, come, dear Lord, and place your hands upon them . . . that faith is still weak which requires the placing of the hands over it, but it already is honourable, for it prays. The weak soul living in temptation shall not be amazed at being weak; but it shall pray, it shall beg; in time it will be stronger.

(c) "*Some come from the ruler of the synagogue's house, Thy daughter is dead: why dost thou trouble the master any further? . . . Jesus . . . saith to the ruler of the synagogue: Fear not, only believe!*" (*Mark* v. 35.) Man quickly says: Enough; do not trouble the Master! But the Master goes towards the bier and the grave. Do not be afraid, only believe; she will live! But, of course, we are afraid! We are afraid of death; it hurts to tear ourselves away; it is terrible to slide down the unknown, roaring depth. How will we find our way home there? Let us have no fear, Jesus guides. To the water it is the same whether it flows by day or by night, the depth draws it on; we are drawn by God in death also; we go rightly and find our way if our heart is pure. Let us not be afraid, but believe and love! Our death will be a magic awakening from deep sleep!

(*d*) "*And they come to the house of the ruler . . . and he seeth a tumult, and people weeping and wailing much. And going in, he saith to them : Why make you this ado, and weep? the damsel is not dead but sleepeth. And they laughed him to scorn. . . . And taking the damsel by the hand, he saith to her : Talitha cumi. . . . And immediately the damsel rose up and walked.*" The mourners weep, sew garments, weave wreaths, and prepare for the funeral ; their hearts are filled with despair. The divine Saviour steps among this downcast crowd as life and strength itself. He thinks differently and sees other things ; He sees no dead, only one asleep. From death, from the threshold of eternal life He recalls the soul of the damsel ; He beckons to her and she obeys. Worldly mourning, which does not care about the soul, is a vain show. We look at the dead with the eyes of Jesus ; we arrange our cemetery for ". the resurrection."

HEALING OF THE WOMAN WITH AN ISSUE OF BLOOD. I

"*And a woman who was under an issue of blood twelve years, and had suffered many things from many physicians, and had spent all that she had, and was nothing the better, but rather worse, when she had heard of Jesus, came in the crowd behind him, and touched his garment. For she said : If I shall touch but his garment, I shall be whole.*" (*Mark* v. 25.)

(*a*) The woman who had the issue of blood, loved life, sunshine, and flowers ; she tried everything, but in vain ; sweet life flowed away ! We also love life, but we have to love the whole of it, the flowers as well as the depth, austere sublimity as well as beauty. Life is not pleasant and attractive, it contains also rain, fog, and storm; it is duty as well as joy; bravery, strength, and strife, but also simplicity, purity, humility, and intimacy. "Blue sky, red roses, white marble, and scented air" is only one side of existence! What about the rocks and abysses of the Alps? . . . What about the heights of duty, the depths of sacrifice? . . . We have   place ourselves in complete harmony with the world; this we are only able to do with strength and discipline!

(b) There is much pain, illness, and trouble, and it is difficult to bring these bitternesses in accord with the conception of the good God. But do not let us blame the Lord; do not let us be indignant with the God of pain. Christ does not say that we are to suffer as much as possible, that virtue and perfection are to be found in suffering alone; but He includes pain in His programme; He sees that it is a problem which has to be solved; and teaches us how to solve it. In the land of death, Achilles thinks of the sunshiny, beautiful world and sighs that he would rather be a beggar on earth than king in Hades. The complaint is of no use, the lovely world passes away and we have to help the soul which does not pass away. We must learn how to suffer for God and the beauty of the soul.

(c) The woman recognized Jesus; she formed the right idea about Him. She might have formed a wrong one; she might have been sceptical. And if she had had no trouble, maybe she would not have cared about Christ. How much becomes woven into the views of men, how many unconscious and conscious, well-controlled and smuggled elements! We are to guard the customs-barrier and disinfect all that enters the soul; dirt, rags, poison, and daggers are forbidden. Yet how much enters the

soul by way of bad example, conversation, and reading !
Let us also take care of the different influences. We must
beware of one-sidedness ; temperance, justice, fairness,
and humility are our safeguards. What conception has
Nietzsche about Christ ? Who inspired that ? And what a
misfortune it is to pass that on and poison souls ! Who is
responsible for this ?

(d) The woman has a simple, childish trust : if she only
touches his garment . . . The instinct of our soul is to
approach, to touch, to come into contact. That is why
God became man, that is why He came near us, that we
might everywhere come near the edge of His garment.
Nature is also His flowery, starry, gleaming edge, but it is
chiefly in the Eucharist and in His Sacraments that we
can touch the Lord ! . . . How often does the Lord
pass close by us, how often His garment touches us !
How often do we feel Him near us and in us and clasp
Him to us ! Our little acts of attachment, such as visiting
the Blessed Sacrament, short prayers, the use of holy
water, promote our attachment to the Lord. We also
touch the hem of His garment.

HEALING OF THE WOMAN WITH AN ISSUE OF BLOOD. II

" *And forthwith the fountain of her blood was dried up, and
she felt in her body that she was healed of the evil. And immediately Jesus knowing in himself the virtue that had proceeded
from him, turning to the multitude, said : Who hath touched
my garments ? And his disciples said to him : Thou seest the
multitude thronging thee, and sayest thou who hath touched
me ?* " (*Mark* v. 29.)

(*a*) The throng nearly crushes the Lord, but this is the touch of the body. There is also a touch of the soul. We touch each other with love, trust, reverence, or with hate and coldness ; the warm hand and loving eye is a human touch. And we touch God with faith and trust. Magdalen touched Jesus not only with her hands but with her soul ; Veronica also touched the Lord, so did the woman who had an issue of blood. The sunshine also touches the buds of flowers and the rain reaches the roots. . . . In Holy Communion we touch, taste, and enjoy Christ : "*mel et lac ex ore ejus accepi*," His kiss is like milk and honey to us.

(*b*) "*And he looked about to see her who had done this.*" No one, no one. Everyone draws back and is afraid ; many have touched Him and now they are perhaps afraid of His wrath and make excuses and perhaps deny it. We are often thoughtlessly cowardly and false, and we also tell lies ; we make excuses and screen ourselves. For our part we also have to educate ourselves to discipline concerning instinctive cowardice, and we always have to speak straightforwardly and openly. If we are questioned we even have to vent our subjective views and differing opinions sincerely. An open, straightforward frame of mind and disposition is beautiful indeed, because it is pure and strong.

(*c*) "*But the woman fearing and trembling, knowing what was done in her, came and fell down before him, and told him all the truth. And he said to her : Daughter, thy faith hath made thee whole.*" There the good woman trembles ; she is afraid, for she was bold and dared to touch the Son of God, she the impure one. What a dear, humble soul ! Often Saints are afraid to approach Jesus, to commune '

with Him ; they think too little of their merits, and find
that their garments are shoddy. They feel their frailty !
God'delights in this. Let us also feel all this, but let us
approach Him with trust in spite of our insufficiencies ;
God accepts us with love and assures us that faith is a
healing force in us also.

JESUS IN THE SYNAGOGUE AT NAZARETH

*" And he came to Nazareth where he was brought up : and
he went into the synagogue according to his custom on the sabbath-
day ; and he rose up to read, and the book of Isaias the prophet
was delivered unto him. And as he unfolded the book, he found
the place where it was written : The spirit of the Lord is upon
me, wherefore he hath anointed me, to preach the gospel to the
poor he hath sent me, to heal the contrite of heart." (Luke iv. 16).*

(*a*) The first appearance of Jesus, of the Messiah recorded
in the Holy Scripture ! He introduces Himself as anointed
by the Holy Ghost and overflowing with grace. " This
day is this scripture fulfilled in your ears." This is the
great fact, that God incarnate came into the world, as a
mountain of crystal, upon which the sun sparkles and out
of which wells spring forth. This is how the preacher
of the Gospel is to be . . . anointed with faith, hope, and
grace ; words shall be sweet upon his lips. The object
of the Gospel shall be shown in him. To carry news of
joy, to heal, to help . . . this is following in the steps of
Christ. " And they wondered at the gracious words. . . ."
These are Christ-like words ; not to scold, but to raise
and to warm.

(*b*) " *And they said : Is not this the son of Joseph ?* " The son of the carpenter ! Behold the human thought which is taken aback by blood, garment, and appearance, and over-clouds the divine, the spiritual. Do not look to see if He is the Son of the carpenter, but whether Soul streams from Him. There was Soul in the bookbinder apprentice Faraday ; and without soul, kingship and academy are worthless. Soul give us, dear Jesus, give soul to our earthly dwellings. Give us soul to hear the Gospel, and soul before the Sacrament of the Altar. Give soul to our daily life, and to public life. Then life will not be empty however it is spent.

(*c*) " *And he said : Amen I say to you, no prophet is accepted in his own country.*" With reverence and humility has the Sublime to be approached. We are not allowed to dispute and quarrel with it. Thus it had already come to pass that Elias put up at the heathen widow's and that Eliseus healed the heathen Naaman and not the Jews. Those who open their hearts, to those I speak. We do not break open doors, we only knock ; brother, let me in ! Oh, my God, where has the word of God and His grace to take refuge from the sages of the world, where ? With a widow of Sareppta. . . . What was more, man was arbitrary with God " and thrust him out of the city, and led him unto the brow of the hill . . . that they might cast him down." On such occasions the prophet becomes dumb . . . and " passing through the midst of them went his way." O Lord, we open gate and door to Thee and accept Thee ; down on our knees, we beg Thee to speak to us. We obey Thee, we will be Thy faithful servants.

PERSECUTION OF THE CHOSEN

"*But beware of men. For they will deliver you up in councils . . . and you shall be brought before governors, and before kings for my sake . . . but when they shall deliver you up, take no thought how or what to speak.*" (*Matt.* x. 17.)

(*a*) Do not let us worry much. Let us do our best in what depends on us and not lament or fear the difficulties. It is not we that direct the world, but the Lord. And the Lord placed us here, so here we are to stand. Those who have faith in the Lord are like the mount of Zion; "and will never waver." The martyrs were also men and stood their ground. Trust is the furthering and development of our own strength with the aid of the strength of God. What we are capable of, that we give completely, God will add to it. St. Ignatius said that we are to trust as if God would do all, and act as if we would have to do all. St. Francis of Sales said: If I were to be born again, I would trust in God still more.

(*b*) "*For it shall be given you in that hour what to speak.*" When it is necessary, the Lord helps in that same hour! Now, maybe, we feel ourselves weak and think that in case of this or that temptation we would fall! This is not the right psychology and still worse theology. For now help is not wanted; if it will be wanted, then it will come and we shall feel differently. How many men became persevering, great, strong, and heroes in that same hour. We sometimes have to pass through queer hours and weak moments, but because of our own faults; because we do not discipline and educate ourselves and say: Here and now we can be heroes, we can be noble-minded,

if we do not let ourselves go . . . let us begin the work
and do not let us yield.

(c) "*For it is not you that speak, but the spirit of your
Father that speaketh in you.*" He is the wise, inventive,
brave, inspiring Spirit, and not ye, ye low-lying, capricious
shadows ; the Spirit is your consolation, your teacher,
whom I send in My stead, who accuses and judges the
world. The Spirit of your Father, who created you and
does not abandon you ; therefore He sustains with the
Spirit and anoints " kings, prophets, priests and martyrs "
with it. We adore the Holy Ghost, who inspires, warms,
cools, and consoles us. With Christ the Man here and
now, we cannot speak ; but with His Holy Spirit we can
indeed speak.

FEAR NOT THEM THAT KILL THE BODY

"*And fear ye not them that kill the body, and are not able to
kill the soul, but rather fear him that can destroy both soul and
body into hell.*" (*Matt.* x. 28.)

(a) There exist evil, illness, suffering, outrage, death ;
but all this is not the real evil ; evil is damnation. Its
abysmal depths are so great, its immense agonies so
tremendous, that in face of them these chains, prison, and
iron bars, and death melt away. The motives of infinity
and eternity tremble in these words of Jesus ; they are the
basis of that Christian temperament which belittles every
evil and by so doing gains victory over it. The infinite
value of the soul and the weight of eternity gives that
energy which conquers everything. It shows us SS. Law-
rence, Agnes, Cæcilia. . . . Their tremendous strength
consisted of their having no fear of flames, fetters, swords,

suffering, and death! They belong to the generation of amazing heroes trained by Christ. He trains us also; we are to fear nothing but the infinite evil of sin.

(b) In this declaration of Jesus' we adore God's unbending, holy will. He puts before us the good and the evil and says: here am I, there is the evil. . . . The immense seriousness of life is that God loves us, honours and lifts us up, and He loves us forcefully; His love is no sugar-water, no effusiveness; His love is force, creation, and exertion; His love inspires heroic temperaments and nobility; He inspires us with magnanimous feelings, which enable us to conquer pain and death and to fear nothing. In nature also God has placed the continuity of strife, battle, and contest. Immense contrasts appear everywhere: life and death, sunshine and night, beauty and decay, and in all this He is the sovereign sublimity. Let us therefore correct our soft feelings and human ideas about God and His love. Our age is much too soft, therefore it errs; it gives up striving to assert its strength and denounces the only rightfulness of virtue. This is not in the least divine but flatly and tediously human. Let us take care not to be mistaken and not to err.

(c) "*Are not two sparrows sold for a farthing: and not one of them shall fall on the ground without your Father. But the very hairs of your head are all numbered. Fear not therefore . . .*" God takes care of us, but according to His conception. He has said and told us what we are to fear, what the real evil is and what counts as lesser evil. Illness, persecution, anguish, and shame may all be our portion; it was also that of the martyrs. There are indeed dreadful things; but we are not to view even these things with pessimism and despair. In every trouble let us hear the words.

"Do not fear those who kill and defame the body," and let us believe that Providence will lead us through these troubles so that we may possess the eternal good. It is the victory of Providence if we struggle through our troubles to repose in God. God knows about us, God guides, God helps us across earthly hell among devilish souls to arrive at Him. Christ did likewise. He is our example. This is how we are to think about evil; this is how good comes of it to us. What is more, it becomes our glory!

JESUS BRINGS NOT PEACE BUT A SWORD

"Do not think that I came to send peace upon earth: I came not to send peace, but the sword." (Matt. x. 34.)

(*a*) Peace as well as the sword. "Peace upon earth to men of goodwill," is what the angels sang. "My peace I give to you" is what Christ says elsewhere. But He also brings the sword, that men should develop goodwill in battle and be able to enjoy peace. Goodwill is a strong will, and this will has to struggle a great deal against the flesh and the world till it brings the divine will to victory in itself. Because we love peace and want to be good-willed, therefore we take the sword and struggle against all that is against the truly good, correct, faithful will.

(*b*) Progress goes everywhere upon freshly broken ground. Until man breaks and conquers nature, he has no culture. This arises when man pours his ideas on to stone, wood, and iron; this plough, hammer, sword, must be used with an effort. From this the Parthenon and the cathedral at Cologne arise. We carry the ideas of God and the traits of Christ over to the instinctive, rough, sensual man. We want the beautiful, pure, spiritual, soul-world— real culture—we wish to create this. The ideal shines before us; let us rejoice that we are able to form a better, finer man from ourselves.

(c) Therefore the saying: " Back to nature," is an erroneous one, if by this we mean life without culture and the world of unruly passions and instincts. " I am come to send a sword "—that is, we have to go forward and not backwards. We have to put much work into our nature, yet we must not spoil it but develop it. We are not to weaken strength but to give it form. Culture often takes from us our natural force and that is not right; but virtue is to keep strength and to render it more noble. Pure, self-disciplined, moderate life which is self-denied in a reasonable manner does not weaken but strengthens man. The sword which Jesus brought never kills; this battle is always fought for the valuable, better life.

BEHEADING OF JOHN THE BAPTIST

" For Herod had apprehended John and bound him, and put him into prison, because of Herodias, his brother's wife. For John said to him: It is not lawful for thee to have her." (Matt. xiv. 3.)

(a) " It is not allowed "; what a blessing it is, if we know exactly what is allowed, what is lawful, and what is not; if we know the sublime, divine will. This knowledge " is the glory of thy face." We see the amoral confusion of the modern world; sophists put a false construction on everything. If mankind is freely to give its opinions about what are the good and bad sides of love, respect, murder, stealing, and adultery, we should find ourselves in the "*selva oscura*" of Dante. Compared to this, how strong we are, for we know that this is allowed, and that not. This is not a yoke to us, but a fence on the brink of the abyss, the flowery bank of the roaring torrent. It is not a bare command, not the imperative gesture of the corporal's stick, but the radiation of perfection and idealism which lifts and warms us and renders obedience easy. It is a sweet yoke and a light burden.

(*b*) "*But on Herod's birthday, the daughter of Herodias danced before them : and pleased Herod. Whereupon he promised with an oath, to give her whatsoever she would ask.*" The girl dances and pleases, and the beauty of the body charms the sensual man ; he becomes drunk with it and pays her homage. Forgetting himself, he says : I give up all for thee. . . . And the end is that he sees to what beastliness his unholy passion has brought him, and "he becomes sad." Ghosts haunt him, and he says, "John the Baptist is risen from the dead and miraculous forces are in him." Failure, sadness, fear—it is to these the broad way and the broad gate lead ; this is the lees of the cup of pleasure and the final end of sinful life.

(*c*) "*Give me here in a dish the head of John the Baptist. . . . And he sent and beheaded John in the prison. And his head was brought in a dish : and it was given to the damsel.*" Behold the pretty, merry dancing-girl's cruel, ugly wish, and how her body becomes distorted before our spiritual eyes, what a pit her heart is in which a base, empty soul resides. But now this beast conquers, that is, she murders and serves up a bloody head to the contemptible troop of guests. And this is the power and mastery of the world ! But the

veritable feast is celebrated by the confessor who held
fast to his strength and faithfulness, which in the world is
not conquered either by fear, prison, or hatchet. There is
a birthday here also, that of the saint ! Our duty is to be
faithful to the end ; to persevere through thick and thin.
This is what exalts God and glorifies man. Prison and
hatchet shall not sadden us, but our faithfulness and
devoted love shall be our consolation. This is how we have
to perform the holy will of God !

" COME APART "

" *And he said to them : Come apart into a desert place, and
rest a little . . . and going up into a ship, they went into a
desert place apart.*" (*Mark* vi. 31.)

(*a*) Jesus draws us on : Come, let us go out to see the
quiet shores beyond which beckon to us, to the proximity
of God . . . come away from the market of the world,
from supercilious carelessness, where none but such
sufferers walk as rattle the chains of custom and human
views—come away from the circle of these tired, faded,
withered, human faces—from this continual search after
self-interest and yet general self-forgetfulness—from this
bustle and this Vanity Fair—away, away from this dirt,
from this stuffy atmosphere ; let the oars work, let oceans
come between us, let us go ! God calls us, our Creator,
our Redeemer, our eternal Judge. The Almighty calls,
the merciful One. What an immense grace this is and
with what a pleased, beating heart we set out for the feasts
of retirement, solitude, and devotional exercise !

(*b*) " *Come apart.*" . . . There is a world where there is

only God and I! Only? Is not God all, all and the
original reality of infinite worlds? God and I! There
His light is, His strength and creating, regenerating power,
His purifying spirit which breathes upon us, and there our
soul softens and becomes annihilated and yet grows into
the infinite. Our continual awakenings bring us the
freshness and strength of dawn; our soul becomes
darkened and overclouded from the accusations of our
conscience, but it rises all the more transparently and
purely. This is the world of God, this is His abode; here
it is that the wells of His grace gush forth; in this silence
we hear His footsteps and His voice. We have to take our
sandals off, for this is holy ground. Let us kneel and
prostrate ourselves. This is the land where God trains
His Prophets and Saints. Let this be our native country
also. We shall love and value it!

(c) "*And rest.*" If you are rested and the noise and
excitement has subsided in your souls, you will awake to
the mysterious fact of your lives and you will find yourselves standing before the locked gates of eternity and
you have not thought about opening them. We seek God
and He does not show Himself, but continually passes
us; we expect a face, but His face is the content of life
in faith, hope, love and purity; we have to feel and
experience that we live and breathe in Him. If we deepen
and strengthen this fact we will become saints. We are
to wake to the consciousness that to-day, and always, we
are living an immortal life, consequently, step for step,
we give this incomprehensible world sense and soul.
Let us wake to the consciousness of the soul's hidden,
inner world and let us develop it. Only faith and the
original force of creative love is capable of this. Here it is

that we meditate, and join God ; here we work with mind, heart, feeling, and will. And we make use of this " for a while " as the doomed ones would make use of it if this " while " were given to them to make good their lost life.

FEEDING OF THE FIVE THOUSAND

" In those days again when there was a great multitude, and they had nothing to eat ; calling his disciples together, he saith to them : I have compassion on the multitude, for behold they have now been with me three days, and have nothing to eat." (*Mark* viii. 1.)

(*a*) Five thousand men assemble around Jesus ; they follow Him with trust and zeal, for He is the leader and master of their soul. All this enthusiasm is surrounded by hunger and desert. They are souls in hungry bodies ; therefore they need bread ; the desert does not give it to them. God gives it. The germs, seeds, and energies are from God ; these are the divine mysteries ; from Him as from the bottomless depth comes this heaving, expanding life. What a mystery all this is ; we feel strangers upon earth when we think of all this ; our heart misgives us, when we look into these depths and into this never tiring stream—incomprehensible, holy stream. " And he asked them, how many loaves have ye ? And they said : seven." And He took the seven loaves, and gave thanks and distributed them, and all of them ate. . . . This also is an incomprehensible, divine fact ; this is directly divine ; the natural crop of wheat is only indirectly so. We adore the Lord in both. Give us bread, we ask, Thou feedest the little birds, they turn their beaks towards Thee ; feed us also. Deep loathing fills us concerning the intemperance with which the undisciplined man disturbs the divine order; they abuse the mysteries of God and derive death from them, not life. We honour the divine flow of life; we do not disturb it and render it unclean. It is holy to us; the function of eating and drinking is also holy to us.

(b) Seeing the miracle, the people want to declare Him king. The divine made a victorious entry into the consciousness of the people conqueringly; to perceive this is to be enthusiastic about it. The divine appears to us in the figure of Christ sublimely and conqueringly. The whole of life with its deep ties and mysterious meaning and significance becomes ennobled in a hallowed, magnified, and enhanced way; the desert and the battlefield change to a kingdom. Hail Thou, our King, who renderest us kings also. We cannot evade this if we follow Christ. Let the Lord Jesus be our King; He accepts the kingdom of the heart; but not another one.

(c) " . . . *he went up to the mountain to pray.*" Jesus leaves the crowd which offers Him an earthly kingdom; a weak kingdom is that; a kingdom over that people which seeks bodily good and is apathetic towards the good of the spirit; which has no idea of His great plans and hardly understands His great struggles. Jesus has no wish for such a kingdom. He goes on to the mountain to pray and with this He also indicates the sources of real values and the enthusiasm which conquers the formalisms of the world. Up there His soul expands and revives. " *A summo cælo,*" from the high heavens, He always makes His start, so as to raise the earth. He did not come to reign and oppress, but to raise and educate rulers. We comprehend Thee, O Lord, and are filled with this ambition; this helps us to endure defeat and ill-success.

JESUS WALKS ON THE SEA

" *And immediately he obliged his disciples to go into the ship. . . . And when he had dismissed them he went up to the mountain to pray. And when it was late, the ship was in the midst of the sea, and himself alone on the land. And seeing them labouring in rowing (for the wind was against them) . . . he cometh to them walking upon the sea.*" (*Mark* vi. 45.)

(*a*) The disciples struggle with the waves ; it is night and there is a storm ; hard, disagreeable, and dangerous is the life of the sailors, bitter is their work. Their soul also easily becomes as bitter as the cruel, hostile waves ; yet Jesus knows about them ; He walks upon the sea ; walks hidden in darkness, but full of goodwill. God walks invisibly amongst us. From Him existence continually rises, souls are in contact with Him with their deepest roots ; He reaches and flows into our life. However the moral world that is the conscious human life fluctuates, it is the way of the footsteps of God. A mysterious thing indeed, but a fact ! We easily neglect this hidden God, this power which asserts itself in His works and which is shown in Nature as supernatural power. Because of the veil of nature and the fluctuation of the moral world and the stormy pace of progress we ignore Him, and maybe, behave with enmity towards Him. Let us endeavour to get deeper . . . in our heart we find Him. Let us come into contact with Him, as anyhow we are connected with Him metaphysically. O Lord, speak, catch hold of us, draw us more forcefully, that we may come to know Thee, that we may see Thee in the mirage of the world and its culture.

(b) " *But they seeing him walking upon the sea, thought it was an apparition, and they cried out.*" They see and are frightened. Strangely, one might say terrifyingly, does the Lord appear. They imagine the apparition to be a hallucination, a spectre. They knew Him to be on the mountain, praying, they did not believe that the Lord could be here amidst the billows and their struggles, and that He could smoothe away the billows and struggles. We believe God, we believe that He is in our churches, and is effective in our Sacraments, but that He should be here, here in the cruel, dreary strifes of life and influence them, and that all this is His territory upon which He wishes to assert Himself—this has a strange effect on us. Let us believe that Jesus wishes to annex the entire life of culture. He is amongst us ; our whole life has to be Christ-like in profession, trade, industry, administration, in public and private relations.

(c) " *And immediately he spoke with them, and said to them : Have a good heart, it is I, fear ye not.*" Jesus assures His disciples that it is He, that they are not to be afraid, that He is concerned with these waves and this tiring struggle, and He has one great proof : He calls Peter to Him and makes him walk on the sea, as if He would say : It is I, here am I, and I give you strength that ye also should walk victoriously. Yes, Our Lord, this is Thy proof ; Thou givest strength and we persevere and conquer. We believe that without Thy grace we are not capable of struggling ; but with Thee we are capable indeed, even if the world falls to pieces ! The proof of Jesus is the pure life which comes from grace. With Jesus it is possible to keep the whole moral law, without Him, not. The more we hold on to this the surer we can be that He is with us.

(*d*) " *And Peter making answer said : Lord, if it be thou, bid me come to thee upon the waters. . . . And Peter going down out of the boat, walked upon the water . . . seeing the wind strong, he was afraid.*" (*Matt.* xiv. 28.) When Peter sees the mighty waves, he is afraid, he loses confidence and sinks. The bottomless depth which gapes below our feet is our nothingness. If we view ourselves we come upon deeper and deeper dark abysses and we lose the ground below our feet. We are creatures and we depend on God, without His grace we can do no meritorious good. The weight of our sins, the millstone of hell is round our neck, and how graciously the Lord comes towards us. Into what depths of mercy and grace we look when we think of His Holy Cross or the Sacrament of the Altar. Behold the depths below our feet. And around us the mountainous waves of difficulties are seething. Yet it would be vile of us if we were to doubt. God keeps us above the depths, He lifts us above the mountainous waves. Those who go through life arguing and not praying, who go sceptically and not trusting in God, those will go under. God is our philosophy and our strength !

(*e*) " *And when he began to sink, he cried out, saying : Lord, save me. And immediately Jesus . . . took hold of him.*" Peter *doubts*, that is why he sinks ; but his instinct rouses him and with the love of life and the feeling of the impossibility of senseless perishing he cries : Lord, help. . . . Scepticism, mistrust, and pessimism . . . these are all false doctrines. Existence and life place strength at our disposal, and if it is not found in us, it will be found in the living, strong God, who is near us and helps us. To Thee, O God, we cry for help !

PROMISE OF THE EUCHARIST

" *When therefore the multitude saw that Jesus was not there* . . . *they took shipping, and came to Capharnaum* . . . *Jesus* . . . *said : Amen, amen* . . . *you seek me* . . . *because you did eat of the loaves, and were filled. Labour not for the meat which perisheth, but for that which endureth unto life everlasting.*" (*John* vi. 24.)

(*a*) They seek Him and speak with Him ; they are excited by the prospects of the "*regnum mundi.*" Christ who had taken refuge on the mountain to pray and who had descended from it again addresses them. It is bread, ye need, is it not ? but I did not come to give ye the bread of earthly life, I came to feed your spiritual life, and for this part I necessarily *do not* give bread ; I *am* the bread. He who gives life, warms, and incites, He is the bread of men, and what could be more *living bread ?* Every soul who enlightens and encourages others, upon whom many depend and grow great, is their living bread. Jesus is the living bread of the world. This is felt by those who have tasted of the world and its honey and gall ; those know this who have searched for food for their soul and have begged from authors and philosophers ; those have experienced this who go along the world with the hunger of life and taste and search for satisfaction, strength, and health. Behold here is the bread of life, the living bread ; this was the living bread in the times of classic Roman law and politics, and this it is now in the times of modern social reform. Thou art our bread, O Lord, through Thee we grow to be great and strong.

(*b*) " *For my flesh is meat indeed, and my blood is drink indeed.*" (*John* vi. 56.) "*Except ye eat the flesh of the Son of man and drink his blood, ye have no life in you.*" We have to eat and we have to drink, we have to take Jesus to us, we have to live on Him! What a forcible, mighty way of expressing the eternal longing of the human soul after God! According to Homer, man opens his soul after the infinite as the bird opens wide its beak. In the Psalms the desire and longing of the soul break forth repeatedly, and the Psalms do not fall into abeyance. Descartes prays this way, and also Nietzsche says: "We can bear it no longer." Tolstoy writes: "As the young bird which falls out of the nest, so the soul cries after God." And Jesus sanctifies and increases the ardent longing and says: Yes, yes, indeed ye have to eat and drink God; that is also why I took a body, that I might not only be your brother but the food of your body and soul. Eat and drink It; let It remain in you, be united with It. The passionate hunger of the generation and its piteous longing will be smoothed over in your souls, and an infinite, sweet, strong feeling will make you happy. How gracious and powerful Jesus is to still such hunger and satisfy such longing!

(*c*) Each eats, and each is united and lives separately with Jesus. All that is public and external is necessarily superficial; depth is internal. Nothing is deep that we do not feel and experience, and from our feelings we become deeper and purer. The intimate soul is a bottomless depth: this is where Jesus goes when He is united with us. Especially in Holy Communion do we go with Jesus to the depth of our feelings and joys. Jesus and I. In silence and sunshine two blue depths surround us; the ocean of the soul and God's blue sky. On such occasions He reassures us (*a*) concerning our sins; He quietens our troubles ; upon His heart we feel that He forgives ; (*b*) concerning our spiritual struggles, which appear to us at their true value, for here we obtain the reward for them and lay our victories at His feet ; (*c*) concerning our future strifes, for He helps us. And we derive strength from Him, for we are allowed to enjoy Him and to become refreshed in Him.

"I AM THE LIVING BREAD"

"*I am the living bread, which came down from heaven.*" (*John* vi. 51.)

(*a*) Good bread it is and we enjoy it ; "*pinguis panis Christi*," the food of souls, the bread of angels. Every taste is to be found in it, according to the sense and necessity of the individual, and it chiefly contains the taste of immortality. Who wishes for humility partakes of it ; who seeks for patience and purity tastes it ; who needs valour, perseverance, joy for work, wins it ; like honey from the rock, so we gain from this unpretentious bread, soul. We do not so much believe but rather experience this.

(*b*) It warms, renders us enthusiastic, willing, and fresh. The Holy Virgin hurriedly starts for the mountains of Judea, after she has received the Lord. So we also, strengthened by the Holy Eucharist, hasten towards the mountains of difficulties ; if necessary, to the martyr's arena also. Without the strength derived from the Holy Sacrament no one was allowed into the arena of martyrdom, for it was feared that he would break down! Oh, beautiful, sweet, lily-like Church, "*erat antea in operibus fratrum candida, nunc facta est in martyrum sanguine purpurea !* " The Church will shine with the virtue of its children, it will be purple with the blood of its martyrs, but all this will be achieved by the strength of the Holy Sacrament !

(*c*) Visiting generally goes with joy and good spirits ; in the Holy Sacrament Jesus does not spare the " *oleum lætitiæ.*" He pours holy consolation into our soul. " *O sacrum convivium,*" give us enthusiasm for what is good ; let us enjoy the good we do.

(*d*) It also affects the body. The soul reacts on the body, on its feelings and instincts ; lower nature becomes refined and nobler from the nobleness of the surroundings ; higher enjoyment strangles the lowly wishes. In this sense it is true that this vine nourishes virginal blood and that this bread educates a chosen, nobler, generation. We continually hear that nature is unconquerable ; but let it be filled with the conscious soul which wishes to shape it and we will see that the body is also material which takes shape ! Blue blood is no fairy story ; neither is the Divine Blood !

"MY WORDS ARE SPIRIT AND LIFE"

" *It is the spirit that quickeneth : the flesh profiteth nothing. The words that I have spoken to you, are spirit and life.*" (*John* vi. 64.)

(*a*) The Jews doubt, they do not understand at all ; the Apostles are taken aback. But Jesus is firm as the rock and even if all depart He declares : Yes, My flesh is meat indeed, you will eat that and when I become man I will even give Myself up so. This is the law of My heart and also of your hearts, for it is the exigence of love. That love wishes firstly for *presence :* " to be with Him," this is the element of its existence. I Myself will be with you, says the Lord. Our heart wishes for the same ; in the hours of suffering and restlessness just as much as in the heat of ardour. Oh, to think that we possess this, that it is here, where men live and struggle ! He is our great common good and bond of union !

(*b*) Presence does not suffice, love demands union. For this purpose the substance of the bread is changed into the glorified body of the Lord Jesus ; by this transformation He approaches us and satisfies one of the heart's most secret and most wonderful longings, that He should be in us, and we in Him. We have also to be transformed, we have to break ourselves and become purer. We have to be filled with the heat of zeal, with divine longing, with thirst for Christ, this is how we are to receive the Lord, and when He becomes dissolved in us, then the following conscious thought shall seize us : " *Est Deus in nobis, agitante calescimus illo,*" God is in us who warms us and makes us live.

(*c*) He not only wishes to be united with us but wants to be the *principium* of our activity. In the soul God throbs with the pulse of stronger, more glorious life. It is of this pulse and surge of finer and more spiritual consciousness that we need more and more. Jesus comes and assures us : I live in you, He says, I impart My life to you. As I live divine life out of God, so ye out of Me ; My life grows in you and blossoms forth. Our soul has to catch the touch of God ; this is how we will live divinely out of Him. *Deo gratias.*

" HE THAT EATETH ME SHALL LIVE "

" He that eateth me, the same also shall live by me."
(*John* vi. 58.)

(*a*) Philosophy and culture seek for the more beautiful, stronger life. Jesus says : This is what I give you in the Holy Eucharist. He shaped the divine-human life in Himself : the ideas of God in the human soul, divine feelings, intentions, and spirituality in the human heart. As the air streams through the organ and swells into music, and the eyes change the quiver of the ether to colours, so through the soul of Jesus the divine poured forth in beautiful, strong, human life. From it we have to derive life. For this the motto is " union." We have to cling to Him receptively and to acquire ruling, ineradicable ideas and thoughts which rest in Jesus. Union renders us capable of this, for it makes us intimate. Betrothed united with betrothed, friend with friend, and mother with child live in intimate, soft, sweet, connection. The Holy Eucharist also trains us for this intimate love ; with fire it burns into us and with tears it imparts to us the ideas and feelings of Jesus.

(*b*) Strong, Christ-like love transfers us to a bright, sunny atmosphere. If we come from the atmosphere of factories, where we breathe soot and dust, where the machines and human faces are oily and we do not see the sunshine ; or from where the world is noisy, into pine-forests, then our lungs get clearer, our blood stirs, and the fatigued, stooping man stretches and straightens himself. Pedagogy and hygiene help this new man. Jesus works in a similar manner, especially by placing the selfish, instinctive, animal, conscienceless, violent, Utopian man into His own pure vigorous world of feelings. He lifts man out from Roman imperialism, from arrogance, from the beastliness of violence, from the tepid stupor of sensuality. Faust and Nietzsche sigh for the strong man, Rousseau seeks him among the bushmen; Tannhäuser also turns his back on the Venusberg in search of what is nobler. Jesus is Master of the eminent, excelling, more perfect life; let us endeavour to feel according to Him!

(c) Vigorous life perseveres and makes sacrifices; so does the strife of the vigorous individuality; for this we also need the warm unity with Jesus. He teaches us to take part in His suffering and so does He partake of ours when we embrace Him. The thorn which pricks us is from His wreath of thorns. Furthermore, that wreath encircles two heads, and the wounds pierce two hands and two hearts : His and ours. Here is the source of sacrificial love; this is whence Christianity derives : " *inter consolationes Dei et tribulationes mundi ambulat Ecclesia*," on the thorny road God consoles us with His person. The spirit of sacrifice comes from Him and it is in the strength of sacrifice that the beautiful souls, the " *anima sublimiores*," become formed (*Pontif. Rom.*). We derive this spirituality and frame of mind from the blood of Jesus and from His kiss.

THE HEART THE FOUNT OF EVIL

" *For from the heart come forth evil thoughts, murders, adulteries . . . these are the things that defile a man.*" (*Matt.* xv. 19.)

(a) Do not let us trust ourselves, but let us look with a

deep searching glance into our heart. We see a world there which is full of ravines and precipices; it is an uncertain, unsteady, "quaking" ground. When we pray, our heart warms and an agreeable warmth of life runs through us; we do not think of those many bad feelings and the passions of cold, indifferent envy which rest at the bottom of our soul or which hide like snakes below our flowering feelings. But how rapidly spring changes to winter in our soul and flowers to colourless, rattling seeds. Therefore, when we pray, this consciousness should also accompany us; when we kneel in front of the cross and hold the rosary we must realize what we are, and in our zeal we bind our *cilicium*. Through this we become objective praying beings and through our prayers we become really better.

(*b*) It may be that our soul is quiet; that our thoughts are charged with electricity, that our heart seems willing; but this is a relative and easily upset equilibrium. How many different sympathetic and antipathetic men surround us! Many would pick a quarrel with us. No matter, we know this, but we are not disturbed by it. Opposition, strife, and struggle is our fate; ideals, goods, and rights are one-sided; some have to be broken down that better ones should take their place. We will be magnanimous, for we know that there is much prejudice and partiality "*extra et intra muros.*" If we pray in this way, we grow out of our surroundings and will be superior to them and consequently reasonable souls.

(*c*) In our judgments we are often conceited and fall in love with one or the other of our ideas. We make plans and dream! Oh, how many weavers sit with us at the loom of the same life, who do not accommodate themselves to us ! So our plans come to naught, our dreams disperse, and our soul falls into despondency ; it sinks as the badly leavened dough. Let us look upon our notions and pet ideas with humility. Often a revision and restoration of ideas is wanted. But those who pray well possess an elasticity of soul and are capable of being refreshed and renewed. The youth of the Saints is restored in life-reforming prayer.

(d) In our enthusiasm we often do not see the difficulties. We set out for life with youthful strength, but with little humility. For what is man even in a town, what in history, and what in Nature ? We have to keep our place amongst the wheels of mechanism, and also amongst the storms of centuries. Of this we will only be capable if we raise ourselves in faith, beyond our extent, beyond our span of time, when we are capable of viewing the unfathomable perspectives of world-development. In this holy dusk we come upon ourselves and, quite near to us, upon the Lord. We know that He is God and we a finite speck of dust, but it is our good fortune that we can cling to His feet and, being attached to Him, can walk the ways of eternity.

THE WOMAN OF CANAAN

" *And Jesus . . . retired into the coasts of Tyre and Sidon. And behold a woman of Canaan who came out of those coasts, crying out said to him : Have mercy on me, O Lord, thou son of David : my daughter is grievously troubled by a devil.*" (*Matt.* xv. 21.)

(a) Every argument is futile which says that man is kept down by the steel web of the forces and instincts of nature and that he is incapable of going against and rising out of them. This argument is futile, for his heart cries out and his consciousness says : Of course you will rise out of it ! You are faced with a mechanical power, but do you not look down upon it and invoke a higher power ? Go on, cry out, it has to exist and it has to help you. This world is only something, not everything ; and our soul reaches beyond the something ; therefore we pray ! The prayer of the woman, the " have mercy on me " asks for the sovereign action of the Lord which another cannot achieve. Thou, O Lord, Thou shall act ; Thou shalt condescend ; have mercy, and will ; our strength, merits, and endeavour do not make up for this. This is the psychology of the humility of prayer ; that is why the woman continually cries and kneels ; she is rejected and again comes forward and approaches and prays and adores, and her praying will conquers !

(b) " *Who answered her not a word. And his disciples came and besought him, saying : Send her away ; for she crieth after us. And he answering, said : I was not sent but to the sheep that are lost of the house of Israel ! . . . It is not good to take the bread of the children, and to cast it to the dogs.*" The hardness of Jesus nearly embarrasses us ; it is cold and deaf, and it rejects. The " heathen " world turned away from the love of God, it obstinately went its own way, that is why the heart of God was cold towards it. With dread we see the " *mysterium iniquitatis* " in death, pain, suffering, decay, decadence, and darkening ; man does this against God. " But he answered not a word." In His soul how Jesus viewed the devastation of the heathen spirit ; His heart contracted from it and His lips became dumb. The sons of God became dogs, how true it is ! But the time of mercy will come, it is not here yet. The mustard seed has first to be sown in the ground, only then the birds of heaven can rest in its boughs, the souls without difference of nationality! There is to be no heathen spirit in us; no cold, irreverent, rebellious, distrustful disposition. Towards such God is deaf as well as dumb.

(c) "*But she said: Yea, Lord: for the whelps also eat of the crumbs that fall from the table of their masters. Then Jesus answering, said to her: O woman, great is thy faith: be it done to thee even as thou wilt: and her daughter was cured from that hour.*" The frank and straightforward recognition of our own sinfulness and impotence contrasted with the saving and merciful will of God is the way of our salvation. Here self-respect and honour is forfeited, here absolute homage is wanted; this is what sovereign mercy corresponds with. We can only then be heroic, magnanimous souls if we first pay homage to God for life and death in dust and ashes. In us the basis is " *miseria* " and in God it is " *misericordia*," but further there are heroism, virginity, martyrdom, and divinity for us. Do not let us mistake the Christian psychology.

HEALING OF THE DEAF AND DUMB

"*And again going out of the coasts of Tyre, he came . . . to the sea of Galilee . . . and they bring to him one deaf and dumb; and they besought him that he would lay his hand upon him.*" (*Mark* vii. 31.)

We have to look into the soul of Jesus; there He stands opposite the deaf and dumb man; opposite this sad figure of dull, stupid, animal existence and He is moved to mercy. He begs Him to help. Therefore He takes him aside and puts his fingers into his ears and spits and touches his tongue. He sighs and says with strong will as if He would pour His soul upon him : Be opened.

(*a*) We have to approach others with a strong, healthy, beautiful soul and impart to them our life and feelings. Spittle is one of the elements of life and health ; but the spittle of a furious or tired man is poisonous, it infects ; that of the healthy one serves life. Jesus touches the tongue of the ailing one with spittle, with His strong life. The weak, ailing, doubting, dark, mistrusting souls do not heal ; their disposition and spirituality infect ; whereas the influence of the noble-minded upon the soul is like the impression of well-grown, powerful trees, flowers, or the firmament. The beauty and goodness of souls is public good, like the sunshine and the breath of the forest.

(*b*) "*And taking him from the multitude apart, he put his fingers into his ears, and spitting, he touched his tongue ; and looking up to heaven, he groaned.*" Jesus sighs ; He helps with the deep emotion of the soul ; with tears, fire, and longing He lifts the soul out of its stupidity. Energies are wanted for breaking down recklessness and dullness ; a scorching soul has to be poured upon the languid souls. We have to be white-hot with prayer ; from out of the depths have we to start if we want to help and move souls effectively. This is also how we have to endeavour to move our own souls ; we have to sigh with elemental force ; we have to cry out from the depths ! This is what Eliseus did, he bent over the dead, placed his lips to the lips of the dead and his heart to the heart of the other and deeply sighed : Stretch yourself, live !

(*c*) "*And said to him : Ephpheta, which is, Be thou opened. And immediately his ears were opened, and the string of his tongue was loosed.*" Be opened ; says Jesus. Here where physical trouble is the point He breaks down every obstacle with His words of command ; He wills it and so it is. This is how He sometimes helps the deaf and dumb soul, He turns and changes it ; He cries out and His voice is heard even by those who do not wish to hear ; but this is not His usual way. He generally moves us and knocks at the door of our soul, so that He expects interest, goodwill, and attention on our part also. He wants us to hear, understand, and follow his advice. "*Open* the door to me, my brother, my betrothed," He says, "and let me in ; I do not break in and smash doors ; I ask for goodwill and love ; that cannot be stolen, that has to be given freely." Let us listen to the encouraging, stimulating promptings of Jesus which guard and attract ; this is the assertion of strength and life in us ; let us always co-operate with grace which precedes us and shows us the way.

BEWARE OF THE LEAVEN OF THE PHARISEES

"*Take heed and beware of the leaven of the Pharisees and Sadducees.*" (*Matt.* xvi. 6.)

(*a*) There is much darkness and many shadows upon the soul, but we are not allowed to weaken our life with them. We have to conquer darkness with light. The source of our darkness is our poor, unstable self. In the deficient garb of narrow-mindedness it is as weak and freezing as a child of the South in a hard winter. The night-light of the sick-room is its special light. The unhealthy dusk of selfishness broods in it, from which the soul becomes wearisome, lazy, and depressed. It is sometimes disgusted with itself. Disgust sometimes appears also in ardent souls. Prayers and the Sacraments do not stimulate them. They lament and complain as if they were living on the outskirts of the lake of Bethesda. They hate themselves and have no spirit or inclination to live. What is to conquer after all? Good or evil? Are we to lapse into complete despondency or are we to break with this helpless " asceticism " ? What is this dark, helpless self-degradation for? What is this cave-life for? What we need is the height of the Alps ; our nature demands the fresh air, the sunshiny peaks, roaring brooks, scented pines, dewy ferns ; not this fearsome, chilly way of lamentation.

(b) Strong natures have an instinctive aversion for such a weak, overclouded view of life and look at Christianity also as gloomy. How far are they right about it? We cannot disperse the shadows and scratch off the birth-marks of our nature ; with original sin many ignoble things are woven into us. But we cannot rest content with this, for we know that good, and not evil, conquers. Good is always much more plentiful than evil. Evil is barely a shadow, the shadow of finiteness ; but it is not the frame of life ; therefore evil is a servile power ; it always serves and is always a tool. Through this shadow we struggle into brightness, into the light where we may develop.

(c) Spiritual life needs brightness and light ; it derives this from the natural brain and from faith, when it sees the ideas of God also in nature but which have to be ennobled ; and sees them in the instincts, inclinations, necessities of life and in physical life also. Do not let us loathe nature; this loathing is not true, not real, not realistic! Do not let us loathe humanity; we have to be superior to the sons of the world, we have to stand high, but we are not allowed to look down upon and despise anyone. He who despises is a dark soul. Nothing develops in darkness; not even the tadpole grows to a frog in the dark; many solutions do not crystallize in the dark. We will possess light and brightness if we see the ideas of God in nature and grace; if we look upon God and His works with love and rejoice in them!

(*d*) Light and brightness are the intercourse of feelings with God. If we get to know the creative ideas of God, then by this we are already near to Him, but what a different proximity is that of living attachment, and chiefly the intimacy which shines forth from the Holy Sacrament. Maybe a feeling seizes us that this is superfluous; perhaps we content ourselves with knowledge; but in such case we would neither understand the Lord nor ourselves. He descended to us upon the wings of the heart; He did not deny the idea, the thought, but He gave a warm basis to thought and drove into its service the indispensable forces of life, its instincts and inclinations, the passions of the heart, and the consolations of actual presence. From the cold brain He leads our heart into warm life, our heart which faltered in the transparent, cold atmosphere of the high regions of the intellect; here it becomes warmed. Proximity, unreservedness, coexistence, real union, this wonderful, natural connection carries us off into the life and friendship of Jesus, into contact with Him. Such a soul verily says: " *Mea nox obscurum non habet* " : my night is not dark.

WHOM DO MEN SAY THAT THE SON OF MAN IS?

"And Jesus came into the quarters of Cæsarea Philippi : and he asked his disciples, saying : Whom do men say that the son of man is? But they said : Some John the Baptist, and other some Elias, and others Jeremias, or one of the prophets." (*Matt.* xvi. 13.)

(*a*) For whom do men take the Son of man? They take Him for man, for a great, prophetic, fiery-souled man, for a Holy, wonderful man, but for a man. Similar to Elias, Jeremias, John the Baptist, similar to the noble-minded, great-hearted men such as have already existed and will exist; similar to men who are related to God, in whom depths open, and who walk the heights and help others to arrive there also, who are productive, who create and shape, who are the blessing and pride of humanity, but are bone of their bone, blood of their blood. Man recognizes the man in Christ. But there exists another knowledge which has a higher origin and deeper effect, which recognizes another reality in the imperial, historical figure; this is the faith. This not man inspires, but God; it does not start on human paths but on the finger-prints of God. We are men but we also listen to God; we have faith and believe; our spiritual world is in contact with Him, receives His impressions, and becomes enriched by them.

(*b*) *" But whom do you say that I am? Simon Peter answered : Thou art Christ the Son of the living God."* Thou, an historical personage, art God. Thou hast a soul, eyes, and mouth, but at the bottom of Thy soul Thou art one

2-N

with the Son of God; Thou art He! Thy soul sees the infinite although it is a finite, created, human soul; it sees the gleam of the Truth, God, the infinite Act; it sees how everything has its source in Him. The soul of Christ sees with delight the fullness of the Divine Being, it sees also the secret of its being united with the Son of God. It is from this consciousness and from the tides of eternal life that the soul of Jesus is fresh, magical, deep, enchanting, strong, and rejoicing. It is the connecting point of God and the world! His flesh and blood correspond with this life-integrity. His immaculate origin and kingly blood were conceived by the Holy Ghost; "Christus" is He, that is, anointed, and the iridescent wreath of the Holy Ghost's grace is upon His head. Great, lovable, and undauntable is He. God we adore in Him, greatness we admire, lovableness gives us courage, and we acquiesce in the undauntable. Jesus our Lord, bread of life, milk of life, our source of life art Thou!

(c) " *Blessed art thou Simon Bar-Jona: because flesh and blood hath not revealed it to thee, but my Father who is in heaven.*" Simon, thou art the son of man and this faith will strengthen, raise, and direct thee and help thee to salvation. Without this there is no happiness; for the reason that without it there is no view of life, no hope, no courage. We grope about uncertainly without Christ, and the weight of our sins without deliverance is a tombstone below which we die alive. Science does not render the soul happy, art and love do not fill it; what we want is strong, rich, immortal, happy existence; this we do not find in empiricism. The sceptic is not happy, nor the one who doubts, nor the decadent, blasé one. We believe Christ, that with the son of Jona we also will find happiness in strong, brave faith. This we will not abandon. If we experience it we will not doubt. Therefore we will not look upon and criticize faith from the outside, just as we do not look at the glass-paintings of a Gothic cathedral from the outside, but experience it from the inside. We view its beauty and enjoy its strength in ourselves ; this is how we will be happy.

PETER THE ROCK

" *And I say to thee : That thou art Peter ; and upon this rock I will build my church, and the gates of hell shall not prevail against it. And I will give to thee the keys of the kingdom of heaven. And whatsoever thou shalt bind upon earth, it shall be bound also in heaven ; and whatsoever thou shalt loose on earth, it shall be loosed also in heaven.*" (*Matt.* xvi. 18.)

(*a*) And I say also unto thee, and say it so that I also do it, I make thee a rock. The house of Christ is a house built upon the rock. The rock means strength which is not upset, it means strong resistance which is not softened. The Lord wished to assure us faith, its Gospel, its doctrine, its spirit and grace ; these He did not entrust to letters which kill ; not to books which are torn asunder ; not to science which the human brain distorts ; but He entrusted it to an institution, to the Church, and that that might be strong, He makes a rock of its head ; makes him strong and infallible in faith and teaching. Behold the house and home of my soul ; the sweet light of truth does not go out in it ; its first eminence is its foundation on a cliff. This is from where we view the waves of the ocean, the chaos of opinions, the strife of spirits. It is good to be in this house ! We love and honour this rock ; we kiss its feet.

This rock is our Holy Father, in whom Peter lives, upon whom the Church, the home of our soul, stands.

(*b*) In this house our other treasures are deposited. Here are we reborn, here educated and anointed heroes ; here is its table with the Bread of the Angels ; here floats His breath with which He breathed upon His Apostles and said : Receive the Holy Ghost. This is where our soul is healed from its wounds ; in one word this is the house of the children of God. In this house Jesus invisibly surrounds us ; His blessing trembles upon the Holy water, the incense, the candles, the palm-branches ; it floats in the peal of the church-bells. And behold the foundation, the head and steward of the house, behold Peter. Jesus entrusted His treasures to his hands and gave him His keys, and these keys open the gates of heaven. The Apostolic mission with which he sends bishops and priests into the world is all entrusted to him. He opens and closes, he binds and loosens. He is the link between the many tongues and races of Christendom, the living centre of religious life and life of faith. How then should we not protect and help him to the best of our ability ?

(*c*) "*I say : Thou art Peter . . . this rock.*" Thou art strong by My grace and not by thy own strength ; thou art strong by the blessing of My prayer, for Simon, Simon, the devil wanted to have thee so as to tear thee away from Me, but I prayed for thee that thy faith should not decline and that thy brothers should be attached to Me through thee. Christ provides for His Church and its rock-foundation, that it should not crumble. This is the ambition of Christ. He conducts affairs so that the Pope should not be mistaken when teaching. What a grace the care of the Good Shepherd for us is ; whether

He takes us upon His shoulder or conducts us to this house of His. We give Thee thanks, dear Shepherd. Your prayers we also enjoy ; we live from them ! Behold at every step we meet with the invisible figure of Christ and His blessing in this sweet, holy House, in the Church.

THE HOLY CHURCH OF CHRIST

" *I will build my church* . . ." (*Matt.* xvi. 18.)

(*a*) This is the great house. It is meant for and open to all peoples ; it is not restricted to Rome, not to one country or one part of the globe. Where the Apostolic creed is said and the Church is mentioned there it is as much at home as the brethren themselves. Neither is the Pope a stranger there, just as faith and eternal hope which live in the heart are not strangers. He is their foundation, their rock, their steward, and their head. This faith induces nations to pay homage to this House and the attachment to this House is not diminished either by space, time, nor by the varying grades of culture. It stands above national enmities, this unique, great House, the home of souls. Nations have attached the foundations of their existence to the rock of this House ; it is from the steward of this House that they asked for crowns for their kings ; on the other hand they helped him to obtain reverence, power, law, and riches. This house was the tower of morals and ideals against violence and barbarism.

(*b*) It is a holy House. It breathes and educates holiness. Its breath comes out of the heart of Jesus. Its aim, value, and mission are pure morality ; its birthmark is holiness. Its value is measured upon the scale of moral effects by the

Holy Scripture and history of culture. Its glory and strength has always lain in its seeking for, loving, and instilling morality. Tertullian said that in the prisons Christians are only to be found for their faith and never because of their morals and that their daughters " *magis timent, si ad lenones, quam si ad leones damnantur* " : they rather fear panders, than lions. This is the wreath which was upon the head of the Church in America, India, China, Japan ; it is by this that it has to be recognized now also. What a duty we have to strive for holiness and upon what a decay we work if by our morals we compromise this holy House ! We are inspired by the immaculateness of Christ's betrothed, and are prepared to sacrifice ourselves for it.

(*c*) It is a sublime House. Its organism is divine, Christ created it. He set up divine authority in it and this stands victoriously against epochs, culture, problems, and conflicts. Let us love and trust this authority and at the same time let us fill our life in the church with the content of our ideals. Let us partake of the duties of the present age and everyday life and let us apply our energy to them. Do not let us fear that we do not comply with faith, if we occupy ourselves with the soil ; the spirit has to evolve through material development. The problems of to-day are new signs of the wounds of the man fallen into the hands of scoundrels, but the Samaritan shall be the same as of old, the same Christ-like spirit, the same Catholic zeal.

(*d*) It is a universal House. The continuation of Christ upon earth is the Church ; its characteristic is that it was given to entire humanity as opposed to philosophy which belongs to few. This belongs to all of us ; through it we all become wise, rich, and strong. And if it has many unstable children, we are not to be scandalized by this. The sun has lost none of its brilliance, beauty, and energy, since men have known that it has solar spots. So be it also with the Church; let us love it and permit its sweet, strong energy to develop in us.

(e) It is an Apostolic House. Owing to legal succession every cell of it is connected with the Apostles and through them with the Lord. Whether we live in the second, the sixth, or the twentieth century is all the same; Apostolic mission, Apostolic doctrine, Apostolic power, pulse in every vein of this sublime, beautiful body. It does not become old; it becomes more grave, but is always beautiful. The Mass to-day is in essence the same as the Mass of St. Paul or St. John, and in the absolution of the mendicant friar we recognize the power of St. Peter. With this faith we come and go; we receive Apostolic doctrine, we win Apostolic consolation, and to-day, as ever, we recognize the traits of beauty of the Apostolic Church.

CALL TO FOLLOW JESUS

"*If any man will come after me, let him deny himself, and take up his cross, and follow me.*" (*Matt.* xvi. 24.)

(a) Jesus beckons; He wishes us to follow Him, wishes us to take up our cross and follow. The idea comes to us: Does He wish us to go with Him? We ask this because we see how much He loves the solitary ways. He came alone, in quiet night did He come into the world; He walked solitarily, no one knew the depths of His soul; unaided He carried His cross to Golgotha; alone He rose from the dead, and descended into hell and ascended into heaven. He had to walk these great ways by Himself; for the ways of great souls are solitary ways. They are not understood. The ways of our souls are also solitary ways; others may love, support, and encourage us, but after all in the world of our consciousness and its depths and wastes we walk alone. Only God whom we see at the bottom of our soul and out of whom we also are, only He is with us; He is the soul of our soul; He is in me, and I in Him! We have to be absorbed in Him, that we may progress; to grow into Him that we may develop. We have to imbibe His strength and grace so as to live a divine life. Indeed it is on to this solitary path that the Lord beckons to us. Here it is where we are to be reborn, here we are to suffer and crucify our sensuality, here descend to hell for the salvation of our soul. Here let us rise from our grave, and here ascend to heaven. *Deus meus et omnia!* My God, Thou my rich world; my God, Thou my deep, forceful, sublime life! My God, Thou my All!

(*b*) These inner depths are terrible; life is such a mystery that we are not able to endure it, and some sort of deep mistrust overpowers us, especially when we view the errors and enormities of the soul. The depths of life are filled with the disappointments of subjectivity. Therefore we are in need of outward instructions which point out divine life to us objectively, and this is the example of Christ, His feeling, disposition, frame of mind, passion, intimacy, prayer, His words, His talk, His longing, and His strife. . . . Behold the pattern of divine life; come, follow Me in these footsteps. Thou wouldst not well understand divine life. Around this problem your philosophers becomes lost like the flies on the fly-paper; your Prometheus goes mad, and your Don Juans rot

away but do not teach you life. I am the giver and
reformer of life ; I gave the ideal unto ye : this ideal is
Christ. He is your born interpreter : *splendor gloriæ*,
figura substantiæ, shaping, development of divine life.
O Jesus, our soul turns to Thee with the mission of
eternal life ; we glow with enthusiasm for Thee ! Sweet
art Thou to us, Thou who hast been born for us and
hast come for us and to us. How strongly we attach
and bind ourselves to Thee, O Thou our strong cedar,
our palm and olive tree ; the tendrils of our soul would
creep in the dust and be trodden down upon the ways
of the world, if Thou didst not stand before us and at
our side and if Thou didst not say : Clasp me, I am thy
Lord, thy ideal and strength.

(*c*) Strong and mighty modeller and model of our life,
our way and pioneer art Thou, Lord Jesus : " Who of God
is made unto us wisdom and righteousness, and sanctifica-
tion, and redemption " (1 *Cor.* i. 30), who captureth souls
and placeth them upon the way of strife that they might
progress. Thou art the kingly way of souls ; the systems
of others are wrong ways, pathless desert-tracks, rattle-
snakes rattle upon them with great noise and bewitch
humming-birds and finches. Thou art the way of life !
Elsewhere Thou sayest that the path of salvation is a
narrow one ; but allow us ardently to avow : Thy way is
verily the way of troops, troops of souls proceed upon it
and not one dislodges or oppresses the other, not one !
It is not narrow for souls, but we understand Thee,
it is narrow for bodies. There is room for millions upon
it but without the baggage ! Thou art also the way
of nations, " *via nationum*," the way of progress and welfare
for the peoples. And it is extraordinary that this way is

bordered by many beggars, lame and blind ones ; they sit by the roadside and criticize ; they criticize the direction of the road, its stones, elevations, and bridges ; they criticize the passers-by ; they call them cranks, tainted ones, and ailing, but they do not even move and with all their wisdom do not get on in the least. Let us leave the beggars and go onward. Jesus beckons : *Sequere me !* follow me !

"HE THAT WILL SAVE HIS LIFE SHALL LOSE IT"

" For he that will save his life, shall lose it : and he that shall lose his life for my sake, shall find it. For what doth it profit a man if he gain the whole world, and suffer the loss of his own soul ? " (*Matt.* xvi. 25-26.)

(*a*) Our chief aim is : to discover life ; that qualitative, eternal life which man lives already here on earth. For we live eternal life indeed ; we have already started it here ; the question is, how are we to live it, so that we may live it strongly and happily ? First of all, let us discover our soul. Astronomy has placed the centre of the world in the sun, philosophy has placed it in the " I " ; how much more have " my world," my moral life, and all my values their centre and essence in my soul. My soul is the pearl of the universe ; even the universe is too small for it ; it is enough for its grave, but not sufficient for the spreading of its wings ; time is a negligible, small quantity, a bond twixt two infinities ! Oh, my God, what a sublimity the soul is, this eternity and infinity dressed in space and time as in a disguise. We know it is not infinite, but a relation, a son of infinity, there it belongs ; that is

why the world and universe are too small for it. I respect
the soul! When I look into myself I am filled with
foreboding; I stand before eternal gates and my soul
becomes alive from the throb of another life. Strength
and longing seizes me.

(*b*) In consequence I infinitely value the soul and do not
give it away for anything. Sin I will not commit, for that
would be madness and it is my passion and joy to rid
myself of sin! In my faith I attach myself to God as to
my Father . . . to beauty, to strength, happiness. I
attach myself in the hope that He helps and I trust. I
attach myself in love and this is more than if I spoke the
tongue of angels . . . and were a prophet . . . and
knew everything. This is more, for this is the assertion of
" God in me," and " filled with God "; this is that sweet
and strong devoutness and reassurance. . . . How much
such a divine soul towers above every science, culture,
and power, above these impersonal greatnesses.

(*c*) It is from the faith of the infinite value of the soul
that the saints and our culture originate. They asserted
this infinite value in institutions, laws, and liberty. A
conquering force is that world-despising consciousness
which feels that it is more than everything else. . . . This
is the plough which ploughed the rocks of tyranny into
fertile soil. This consciousness will develop and build up
my soul-world also : I will be noble, pure, strong, and
chivalrous for the sake of my soul!

VALUE OF THE SOUL. I

" *For what doth it profit a man, if he gain the whole world,
and suffer the loss of his own soul?* " (*Matt.* xvi. 26.)

(*a*) The value of man is not science, not art, not culture, not political power. Man stepped into the world with the consciousness of his strength and opposed it to Nature. " I," said he to himself, " exist, I have knowledge, I possess, I will, I act," and he placed his hand upon the world and asserted himself in knowledge—and created a beautiful world in Greece, and raised Rome to the height of power. But this greatness is not sufficient if his works do not release him, but disable him ; if knowledge becomes an agony and man turns into a Prometheus—if the beautiful earth becomes his prison which restricts and locks him in— when power expropriates the individual and makes a slave of him, namely, when man becomes less than his work and when this work is a burden and obstruction to him ; man becomes a function ; he works upon the immeasurable building of culture until his coals and metal last ; he works, but from the comprehended, modelled, and hammered world he cannot extract its value ; for it is he that gives it value, his heart, his brain, his arm, his hand. Behold, therefore, not the elaborated, worked-out world of science, art, and culture gives us value, but its value is from us and through us : how much more will our value be in ourselves !

(*b*) The Gospel points out the soul as an infinite treasure : What is a man profited, if he shall gain the whole world . . . as if it would say : " What worth is the whole world compared to you ? " Nothing. Our Saviour's words awake in us an immense consciousness which considers the world as nothing. Seek the kingdom of God, " *et hæc omnia*," and all the rest—that certain " all else " that is not even worth mentioning—will be added to you. That will be given you into the bargain. The Gospel

makes an urgent exhortation to perfection : "Be perfect,"
it says, " . . . Have no fear, for God enlightens and
helps ye : *sicut lucerna fulgoris illuminabit te*." . . . It
asserts great, irreconcilable contrasts : " No one can serve
two masters "; as if it would say : " either or." But
give your entire soul, the whole of it ; I will not excuse
the slightest part of it. It wishes us to live a strong,
enthusiastic life and not to shrivel. Let us go through the
world with divine consciousness : " *Considerate volucres
cæli* : behold the vultures of heaven . . ." Freedom I
wish you.

(*c*) Oh, sweet, strong, blissful sentiment ; sentiment and
consciousness of the infinite value. This we have from
Thee, dear Jesus. Thou hast lifted our head, Thou hast
placed a wreath upon it. Thou hast urged and questioned
me : Answer, who art thou ? and I stammered : I am
a man. Thou saidst : It is not enough what thou hast said,
say more. And I said : I am Thy brother. And Thou
wast not satisfied even with that ; I had to say more and
I dared to say it : I am divine ! Yes, this they did not
know either in Rome, Greece, or Babylon, and there
are still many in Europe who do not know it ! Men seek
and guess ; they long to be like Prometheus, Oedipus,
Cæsar, and the Borgias ! We loathe all this ; we are
Christ-like. We love knowledge as well as art and culture,
but we look upon them with the eyes of Jesus and with the
heart of Jesus we ascend these as steps towards the more
perfect and divine existence !

VALUE OF THE SOUL. II

"*What doth it profit . . . if he suffer the loss of his own
soul.*" (*Matt.* xvi. 26.)

(*a*) We must not lose our soul, for that is an immortal entity worth more than the world; it is our own self. We, who awake to the consciousness of ourselves and the world, of strength, law, necessity, and freedom, and by so doing stand above the whole. We and the whole— is what we say to ourselves—we are more, the whole is mere confusion. This world is mere confusion, a numberless crowd, a jostling throng, each member of which is unknown to the other, though each stands next to each other. And opposite these strange unknown others here am I; I also am existence and reality, like those numberless others, but my reality is reality in spiritual form, it is transfigured existence; I am a unity which joins the throng, which notices in the many unknown others time and space, but rises above time and space, as indivisible I am one in space, and as immortal the same in time. Behold the strong, higher existence and reality . . . behold the soul. According to its reality and nature it is transfigured existence, the " other world." Its functions are called sight, knowledge, will, but the functions are only functions. It is the " I " that forms the chain of ideas; it is the " I " that bears within itself the expressions of will. The soul is not an idea, a thought, but the soul thinks the idea, the thought. The soul is not a survey, but the soul surveys. Thoughts change and pass by; I think the thoughts. O soul, unconquerable soul, how many have denied thee! They wanted to dissolve thee into infinity, to submerge thee in the stream of ideas (Spinoza); they wanted to identify thee with the idea itself and called thee the point of intersection of thoughts and feelings (Mach), but all this is insufficient. We rejoice in the mysterious, deep reality; in this earthly manifestation of infinity and eternity. We rejoice; we thank Thee, our God, that Thou hast created us as such, created us superior to the whole world—created us as immortals. We look upon the world in which we live and above which we are forced to rise with consciousness, superiority, and triumph. Our centre of gravity is different! Different instincts and inclinations awake in us, longings for immortality and eternal life. Let us repeatedly rejoice in our immortality and thank God for it. He is our sun, to Him we turn. Let us likewise look upon every individual with reverence; the high esteem in which we hold our soul teaches us to do so. The higher we value our soul the greater honour we have for man and we hate all the more everything which degrades man, the individual just as much as society: unbelief, pauperism, prostitution, war, alcoholism, etc.

(b) In life we see, on the one hand, the inevitable sequence of things, the law by which certain reactions are brought about, and we marvel at the tremendous mechanism by which multiplicity is held together in a certain unity. Alongside this there is also an activity which originates within myself, which enters my consciousness independently of every reflex movement, every stimulus, every external exertion, which manifests itself as an act of feeling or will. This is the world of spirit. It contains depth and intimacy. Philosophers and poets measure its depths and guess at its heights; an immense spiritual labour goes on in this world which asserts itself in logical creations, in the types of individuals, in the power of liberty, and in the beauty of morality. Everything here raises man and awakes in him the rejoicing, thankful consciousness of his strength. This is whence the force of will originates, which fights the moral battles. This is the achieving, decisive, creating force. This is constructive, initiative force. I own something—it consciously says—and I will achieve it.

Oh, if we would comprehend and value this inner world, this our life ! If only we were sensible of the superiority of this *inner world*, which is superior to every existence, every treasure and fortune ! If we would only endeavour to assert the forces of this inner world, we would acquire divine consciousness. Whereas we go about bound to the social, legal, and economic questions of the outer world and deserve the complaint of the mediæval mystic: "What doth it profit me to be a king, if I know it not ? " I am king indeed . . . I can work . . . I can will . . . construct . . . create . . . ! We have a will, therefore God, virtue, and happiness may be ours. Oh, what a great power the will is, what a benediction the goodwill. In Thy will, O Lord, we delight, " as in so many riches."

(*c*) Contrasted with mechanical necessity, we see the force of our will asserted in freedom. At every step the law accompanies us, but it merely helps us to realize our freedom more vividly. Only those know the law fully who are free. It is in liberty and freedom that we urge and emphasize law and its accomplishment and it is in liberty that we give shape to activity according to the instructions of the law. Liberty is the spiritualization of the law. The free man fulfils the law of his own accord ; he rises out of the iron-furnace of mechanism and fulfils the law more perfectly than sun, moon, stars, ocean currents, chemical and physical phenomena, fulfils it infinitely more perfectly, for he knows it, wills it, and accomplishes it *freely* ! Oh, ye helpless things, ye revolving, whirling, swarming, moving crowds ; ye suffering figures of existence ; ye do not act but are merely moved. The one who acts am I; I act when I assert my free will. God demands free activity from us, consciously free service, free homage and love. Only such honours Him. The conscious homage of the heart honours and reveres God and serves Him more truly than the sun, moon, and ocean. *Laudamus Te, benedicimus Te, adoramus Te !* O my sublime, kingly, divine soul, feel and experience the nobility of thy race, thou immortal being ! This consciousness is our consolation, our force, and our joy. Do not let us cling to the dust and clod, we have wings, let us soar to our Jesus, to our Lord. Let us whisper trustingly and continually in our prayers : Lord, Thou hast redeemed me. Behold, God values me as much as Thy precious Blood !

THE TRANSFIGURATION

" *And after six days Jesus taketh Peter and James, and John his brother, and bringeth them up into a high mountain apart : and he was transfigured before them. And his face did shine as the sun : and his garments became as white as snow. . . . And Peter answering, said to Jesus : Lord, it is good for us to be here.*" (*Matt.* xvii. 1-4.)

(*a*) The Lord was transfigured by His soul, by His soul glowing with prayer, " and whilst He prayed His countenance was altered." (*Luke* ix. 29.) This is the transfiguration of the soul rendered happy by union with God. Flesh and blood, the difficulty and darkness of earthly existence, puts on soul. We continually strive that more and more soul should suffuse the flesh and instincts, that more soul should be poured upon work and social institutions. The work of the soul which clothes flesh and instincts with superior beauty and light is called prayer. In our prayers we strive to be reshaped, to be purer, nobler, and more spiritual. The first step towards moral transfiguration is the humble, warm, strong, prayer !

(b) When this warm stream is set free in our soul and a higher, sweet light filters into our life, we exclaim with Peter : " Lord, it is good for us to be here ; here upon the high mount of spiritual elevation, here in the regions of divine enlightenments, here in the bright cloud of prayer, here, far from the world and near to God. It is good, good indeed, for us to be here, so let us make use of this spring-blossoming of consolations, but let us keep in mind that we have to descend from this mount to the dusty, flat world. Let us descend as one whose soul is radiant and whose soul is filled with the balmy, spiced air of the heights."

(c) Let us look at the other transfiguration. " And taking with Him Peter and the two sons of Zebedee, He began to grow sorrowful and to be sad and he fell upon his face, praying and saying : . . . My Father, if it be possible, let this chalice pass from me . . . and he cometh to his disciples and findeth them asleep." (Matt. xxvi. 37.) This is the " facies " which sweats blood ; this is the outpouring of the sad soul over the body ; the state of desolation and darkness. The man of earth shrinks from it and sleeps ; he is happy to forget himself. But Christ prays. He struggles but acquiesces in the will of God. Thou dost wish it, my Lord, from Thy hands do I accept this cup ; even if I do not feel consolation, no matter ; I lock the guarantee of glory into my consciousness which assures me that the divine will accomplished at time of desolation is the seed of eternal life and that of every grace.

LORD, IT IS GOOD TO BE HERE

" Lord, it is good for us to be here." (*Matt.* xvii. 4.)

(*a*) Jesus prays, and being transfigured is arrayed in glory. What is the meaning of this ? We generally refer to Christ arriving at the Mount of the Ascension by way of Golgotha ; but we do not pay attention to His having arrived at Golgotha by way of Tabor. He was able to fight His battle victoriously, for evil, pain, and suffering became spiritualized in His soul. His soul stood and lived in light, that is why He could conquer darkness. It is on Tabor that He presented the elevation of His soul, *" ascensus in Deum."* He teaches mankind *spiritual work*, with which it rises above the world, time, want, transitoriness, and weakness. He teaches *work*, with which it releases its heart. He teaches it not to cling to earth. He preaches *work*, through which it keeps its soul elastic in reactions against evil, keeps it vigorous and strong also in sorrow. He preaches *work*, with which man can enlarge his soul in endeavour, longing, and strife. This *work* is prayer. We are to pray so as to rise in our soul, to glorify, bless, and beg the Lord and confess to Him. As the eagle drinks in the sunshine so shall we fill ourselves with divine ideas and enthusiasm. Elevation is the psalm, the impulse, the hymn. Let us talk our affairs over with the Lord, let us question Him and await His answers : *" Loquere, Domine."*

(*b*) And, as He prayed, His countenance was altered ; He was clothed in light and fire and He felt the joys and consolations of God. We become transfigured by divine ideas and feelings—*" species altera."* We become different, better men. The mistrusting, dismayed, earthly man becomes a divine being. The weak one will have strength and the disheartened a soul. With soul he conquers the flesh and the world, evil and temptation. Only such misery conquers to which we oppose no soul; suffering diffused with spirit is not ugly and does not kill; all the more devastating is the one which lacks spirit. A heart capable of opening and speaking with such feeling to God that it continually longs for the better and thwarts evil in himself, verily walks the slopes of Mount Tabor and enjoys the attachments of God. " *Multaberis in virum alienum* "; thou wilt be transfigured—the soul encourages —transfigured to a different man. Longing expands, love dissolves, and discipline reshapes the soul. Let us therefore strive to transfigure our soul, let us awake the appropriate feelings in ourselves. Do not let us wait till the stream carries us away; let us descend to the depths. Let us practise ejaculatory prayers. Let us awake our longings and supplications with the words of Holy Scripture !

JESUS HEALS THE DUMB. I

" *And coming to his disciples, he saw a great multitude about them, and the scribes disputing with them. And presently all the people seeing Jesus, were astonished and struck with fear : and running to him, they saluted him.*" (*Mark* ix. 13.)

(*a*) Up on the mountain Jesus is transfigured in the force of the soul, and imbues His disciples with sweetness, with remoteness from the world. Meanwhile, down below, weak faith disputes. And Jesus asked the Scribes : " What question ye with them ? " And one of the multitude answered and said : " Master, I have brought unto thee my son, which has a dumb spirit . . . and I spake to thy disciples that they should cast him out, and they could not." Thy strength ought to be in Thy disciples, ought it not ? But it is not, and instead of it there is rivalry and questioning. Let us not dispute and question, but enter the world with the spirit of Christ. Let us recall His memory with our individuality and not merely by our words. How very attractive this Christ is ! The people abandon the dispute ; they look upon Him with deep reverence, they run to Him and salute Him. Behold the strength of soul in the traits of Jesus !

(*b*) The father of the sick child begs : " *If thou canst do any thing, help us, having compassion on us. And Jesus saith to him : If thou canst believe, all things are possible to him that believeth.*" Whether miracle accompanies it, or whether the Lord directs us to the ways of patience, faith is always a vital force. It is by faith that we rise from out of the mechanism of the world. We know that God is in us, and that in the moral order He does not permit us to be tempted beyond our strength. We are imbued with courage and trust, and in the struggles of life we do not tear the ropes of patience. This strength will stream forth upon our surroundings and with it we will change " our world." Do not let us continually refer to circumstances and surroundings and the difficulties of them, but let us forcibly assert the soul, assert " our world." Let us believe and trust. There is light and warmth in that. Strength will pour forth from us.

(*c*) In society also " *all things are possible to him that believeth.*" Let us firmly believe that evil cannot conquer and that the Kingdom of God spreads and gains ground not only in the inner world but in the outer one also. It is true that this involves strife, and the clashing of interests involves bitterness. In every age different balances have to be created in economic circumstances, but let us keep our aim before our eyes, according to which the whole world is meant for the development of more good men, and that more valuable, better men should be formed. Do not let us look too gloomily upon the world, upon the feud between classes. We see that in spite of everything we are achieving more; the state of the working-classes and its way of living is improving; a more reasonable public spirit possesses us; love, mercy and charity are livelier. Distrust and despair have no place in the Gospel, which speaks of the Kingdom of God. Let us work for a better world, a better man, a more valuable one. Do not let us be angry with one or another class of society. " All things are possible to him that believeth."

(d) How are we to serve this great aim ? In the question the answer is contained : *with service.* Not with general phrases about people and country ; not with sentimental humanism, but with faith, with belief, backed by reverential, devoted, serving love. Let us place ethics in business, in economics, so that we be not selfish, unjust, and extortionate. Let us lighten the work of man, and encourage honesty, faithfulness, and reliability. These qualities are paid for, yet we always seek for them, for in business we ask first about moral qualities ; we ask whether the man we are interested in is a worthy, good, reliable man. Therefore we have to wish for as much morality as possible, in the world, that is, we wish for more and more good, correct, strong, honest will.

JESUS HEALS THE DUMB.   II

*" He threatened the unclean spirit, saying to him : Deaf and
dumb spirit, I command thee, go out of him . . . and he went
out of him." (Mark ix. 24.)*

(*a*) On Mount Tabor the glorious Christ celebrates the
feast of the soul, which creates heaven on earth and brings
down the Saints, Moses, and Elias amongst us ; whereas
down below feebleness of soul and misery of the body
torments men ; the soul is suffocated, the spirit darkens.
We feel both. The contrast is enormous. But who is to
help the world which struggles in the depths ? Behold
the Apostles standing there : they shrug their shoulders,
they cannot cope with the misery, although they are the
disciples of Christ. This is how it is with us. We are
faced with dark powers and forces. We too are pupils
of Christ and we cannot cope with them. We are humiliated and we suffer. Then comes the command of Jesus :
" Dumb and deaf spirit, I charge thee, come out of him,"
and by this we conquer. Let us always be convinced that
we have to suffer much. We cannot alter this ; but we do
not therefore renounce the good, and in this our humility
also God belongs to us and is ours.

(*b*) *" And when he was come into the house, his disciples
secretly asked him : Why could we not cast him out ? And he
said to them : This kind can go out by nothing but by prayer
and fasting."* The sword is rusty, it is unfit for victorious
strifes. Weak is the soul, therefore it cannot sufficiently
assert the force of God in the world. Two things are
wanted : prayer to God, so that we might be filled with
Him, and self-denial and fasting so that we can be free

from ourselves and the world. It is upon this way that those walked who did great spiritual things. The opposite way was taken by those who compromised the divine upon earth. Let prayers and fasting make us worthy fighters for God.

(c) Many good priests are wanted. Our age abstracts many hearts from God and stifles many souls in materialism. Let us pray and fast on Ember days that good priests may be created. Let us suffer for this. St. Stephen the martyr has procured St. Paul for the world, and St. Alphonso Rodriguez gave us St. Peter Claver. Why have we not more holy priests? The Lord answers this question thus: "Because ye do not beg for it sufficiently."

"UNLESS YOU BECOME AS LITTLE CHILDREN"

"*At that hour the disciples came to Jesus, saying: Who . . . is the greater in the kingdom of heaven? And Jesus calling unto him a little child, set him in the midst of them. Whom when he had embraced he saith to them: Amen, I say to you, unless you be converted, and become as little children, you shall not enter into the kingdom of heaven.*" (*Matt.* xviii. 1 ; *Mark* ix. 35.)

(a) Oh, men, you are filled with fog and imagination and sensitiveness, and there is little of truth and solid virtue in you. Your subjective stupidity renders you deformed, and your vanity makes you ailing. No one shall touch your self-love or else ye cease to serve the most holy interests. If your good intentions are criticized, ye are liable to forget God, for ye seek your own selves.

Ye are further filled with darkness, mire, and earth; the smell of decay is upon your robes and the sadness of the graves upon your being. Ye work for archæology. Contrary to this, Jesus wishes for a purified, noble-minded, superior soul, which has washed the mire out of itself and stands above petty subjectivity. He wishes for a transparent, beautiful, strong, free soul. We must fight against sensitiveness and against the many hidden ways of vanity which appear in us as antipathy and estrangement towards our neighbour. *Pro libertate !*

(b) "*Whosoever therefore shall humble himself as this little child . . . And he that shall receive one such little child in my name, receiveth me. But he that shall scandalize one of these little ones . . . it were better for him that a millstone should be hanged about his neck, and that he should be drowned in the bottom of the sea.*" Jesus sees the beautiful soul of the little child in which God resides, sees its transparency, sees that "*limpidezza*" which has not yet been overclouded by mist, fog, and stench . . . the heavy mist of care is not upon it, nor the slave-like state of labour. And He embraces the little child, He becomes its panegyrist and identifies Himself with it. How much He loves souls ! But at the same time, at seeing the destruction of these heavens, of these pure souls, He expresses His alarm and terrible anger : Woe to those who destroy a pure soul ; woe to the monster which sucks the blood of the soul and turns it into a corpse ! The curse of such a deed draws such ones down, like a millstone, into the depths of God-forsakenness ! The soul is a treasure, we also are such, but if we poison a soul we are objects of loathing and dregs. How can we look Jesus in the eyes ? Can we bear the contradiction which exists between His love for souls and our destruction of them? Jesus is the sun and we would then be corpses rotting below a millstone in a dark abyss. Oh, never let us be the cause of anyone becoming coarse, of his decadence, his unbelief, and distortion. Never, never, will we be a thorn in anyone's eyes. Never will our behaviour cool anyone's love and ardour.

(c) "*Woe to the world because of scandals. For it must needs be that scandals come. . . . And if thy hand, or thy foot, scandalize thee, cut it off. . . . And if thine eye scandalize thee, pluck it out.*" Behold the cry of pain of the soul of Jesus! His heart is heavy for that world which extinguishes the soul and eternal life; heavy for the dark, sad music which renders souls sorrowful in their love of the flesh and the earth. True that this power will assert itself, yet still it is fatal to be pioneer, outrider, and courier of fate. Jesus educates a different generation contrary to this sorrowful necessity; a generation in which the soul is not for sale for any price. What is the use of nimble feet, if they dance to hell? Of beautiful eyes, if they extinguish our light? Only he can be deemed magnanimous and prudent who can do without dance, embrace, bright eyes, so far as these are against virtue, for the sake of the most beautiful, for eternal beauty and love. He is capable of this because He loves intensely and fervently. This is how we also wish to love! It is with this sense that we handle the souls of others. We do not say: it is in vain, all belongs to the devil, but we act as such who wish to draw away everything from the power of the devil.

TRUE CHILDHOOD

"*Unless you . . . become as little children, you shall not enter into the kingdom of heaven.*" (*Matt.* xviii. 3.)

(*a*) There are two kinds of naïveté : the naïveté of *feeling*, and that of *knowledge*. The naïveté of knowledge is no advantage and no virtue, and with all our endeavour we see to it that we rise above the ignorance of childhood with as complete, as rich, and as true knowledge as possible. According to St. Paul : " When I was a child, I spoke as a child, I understood as a child . . . But when I became a man, I put away the things of a child." (1 *Cor*. xiii. 11.) But a naïve disposition, a simple, unpretentious, straight, true feeling, we have to tend and cherish. This is what Christ teaches us when for example, He washes the feet of His disciples. We are not to be children in that we stand on a low grade of knowledge, but in that we show the brightest knowledge and ready homage for the Lord and His holy will.

(*b*) What is more, filial feeling is the innocence of life and the unpretentiousness of ready love. Again, it is St. Paul who says : " Brethren, do not become children in sense ; but *in malice* be children and in sense be perfect." (1 *Cor*. xiv. 20.) The will of the Lord Jesus is to lift us continually to a higher and higher grade of spiritual life and to educate us to be free souls in spirit. We thirst for the spirit of eternal love and beautiful freedom ; we wish to be purified.

(*c*) Filial, childlike feeling is at the same time also trust. We look upon God and the holy dusk of our future and eternal goal with childlike eyes. We run through dark rooms into the arms of our Father . . . we run into Church as the children playing in the square before the Church, run up to the steps of the Altar, speak to our Jesus, and throw Him a kiss. Darkness does not swallow up the rays of trust of the childlike soul.

THE CHURCH TEACHES TRUE CHILDHOOD

"*Unless you . . . become as little children, you shall not
enter into the kingdom of heaven,*" namely, if ye do not possess
a trusting soul, attached to Me, which finds its joy in
Me, ye will not find your happiness !

(*a*) Everything in the Church trains us to this : Jesus
assures us that He is with us and does not forget us and in
this holy secret of unforgettable promise, in the Holy
Eucharist, He continually draws our hearts to Him. There
the motherly soul, the charm of beauty, surround us and
the eyes of the Holy Virgin rest upon us, eyes so often
mentioned : "*Illos tuos misericordes oculos.*" Our soul
cannot be indifferent, dark, and dreary ; the trust in our
prayers, gentleness in our art and feeling, in our songs,
betray the child's soul, voice, and look. . . . Oh, how
good it is for us to be here . . . here in the paternal
house . . . here in the home of God.

(*b*) Children are we, but not soft, weeping puppets, we
are shepherd-boys who do not want a sword and pike
but who have a sling and five sharp stones : the five letters
of the name of Jesus and the infinite trust they give us for
vanquishing the enemy : sin, passion, intrigue, hate,
poverty, illness, and death. Man groans beneath these
forces. He often comes upon victorious evil and nearly
loses spirit. In the world he experiences the self-forgetfulness and meanness which sinks to baseness ; the tor-
menting misunderstanding, inextinguishable hate, and the
alarming shadows of illness and death. He sees how life
fades and would fade even if every meadow were an

elysium and every isle a wonder island. And yet he knows that not evil but good conquers ; that the soul conquers the decaying body and that life lives beyond the grave ; he knows that the soul conquers all, conquers prison, suffering, death, bondage, hate . . . that it conquers as it conquered in the Holy Virgin, in SS. Francis, Agnes, Perpetua, Catherine, that it conquers if it undauntably believes and lovingly and trustingly embraces Jesus. Oh, children of God, ye wonders of God, your eyes are capable of looking into heaven without being overclouded, your child-face smiles even in the breath of death, your child-hands handle the sling and knock Goliaths down. . . . *Venerande puer, fortitudo Dei* : Venerable child, thou strength of God.

(*c*) Such a soul finds joy. Joy comes from victory. *Gaudete in Domino semper . . . Exultent et lætentur in te !* . . . God wishes that we should serve Him with joy : *Jubilate Deo, servite Domino in lætitia,* and that we should feel and experience that " *melior est dies una in atriis tuis super milia* " ; better a day with Thee than elsewhere a whole life. Do not let us be quarrelsome, dejected, suspicious souls. That spoils all : disposition, belief, artistic creation, and life itself ; it darkens the eye, our words and looks. It does not glorify God. The dejected, joyless soul has no perseverance, for it has no strength : " the sorrow of the heart defeats the soul." The dejected man's heart, hand, and arm are of lead and his soul is the hot-bed of suffering. It is joy which made St. Francis sing: " *tanto e il ben, ch'io aspetto, che ogni pen mi par diletto.*" Let us therefore live the " happy life " in the attachment to God and in ready service.

GOD'S ANGEL ACCOMPANIES US

*" See that you despise not one of these little ones : for I say
to you, that their angels in heaven always see the face of my
Father who is in heaven ! "* (*Matt.* xviii. 10.)

(*a*) We are not lonely and forsaken ; the angel of God
walks with us. "*Angeli eorum*," our angel. We would like
to speak with him, to look in his eyes, to embrace him,
but we can only approach him in spirit, for he is in an
" other world " than ours, of which we only feel the
breeze, as Columbus felt the scent of the sassafras tree on
the ocean. We believe that we have a guardian angel, for
there is a spiritual world which we cannot deny. The
fish shall not say : there is no life beyond that of water ;
the beast shall not say : there is none beyond that of the
air. There is life beyond the great world, above the
æther, "*in lumine tuo*" ; there is an invisible, spiritual
world, there are eyes needed for it, eyes of the spirit and
the soul. We believe it and rejoice in it. We cannot
embrace and clasp it, but we understand and love it.

(*b*) How are we to approach this invisible, spiritual
world ? With love and reverence. We reverence it as
great, sublime spirit. We know that in it the force of the
spirit is freed from the guardianship of the senses and it
shines and glitters, whereas our mind—be it even as that of
Leibniz or Kant—is a captive, a prisoner, which builds its
houses from ideas and its bridges from analogies with
which it wants to bridge dark, undiscoverable depths.
Whereas the mind of the spirit is intuitive, its knowledge is bright sunlight. Thy wisdom, O king, is as
the wisdom of angels ; David is told this. And this
wisdom draws and carries upwards, not downwards.

The clods of malignant, intriguing, base passions are not chained to its feet. It is loving wisdom ! Those souls are united with God and filled with grace. Such a pure spirit, a sublime one filled with grace, stands beside us and goes with us ! How highly have we to reverence and value it and to glow with enthusiasm for it ! We have to render ourselves worthy of such company. Angelic proximity . . . what a mighty motive this is for every good !

We have further to have ardent love for the angelic ; for these angels are strong, brave spirits bringing victory at the head of armies, as in the battles of Macchabeus. They are bountiful, merciful, gracious spirits, " the angels of peace, consolation and mercy." They are beautiful, they are sublime. In the hierarchy of existence they mediate the graces of God ; they lead us, take care of us, and encourage us. " I send my angel before thee " ; love him and trust in him, says the Lord. Clemens Brentano wrote a beautiful poem about Louise Hensel under the title of " The Angel of the Desert " ; this angelic soul led him back to faith, out of the desert to the sources of life. We do not walk in a desert if we listen to the words of angels and if we lovingly ask : what dost thou wish of me, thou victorious, sublime, heroic spirit ? Thou wishest me not to grow faint-hearted, not to waver and be afraid, but to love and trust and to call the name of our God for help and for His grace.

PARABLE OF THE CRUEL SERVANT. I

" *Therefore is the kingdom of heaven likened to a king, who would take an account of his servants. And when he had begun to take the account, one was brought to him, that owed him ten thousand talents.*" (*Matt.* xviii. 23.)

(*a*) Everyone is in debt to the life- and bliss-giving God. It is from Him we receive all the good in creation just as in redemption, and we can abuse everything. We commit sins. We abuse the words of Christ, His blood, His grace, His treasures; we oppose God and virtue; we live through conflicts which make our heart bleed; we groan in battles which make us grow weary. The Sublimity approaches me to settle accounts, He who excelled so in creation; He the joy of existence and its completeness, the infinite "*jubilus*" of strength and perfection. Oh, what has become of the strength and life in me? What of grace and beauty? The destitute, miserable pariah has ten thousand talents of debts! He writhes without merits, law, ability, without active and asserting force. Here there is only place for "*indulgentia*" and "*remissio*," place for pardon and remission of sins. If the Sublimity lets me off, then good, if not, I am unable to pay. Therefore I beg the Lord: "Forgive me, let me off"; this is what we pray for, when we confess; this is what we beg for: "Remit my punishment, my Lord." This is our object when we wish to gain indulgences.

(*b*) "*But that servant falling down, besought him, saying: Have patience with me, and I will pay thee all.*" This is our attitude towards the infinite Lord, every confession of ours, the more conscious moments of our zeal, our approach to God, and, above all, the hour of our death, urge us to adopt this attitude. I fall on my knees and with the longing for eternal life, and the ardour of my soul which adores the eternally Sublime and encircles His beauty, I beg Him to act, for only He can do so. I cannot do else but beg and repent and hope; but this I do with the resolution and undaunted trust of my soul. God help me that it be so ! What great forces are humiliation, trust, repentance, and hope !

(c) "*And the lord of that servant being moved with pity, let him go and forgave him the debt.*" The humility of repentance is followed by exaltation, that of kneeling down, by sweet embrace ; the dark brooding of the care of salvation is exchanged for the kiss of compassionate love. On the brink of hell the thorn-crowned Jesus appears. He raises us and encourages. " Come to me," He says, " do not doubt." I wipe out the doubt and misgiving from thy soul. I disperse the shadow of anguish from thy brow. Come, come, I replace sin by grace, my strength relieves thy helplessness and my love thy apostasy. Come, it is I who forgive thee ! I know thy ruin ! Thou didst become a pessimist. Thy philosophy also announces that man is vile ; thy science declares that man wears the signs of beastliness ; I also see an immense debt upon thee. Thy action opposes the moral law ; thou didst break away from the Holy God, and thy moral existence was hazardous. But I forgive thee ! Behold the new creation of God in the moral order ! Behold the merciful power !

(d) But this does not affect us as mirage and enchantment ; it causes a deep fluctuation of the soul. Soul ferments and rises here, bliss comes to it, and the soul grasps it fervently. The breath of the heights and reviving of the moral world touches it ; the beauty and charm of moral purity extricate themselves, and two feelings possess the soul : it feels its own misery and also the helping, saving power of God. God comes and revives me and I revive. Oh, do not let us doubt God and His mercy, for by so doing we would offend Him ! Our undaunted trust will give us strength and heighten our ardour and raise our attachment to passion.

(*e*) The gracious acceptance of this sin-forgiving grace changes life; the wall of partition twixt God and man crumbles down and divine forces stream towards us and into us. We will partake of the strength of Christ, of His reign and glory. We become delivered from the embarrassment of our faint-heartedness, mistrust and small faith, and we go forward bravely. Christ gave Himself and His grace to us; we became relieved and strong. We bravely act and continue to further the work of Christ in ourselves and in others.

PARABLE OF THE CRUEL SERVANT. II

"*But when that servant was gone out, he found one of his fellow servants that owed him an hundred pence : and laying hold of him, he throttled him, saying : Pay what thou owest. And his fellow servant falling down, besought him, saying : Have patience with me, and I will pay thee all. And he would not : but went and cast him into prison. . .*" (*Matt.* xviii. 28.)

(*a*) The servant having gone out to his fellow-servants, having descended from the heights of the Sublime Lord into the region of low feelings where servant and pedlar-souls torment each other, he became cruel, and forgot mercy. Behold the earthiness of the low soul! The soul of Jesus approaches us with the sublimity of the greatest vocation, with the blessing of divine feelings. In His soul the anxiety of the danger of eternal death and the longing of imparting eternal life became a passion. He comes to remove the curse, to unlock the gates of hell, to remit interminable debts. He comes to disperse the darkest worries of life. He comes with strength and power. He comes to us with outpouring soul, with the fire of Pentecost in His eyes, with the honey of Christmas-night upon His lips, He comes to us with the ardour of the Incarnation in His heart; He brought tears, mercy, compassion, purity, strength, and immortality, and servant-man forgets all this and for a hundred pence he tries to strangle, embitters, persecutes, kills . . . and plunges into hell! That is the child of God, this one is the servile type!

(b) "*Now his fellow servants seeing what was done, were very much grieved.*" Those fellow-servants who have not become beast-like by cruel selfishness, those are sorry; the world is their anguish, that low, creeping, snake-world. They fight against it, they work and strive and weep, but God does not wish them to languish, to pass from the heights of the eagles to the tracks of snakes. Let them go confidently after Christ, even if they have tears in their eyes. Let them go and assert His strength and exercise the power of love as far as they are able. Let them frame the dis-harmony of life into songs and hymns. Let them pour out their souls. The rays and outpourings of the soul are truth, sanctity, beauty, strength, joy and life. Let them render the world beautiful; and carry the Christly light which makes the fairy-stories pale, into their huts amongst their rags. Let them spread poetry over the view, meadow, barn and rotten garden-fence, poetry over the bushes. May the enthusiasm of life accompany them in the streets and corridors, in saloons, in attics and basements, and in the midst of their sorrow let them not forget that in reality they are the wine-inspired lords of life and existence! This is not philosophy, but Christianity.

(*c*) " *Then his lord called him : and said to him : Thou wicked servant, I forgave thee all the debt, because thou besoughtest me : shouldst not thou then have had compassion also on thy fellow servant, even as I had compassion on thee ?* " Oh, who can bear this accusation ? How the Lord has given and forgiven us ! How the blood of Christ with which He wiped off my sins burns upon my soul ! How His words pierce my heart " sharper than a sword with double blades " ! What treasures have slipped through our hands, as if they had been grains of sand ! Or perhaps the eternal loss of souls also casts its shadow upon us and behold " I forgave thee all that debt " and thou deceitful, dark, cold soul, thou induceth thy soul not to forgive others but to be cruel with them ? Oh, men, this is baseness indeed ; its track is the way to hell ! Love therefore and be merciful, as I love and am compassionate. Do not have a heavy heart of stone, but forgive offence and meanness !

THE SENDING OF THE DISCIPLES

" *And after these things the Lord appointed also other seventy-two : and he sent them two and two before his face . . . and he said to them : The harvest indeed is great, but the labourers are few.* " (*Luke* x. 1.)

(*a*) The fields grow yellow, the harvest is great. In spirit Jesus looks at the world. He looks into its misery, into the darkness of its sins and sufferings ; He experiences its troubles vividly ; He wishes to help with a sympathising, generous heart, therefore He tells us what we are in greatest need of : Beg God to send you apostolic men. He also indicates what they are to be like : pure-minded, without violence and interest, they are not to be tainted by the temperament of the rapacious, cruel, selfish world. They are to be barefooted, peaceful men, out of whom the soul radiates ; who have only one fact for the world, and that is that it should receive the peace which they give and return them bread for it. Christianity originates from the soul of Jesus ; its spreading and upholding also needs " congenial " men whose soul is like the soul of Jesus. Let us view this Christ-type ; let us look into its crystal-depths ; may this soul also fill us ; if we possess it, then let us look trustingly at the great harvest and whisper to ourselves : God sends us, His soul urges us on ; we go.

(b) " *Pray ye therefore the Lord of the harvest, that he send labourers into his harvest.*" Pray ye for such labourers. " Congenial " souls, in spiritual relation with Christ, have to be prayed and begged for. In the Holy Church the Apostolic succession will exist according to the law, but the law is only an iron wire, from which no wreath can be made ; flowers and morality are wanted for it. Law is a layer of rock, from which no beautiful world will arise ; that needs pines, forests, moss, lawns, meadows ; therefore let us pray and beg for them. Sometimes something of this genius appears amongst us and transports us. We can well imagine that, if this type does not come to us darkly, one-sidedly, with the passivity of Tolstoi, or in the mist of Ibsen ; but if it comes to us in the original beauty of " the Son-of-Man," how truly it will conquer our heart ! Our Saints are variations of this Type. Let us beg and pray for Apostles and Saints, and not only beg for them but educate such. Maybe, if we educate our children for Christ, Christ-like resemblance will appear in them !

(c) Labourers are wanted to create a new world. We

need hard-working and vividly perceptive souls. Work is needed ; rocks have to be pierced, stones to be quarried, harvest has to come and has to be reaped. The Apostles have not to sit in offices and await those who inquire ; this is quite a secondary function. Fiery rain comes down upon the Apostolic men from the censer of the apocalyptic Angel. They have no rest ; their soul expands, their eyes see, their face glows, and their hearts speak. The fire of love and the shadow of care characterize their frame of mind. Children, ailing ones, those who scandalize, those who are in peril, sinners, good souls, school, family, the thousand needs of society swarm before their eyes. They trust, pray, suffer, and persevere.

THE COMMAND OF LOVE. I

" *And behold a certain lawyer stood up, tempting him ; and saying : Master, what must I do to possess eternal life ? But he said to him : What is written in the law ? . . . He answering, said : Thou shalt love the Lord thy God with thy whole heart, and with thy whole soul, and with all thy strength, and with all thy mind, and with thy neighbour as thyself. And he said to him : Thou hast answered right : this do, and thou shalt live.*" (*Luke* x. 25.)

(*a*) Let us love God, our Sublime, Infinite, Sweet All ; that eternal, great good which reveals itself continually more and more ; " *omne esse,*" this swelling ocean of life and existence ; this warm, happy eternal life out of which souls spring forth as well as intuitions and inspirations and the joys of ecstasy ; out of whom the visions of the spirit and the inspirations of art arise, who charms souls and pours rhythm and harmony upon existence. Let us love this most real beauty which is poetry as well as reality ; this productive force which sets the stars in motion, which fills our heart with lofty, sweet feeling. Let us love Him, Him from whom comes material joy ; through whom children are born and flowers blossom ; who inspires every motive of the song of happiness, who drops milk, honey, and wine upon the lips of lovers, poets, prophets and Samaritans ; who brings tears to the eyes and inspires the thrush-songs of quiet joys ; who mingles tears of emotion with suffering and also works with dusk and darkness forming the better, more beautiful life. Let us love Him, Our Lord and our All, who willed us to exist, who wishes us to be better, more beautiful, stronger, fuller, richer souls ; who draws us on and opens the flood-gates of His graces and educates our soul continually to a more beautiful, more conscious spring of life. We have to love Him with heart and strength . . . and is it possible to love Him without feeling, emotion, and passion ? Who does not love Him passionately has not yet looked into His face !

(b) " *Thou shalt love the Lord . . .*" This is the first command of His, not that we should believe, hope, be afraid and expect reward. Thou shalt love, not anyhow, but passionately. Long, start, fly towards Him, thy heart shall leap for Him ; enfold Him, embrace Him, encircle Him in your arms. This command stands first, for love is the most perfect, most moral, most fine and noble will and feeling ; I myself have decided that I give myself over to Him with my entire being ; what else could suit Him and me better ? It is pure morality ; it fills the heart. It is also *first*, because God, the soul of life and perfection, wishes this above all ; He is jealous of the first fruits of our love. It is the *first* command also because it is the sweetest; its element is joy. We may find joy in the obedience, reverence, and glory which we give God, but the sweetest joy is in love! With this we are indeed able to progress, to persevere, to strive and make sacrifices. With this love we are able to surrender; it serves and is good for everything, it conquers all and is capable of everything!

(c) "*But he willing to justify himself, said to Jesus : And who is my neighbour? And Jesus answering, said : A certain man went down from Jerusalem to Jericho, and fell among robbers, who also stripped him, and having wounded him, went away, leaving him half dead. And it chanced that a certain priest went down the same way; and seeing him, passed by. In like manner also a Levite . . . But a certain Samaritan, being on his journey, came near him : and seeing him, was moved with compassion. And going up to him, bound up his wounds, pouring in oil and wine : and setting him upon his own beast, brought him to an inn, and took care of him. . . . Which of these three in thy opinion was neighbour to him that fell among the robbers ? But he said : He that shewed mercy to him. And Jesus said to him : Go, and do thou in like manner.*" (*Luke* x. 29.) First those pass the suffering man whose compassion is restricted and who have not the feeling in common with him, because they are strangers. Priests and Levites hurry perhaps to church or may be have no time because of important public affairs; suffice it to say that he who lies by the wayside is not their brother; they are not moved, and the sight of him does not affect them; in a word, they are strangers. But the Samaritan comes, and " has compassion," and offers his services. He approaches him spiritually and shows that he is concerned at the sight of the wounded man. This is that "*proximus*," the real brother, who is a friend and not only gives, but does ; who puts himself in a loving, helping state towards the sufferer and pours the strength of his soul upon him.

THE COMMAND OF LOVE. II

"*Love the Lord thy God.*"

(*a*) With all thy mind ; think of Him, search for Him, become absorbed in Him, contemplate Him. With all thy soul : thy disposition is able to become immersed, to sing, to shape ; it is able to inspire and enjoy ; turn to Him with all thy soul. Love the Lord thy God with all thy heart, with thy heart which beats and throbs blood, and spreads bounteous warmth and vital strength ; love Him like this and with all thy strength, with the strength and organs of life, with the eyes, ears, lips, and tongue. Love shall be the inspiration of thy heart, thy soul, thy mind ; this shall be the element of thy life. Without this the idea is a mere shadow ; it is a pale, colourless, feeble impetus which does not reach to God. Without love the "*anima*" has no value, it sees not, does not notice anything and reacts not ; and the heart, though it throbs, is like the weed of the swamp.

(*b*) Love . . . love bravely ; have no fear of being disrespectful. The objection against some statues of Our Lady is that the Infant is too closely joined to the breast of its mother and that " its intimate nestling spoils the hieratic appearance." Indeed, theoretically, we object to the anthropomorphistic representation of the " *Dominus*

Deus," which views God as man, but in feeling God is nearer to us than any man. The intimate union and the fusion of God with what is human and the conversion of doctrines into warm life will always be the chief aim of the Gospel! Our soul is poured over the Lord; we do not shrink because of His being Lord; our soul is poured upon its God; that He is God does not make us stiff! We love and love indeed; hieratic stiffness dissolves. The child clings to its mother, even if she be a queen; it would be strange if love were to decrease because of kingship. We comprehend this indeed; we take our feelings seriously, we become more serious in our love; but the "*Dominus Deus*" does not frighten us.

(*c*) Let us love the Lord; He is sublime and high, but not unsociable, for He is full of sunshine. He is deep and abysmal, but life throbs from this depth, and warm blood gushes forth. He is strong and stormy, but He holds flowers in His hands, scatters scent, and sings. He is mysteriously dumb, but becomes loud in the soul; He teaches us psalms, hymns, and the *Gloria ;* He terminates even the "*De profundis*" on a note of encouragement. His eyes are as black as night, but beautiful; the fire of eternal love glitters in this darkness. His visage is veiled, but nature is His mirror and everything symbolizes Him. He bears and educates. He gives joy and enthusiasm to our soul; He is good and true; He stretches out His hands towards us across transitoriness as across a ditch; we spring towards Him, for He raises us. He does not guard us from strife, but continually whispers: Thou art my child, and if thou weepest come to me and cry upon my heart. Oh, our God, our All!

MARY HAS CHOSEN THE BETTER PART

" Now it came to pass as they went, that he entered into a certain town : and a certain woman named Martha received him into her house. And she had a sister called Mary, who sitting also at the Lord's feet heard his word." (*Luke* x. 38.)

(*a*) Martha, the busy one who succeeds in the practical line, receives Jesus into her house and even in His presence she is unable to do else but work. She is busy, she has much to do. Whereas Mary does not work now, but sits at Jesus' feet and opens her soul to Him ! She has been working and will work again later ; but now she adores, loves, glows, and enjoys ; she is happy. In Martha the faulty one-sidedness of life reveals itself which only urges work and work again—which honours strength and perseverance, but which neglects the inner world, the reviving of the soul, the depth of consciousness, its beauty and freshness, neglects the purifying and refreshing of disposition. This is not right ; Martha should also sit down while the Master is there ; she should be absorbed in His soul ; she has time for work afterwards. Neither strength and talent nor production and work can be the content of life. Not on these but on the direction of endeavour and the form which our inner world takes upon itself everything depends, and everything depends on whether we are true to the holy, perfect principles and how we live up to them. Therefore the first requirement of life is content, consciousness, faithfulness, and ardour ; no one is allowed to neglect these but has to devote time, strength, and interest to them.

(*b*) *" But Martha was busy about much serving. Who stood*

and said : Lord, hast thou no care that my sister hath left me alone to serve ? Speak to her therefore, that she help me." This exaggerated, one-sided work renders man irritable, plaintive, dissatisfied, and unjust. Work becomes a yoke and burden which crushes, not a vocation and a duty which ravishes. We would like to shake this yoke off and look enviously and askance at those who work less. Nowadays work is verily a burden which weighs terribly upon humanity ; it has become a yoke of constraint and we serve it. Do not let us allow our soul to become embittered and deformed by work ; let us put our soul in our work and our noble motives and goodwill. This is the oil upon the grating wheels. Let us work for God and man from vocation and do not let us complain, but at the same time let us do our best to see that the present graceless state of labour gives place to a better social order.

(*c*) *And the Lord, answering, said to her : Martha, Martha, thou art careful, and art troubled about many things. But one thing is necessary. Mary hath chosen the best part."* Martha, thou art busy and careth and thinketh for many things, but do not neglect thyself and do not be unjust towards others. " One thing is needful " ; needful and necessary is the frame of mind which is united with God and lives from Him. God shall be thy soul, thy life, and the centre of thy endeavours, and all thy work and endeavour shall be a harmonious outline of this centre ; then there will be symmetry, harmony, peace, and happiness in thee. It is then that thou provest that " thou dost not produce more goods but more happiness." Therefore " one thing is needful " and that is a pure, beautiful, noble soul which loves God. Who chooses this has chosen the best part and this is the only rational, logical procedure. Those who neglect the soul and themselves carry disunion in themselves; their fate is darkness, bitterness, and emptiness. But this does not mean that we should retire, and hide in seclusion; let us remain at our profession and in all our work keep an eye on the " one thing which is needful."

CHRIST AND THE WOMAN TAKEN IN ADULTERY

" *And the scribes and Pharisees bring unto him a woman taken in adultery; and they set her in the midst, and said to him: Master, this woman was even now taken in adultery. Now Moses in the law commanded us to stone such a one. But what sayest thou? And this they said, tempting him, that they might accuse him. But Jesus bowing himself down, wrote with his finger on the ground.*" (*John* viii. 3.)

(*a*) Before Christ stand the adulteress who feels that she has fallen, and her deceitful persecutors, the executors of the law, but these have not come here because of the sanctity of the law, but to ensnare Jesus. Jesus wished to deepen the feeling of morality; He wished that every sinner should first feel his own sin; that with the loathing of sin and the hatred which we feel first towards ourselves we should start out to improve and save others. Blessing only rests upon such a mentality. Let us therefore go into the depths, into ourselves; let us become pure, then we can affect others.

(*b*) "*When therefore they continued asking him, he lifted up himself and said to them: He that is without sin among you, let him cast a stone at her.*" This does not mean that sin

has not to be punished; this would lead to moral enerva-
tion. Jesus does not here adopt a legal attitude, but deals
with the souls of the deceitful men who stand before Him.
He sees through their guile. He sees that they do not
serve morality, but want to ensnare Him. How good it is
to bring such people to the consciousness of that sinfulness
which they want to have punished in others. The woman
is a sinner, but they also are deceitful. Let us purify the
good intention so that base, selfish, sensual, ignoble
elements do not mingle with it.

(c) *" But they hearing this went out one by one . . . and
Jesus alone remained, and the woman standing in the midst.
Then Jesus lifting up himself, said to her : Woman, where are
they that accused thee ? Hath no man condemned thee ? Who
said : No man, Lord. And Jesus said : Neither will I
condemn thee. Go, and now sin no more."* They went away,
they felt that Jesus saw through their deceitfulness. Jesus
and the sinner are left alone. This is as it should be :
street, noise, and passion have no place here. " I do not
condemn thee," says the Lord—I do not crush thy
individuality, live and grow better. I loathe sin, but I wish
thee good. Make good thy sins ; live purely. This is how
" misericordia " speaks to *" miseria."* To despise and
loathe sin, but to wish the sinner good, is the great thing.

CHRIST'S WITNESS TO THE TRUTH

*" Which of you shall convince me of sin ? If I say the truth
to you, why do you not believe me ? "* (John viii. 46.)

(a) The humble Jesus who rejects every homage, who
hurries to the mountain when they wish to proclaim Him

king, who has forbidden those whom He cured to go and tell others, presents Himself here in the greatest sublimity and moral dignity and demands that everyone should acknowledge that He is holy and without sin. This is the greatest sublimity. How nobly Jesus stands out from the poor, sinful world which is full of the lusts of the flesh and eyes and of the haughtiness of life! But this sublimity is the due of the Son of God, who came to take away our sins. What crystal depths open in those pure souls which are filled with God, peace, and joy. Compared with these, genius, power, and riches are mere formalities, which do not render life happy and sweet. Let us endeavour to achieve real purity of heart, that God may not reprove us with our sin. The world may not do so, but that is not sufficient.

(b) " *He that is of God, heareth the words of God. Therefore you hear them not, because you are not of God.*" Behold the great empirical fact : who is of God, is drawn to Him, has a sense for Him and speaks with Him ; who is not of Him is a stranger to Him ; but his being a stranger is his own fault. God gives Himself to everybody ; with His grace He precedes, enlightens, and attracts souls ; if He did not do so no one could go to Him. But the trouble is that we either refuse the grace of the Lord, or do not collaborate with it. O Lord, how much we spoil Thy work ! How have we treated Thy grace and Thy enlightenments ? How do we still treat Thy promptings ? We pray that our mind and soul should become finer concerning God. What wonderful feelings the 119th Psalm shows us about this. " With my whole heart have I sought thee ; O let me not wander from thy commandments. Thy word have I hid in my heart, that I might not sin against thee."

(c) " *Jesus answered . . . I seek not mine own glory ; there is one that seeketh and judgeth. Amen, amen, I say to you : If any man keep my word, he shall not see death for ever.*" Of you I do not seek glory. What could I get from men who do not comprehend God, soul, world, and life ? Yet ye think highly of your opinions, and ye criticize, abuse, and condemn. Contrasted with all this there is one single criterion which I establish : with Me only such words and speech are of any account which pursue death and give life. Ye blame and criticize ; but from this no one will be better, more holy and trusting. Whereas if a man keep my saying, he shall never see death ; the morality of such a one who keeps My word, keeps My saying, is founded on God, his heart is warm, his strength does not run short, and his soul stands in eternal spring. This verdict is not a word but a fact. This is our experi-ence ; why should we dispute ? Rather let us live.

HEALING OF THE MAN BORN BLIND

" *And Jesus passing by, saw a man who was blind from his birth ; and his disciples asked him : Rabbi, who hath sinned, this man, or his parents, that he should be born blind ? Jesus answered : Neither hath this man sinned, nor his parents ; but that the works of God should be made manifest in him.*" (*John* ix. 1.)

(a) Troubles are not only punishments. To see sin behind every trouble is a superficial, bad theology. We are finite, that is, we are limited in everything, therefore in our life-energy also. Our individual organism and our social life are complexes of innumerable forces, in which mistakes easily happen and appear as troubles and suffering.

We are placed into the mechanism of the world, and the development of the world proceeds upon the way of blind force. There is providence, but this does not save us from need, suffering, and mistakes. Do not let us therefore sniff sin everywhere we have to suffer, but let us see to it that "the works of God should be made manifest" in us: in our trust, in our patience, and prudent, moderate behaviour. The book of Job says that one does not only suffer for ungodliness but also for other reasons, and likewise it says that the wicked are often lucky in this world, being reserved for the day of vengeance. Let us wish to glorify the Lord. We do not remonstrate with Him, but endure what He metes out to us upon earth, be it sunshine or night. May the Lord not withhold eternal light from us after death.

(b) "He spat on the ground, and made clay of the spittle, and spread the clay upon his eyes. And said to him: Go, wash in the pool of Siloe. . . . He went therefore, and washed, and he came seeing." The beggar sat on the roadside and begged; many gave something to him; Jesus did not give money to him but He gave his soul strength and sunshine; He gave life and by this freed him also from begging. This is His way: He helps to life; He places us on our feet; He helps us to get on by ourselves. Oh, what a divine gift! It helps us to belief, trust, and bravery. In this respect we all are in want of Jesus' alms. We need great courage to emerge victorious from life's struggles and temptations, and we are not so much in want of alms as good friends. This is how we also have to help the poor: let us help them to trust; let us console them and lift them up.

(c) "The neighbours therefore . . . said: How were thy eyes opened? He answered: That man that is called Jesus made

*clay, and anointed my eyes . . . and I see. Now it was the
sabbath when Jesus made the clay."* Jesus called forth light
with clay, whereas we suppress the divine light in us with
clay, with our earthly, lowly way of thinking. What
darkness there is everywhere . . . in religious souls also,
who do not understand the great ideas of God and who,
for instance, are scandalized because Jesus gives His love
and help on the Sabbath ! What a darkness it is which
forgets the great, free, loving spirit of God because of
empty, senseless formalities, and draws the sublime down
to its own ideas, instead of raising them to it. That is why
it does not recognize God and His works and disputes and
becomes blind, saying : " This man is not of God, because
he keepeth not the sabbath day," even if He loves and does
miracles. O Lord, we wish to rise to Thee, and to Thy
truths. Divest us of our weak, worthless understanding.
Speak, O Lord, Thy servant listens : Speak, we pay Thee
homage. Do not say of me also : " For judgment I am
come into this world, that they which see not might see ;
and that they which see might be made blind."

(*d*) *" Jesus heard that they had cast him out : and when he
had found him, he said to him : Dost thou believe in the Son of
God ? He answered, and said : Who is he, Lord, that I may
believe in him ? And Jesus said to him : Thou hast both seen
him ; and it is he that talketh with thee. And he said : I
believe, Lord. And falling down he adored him."* It is to this
sight that Jesus wishes to open our eyes, that we should
see Him as the Son of God. Similarly He has shown Himself to us in His sublimity, in His life, and miracles. Indeed,
we too see Him, we see the most Sublime. We feel that
He lifts us out of the narrow, lowly world and gives us
strength. With this faith, with this belief, the wings of the

soul grow. From the ethical chaos stirred up by theosophy we rise to pure, divine, strong will. Also our greatest step is falling on to our knees.

WORK WHILE IT IS DAY

"*I must work the works of him that sent me, whilst it is day : the night cometh when no man can work.*" (*John* ix. 4.)

(*a*) Usually we see in work only the stamp of punishment, and we may do so too, for there is some truth in it. It follows us as a dark, gloomy shadow through history. But it is in work that we become like to God, who is eternal activity. Every potentiality, whether it be of the brain or muscle, is meant to spend its strength in activity ; if it does not do so, it fails and becomes ruined. Work, therefore, is the necessary element of life, health, and happiness. Work is a life-developing, life-ennobling factor. Work must not kill and cripple us ; but to avoid this we should perform our work with pleasure and put our soul into it. Whether we work for money or for pleasure, let us think of it thus : This is good for us, this is the fulfilment of our life. We work for God and for the fuller life !

(*b*) Let us work in keeping with our profession : whether behind the plough or in the workshop or in an academical profession. It is better for us to be intelligent, zealous labourers who work for God, than to be bunglers. It is bad when ability and talent is not in its right place, when genius struggles amidst pecuniary worries ; but it is just as bad to rise through protectors and to prove no good there. Therefore vocation is needed ; where God places us there we wish to prove good ; for the chief point is that we should do everything well. This feeling is our sunshine ! We must unite the activity of Martha with the spirit of Mary. It would be best for us to unite a high level of individual education with simple manual labour ; by this many conflicts would be smoothed over, both in ourselves and in our communal life.

(c) We have to work conscientiously, with interest and purposefully. We ought not to undertake too many different things. " *Pauca agas, si tranquillus esse cupis*," do not let us do many kind of things, then we will be calm. Do not let us fear and shirk work ; do not let us put it off for another time. " Procrastination is the thief of time." Let us use our time well, and if our hands do not work, let our soul work. Whether we are at a concert or are going for a walk, let us occupy ourselves with love and consciousness with our own self and our tasks, with God and our difficulties. Let us do this, not feverishly but diligently. Fever and excitement harass, whereas diligence soothes us.

RETURN OF THE DISCIPLES

" *And the seventy-two returned with joy, saying : Lord, the devils also are subject to us in thy name.*" (*Luke* x. 17.)

(a) They come with joy, with the feeling of victory and triumph. Great is their joy, for they have done great good, they have power. Misery and illness fade, the bonds of evil are loosed, and the released sufferers sing their praise. In their tracks there is peace, happiness, holy joy, and thankfulness ; as if there were a pilgrimage of angels upon earth. Even their feet are beautiful, " *speciosi pedes evangelizantium*." Those whom Jesus sends walk this way; power radiates from their face; their soul is strong, they feel that even devils obey them. We also have power and vocation; we act with the strength of our soul, and where there is want and darkness and cold, there we warm and light and help.

(b) " Rejoice not . . . that spirits are subject unto you: but rejoice in this, that your names are written in heaven." Do not rejoice because of your miraculous strength, but rejoice in your unity with God which manifests itself as faith, love, trust, joy, and confidence in the prospect of eternal life. The miracles are not your work, but this soul, this disposition, lift you out and place you in the stream of eternal life. Prophecy, knowledge, and power are advantageous things, but they are merely external gifts which do not render man divine. " Non sum propheta," no matter; but our soul is to be filled with God. We are no savants, but we are able to love and unite ourselves to God. We do not speak angelic language, but we understand the tongue of the loving soul and it is to this that God replies.

(c) " In that same hour he rejoiced in the Holy Ghost, and said: I confess to thee, O Father, Lord of heaven and earth, because thou hast hidden these things from the wise and prudent, and hast revealed them to little ones. Yea, Father, for so it hath seemed good in thy sight." The soul of the Lord is filled with joy at the working of the Spirit in His followers. He rejoices in the Holy Spirit, rejoices more powerfully than poets and prophets; He rejoices more passionately than the seer of Patmos. He sees a world which echoes with " the surging of many waters " and with the flapping of wings of the souls striving towards heaven. He sees culture, sees machines, art, and science; He sees the development of forces and the ascendancy of man on

earth, but as if He would smile at these exertions, saying :
" I thank Thee, O Father, Lord of heaven and earth, that
Thou hast created not this, but that other internal heaven,
and that Thou hast guided souls thither by way of the
sonship of God, humility, and sanctity. Oh, this Thy
kingdom is superior, beautiful, and deep ; its forces and
joy cannot be compared with culture. This Thou hast
created, and Thou shapest it—the excellence and blessing
of Thy hand is upon it."

BLESSED ARE THE EYES THAT SEE THE THINGS WHICH YOU SEE

*" And turning to his disciples, he said : Blessed are the eyes
that see the things which you see. For I say to you that many
prophets and kings have desired to see the things that you see, and
have not seen them ; and to hear the things that you hear, and have
not heard them."* (*Luke* x. 23.)

Blessed are you if you see, not only with the eyes, but
with the soul ; not only with the mind, but with faith.
Blessed are you if you see the world in divine light—if
your eyes not only absorb light but can pour light upon
the world, can pour the " *lumen Christi* " upon it.

(*a*) Man is the soul and heart of creation ; in man
creation turns into emotion and idea ; through him the
world receives sound, colour, and intelligence. Man has
to take in its impressions ; he has to make use of the
oppositions of nature for developing his virtue, energy,
and patience, and he can derive joy and pleasure from the
beauties of the world. These are the impressions of the
outer world upon the soul. On the other hand the soul

has to create its own world ; it has to see God ; it has to see the ideas and love of God and dwell with delight upon His works. Its instinctive feelings about its dependence, its immortality, must, with the aid of divine revelation and the death of Christ on the Cross, build up the theological structure of faith. Behold the light which Jesus kindles in the soul, which shines from out of the soul. It is we who are the lamps of the world, our believing soul is the light of the dark earth. For we always expected light from the world, and it is just the opposite : we pour our light upon the world. O God, our sweet sun, thou shalt shine in our soul ; who looks into thee, shall see heaven ! Look out from our soul, our trusting eye is a star in the night ; it is the star of many who doubt in darkness. . . .

(b) Man is the centre of Nature ; he is placed in the world with his power of feeling ; in him cold and warmth, gloom and brightness, become a feeling ; just as the way of the world arouses in him humble faith in Providence— the mingled chaos of conflicting elements becomes sweet harmony. O Lord, again our heart is the source, the sweet or bitter source ; it may destroy our world with its dark, helpless pessimism, with its impatient, bitter, dis-united spirit, or it may set it in order, discipline and beauty. I, I myself, am the smith of my fortune, I am he who shapes this great work which is called life.

(c) Some see punishment in the blows of fortune. Do they see well ? Is it true that if the crop rots, it rots because souls rot—that if it is withered it is because souls are dry ? It is true, verily true. Blows and troubles are punishment to us because we are sinful ; who feels his sin suffers his punishment in evil. Reverence is due to these fine, enlightened minds and souls. Who does not feel punishment in evil is blunt; such a one is not tortured by sin either. In our sufferings the wound of our soul shall hurt us most of all. Oh, divine, spiritual, fine feeling, where thou comest forward there there is strong life and strong reaction against sin and decay. Oh, possess us, so that spirit and life shall live in us !

COME TO ME

" Come to me, all you that labour, and are burdened, and I will refresh you." (*Matt.* xi. 28.)

(*a*) The bountiful, strong soul of Jesus streams forth in these words. This generosity of heart comes from the soul which makes its sun rise upon good and evil and which gives rain to sinners and saints. This is the noble love which narrow-minded, human truth or wickedness cannot quench. It appears to all of us, whether we be sinful or virtuous and says : Ye all labour and are all heavy laden, come unto me, I will help you. This bounty of soul is indeed a great and good power ; it draws us on, it fascinates and unites us. Its vocation is to draw all of us to Himself and to unite us amongst ourselves. Who is good, does not remain alone ; others attach themselves to him, and a fresh, ruddy, vigorous attraction streams forth from his soul. It is like the mountain stream, it does not get tired and does not lose strength. This is the frame of mind, the disposition, we learn from Jesus. The ideal of antique culture was the fine, many-sided education and civilisation ; the ideal of Christianity is compassion which raises, and strength which turns to the low ones, the sufferers, and suppressed ones. There are many such ; they have to be raised. Jesus helps all of us ; He streamed forth strength and soul. His Apostles shall walk in His footsteps as the generation of the strong ones, which equally raises, helps, and renders happy.

(b) " *All*." What a great undertaking it is to fulfil the claims of all of us ! Especially the claim of lifting " the load of the heart." All these loads gravitate towards the Heart of Jesus, and they who feel the load are already drawn on by the Father. They seek relief, and they find it, but only in Jesus. The centre of gravity of the solar system may be an interesting point, for it is the centre of physical existence. But behold the centre of the loads of the world, it is Jesus ! It is He who carries the load, " He takes away the sins of the world." This load crushes us, if we do not turn it over to Him. It is in His blood that we are refreshed.

(c) What trust this invitation of Jesus awakes in us, especially at our death ! Lord, where are we to go, when we are torn from the world, when the whole world has become estranged from us ? " Come unto me, come," Thou sayest, " and I will give you rest . . . finally and victoriously." *Veni, coronaberis !* This is indeed an invitation ; happy are those who earnestly strive to merit it !

PRAYER IN THE NAME OF JESUS

" *Amen, amen, I say to you : if you ask the Father anything in my name, he will give it you.*" (*John* xvi. 23.)

(a) In distress man looks to God in his sorrows and troubles ; he asks, implores and begs. Here upon earth we also ask each other for help, for we are dependent on each other. With God also we may speak and negotiate; this is prayer. We have to pray, for we believe that God is near us and that He is wise and strong. We believe that He loves us, loves us more than our fathers and mothers do. Therefore our heart and lips open; being rooted to the earth we are in need of bread, sunshine, rain, and grace and we cry out to Him; we disclose our anxieties and everything that endangers our peace. No kind of philosophy, no kind of insight into the mechanism of nature will confuse the genuine instinct of such feeling, striving hearts; nor will we condemn to stupid dumbness our hearts which rise above mechanism and materialism. Prayer is the mother-tongue of our souls; let us never forget that.

(b) " *Whatsoever you shall ask of the Father in my name, he may give it you.*" (*John* xv. 16.) Whatsoever? The mechanism of the world we cannot stop; we are not successful in our prayers for rain or sunshine; for the conversion of the wicked, so what does " whatsoever " mean? Jesus explains: He also begged and prayed, and did not gain what He begged for. What a grace the unanswered prayer of Jesus is to us! To beg in the name of Jesus therefore means as much as to beg according to His example; to beg in this way: Lord, if it be possible . . . if it be Thy will . . . to beg in the name of Jesus means as much as to rise above troubles, adversities, and miseries, so that if we do not get sunshine and rain on the crops we should always receive it on our soul and even if our crop rots we should receive perseverance and strength for life. Jesus also won this hearing. After having prayed, He says: *surgite, eamus;* come, let us go, let us conquer. Let us also understand His reproach: " Hitherto you have not asked anything in my name. Ask, and you shall receive, that your joy may be full." (*John* xvi. 24.)

(*c*) Let us place our longing, imploring soul in this state of praying faith and let us cry to God: (1) for earthly things: Jesus taught us to pray for our daily bread and He prayed that His life might be spared. (2) Let us pray for each other. In the prayer that Jesus taught us He did not use the singular number; He considered all our interests together. The power of evil shall not terrify us, neither the will of the resisting ones; God is strong. He can turn all ill aside. (3) Let us pray with profound exertion. We struggle with ourselves and with the load of worlds weighing upon us, let us cry out to the strong God. Let us seek Him and His consolations as the wounded deer seeks the springs of water. Let us thirst for God and cling to Him. (4) Let us pray with perseverance, for we are in need of the Lord. He is Lord; He is able to give life. We go after Him; let us beg Him seven times a day! (5) Let us pray with resignation; the focus of our prayer is: Thy will be done, O Lord; and even if we sweat blood, let us whisper: Not our will, but Thine be done.

LORD, TEACH US TO PRAY

" *And it came to pass, that as he was in a certain place praying, when he ceased, one of his disciples said to him: Lord, teach us to pray.*" (*Luke* xi. 1.)

(*a*) Teach us to speak to the Infinite and lead us on to those paths upon which our soul finds its way to God so that it is able to talk to Him. Master, we see that Thou

art able to become absorbed and canst speak with God.
We also feel that life must not be allowed to become dull
and formal, our soul must not be allowed to be crushed
by the mechanism of nature.   Often our feeble heart
instinctively longs for original truth, original beauty,
and original strength, for it notices that the world is filled
with form, that is with ideas, with beauty, that is with joy.
God is so near !   We stretch out our arms towards Him,
but we do not trust ourselves and our inspirations.
Therefore, Our Lord, Thou the " seeing " one, Thou the
" Master," who came from God, Thou teach us the mother-
tongue, which God understands as well as we.   Teach us
the sweetest mother-tongue of the soul, which is prayer !

(b) " *And when you are praying, speak not much, as the
heathens . . . thus therefore shall you pray : Our Father who
art in heaven.*"   (*Matt*. vi. 7.)   To pray, that is to turn
towards the Infinite, to awake to the consciousness of the
depths opening in our soul, to be steeped in the radiation
of nature and grace and to seek that word which shall be
our strength, life and joy; this praying word which says all
is : Our Father.   Many only saw darkness and unfriendli-
ness in existence, for their soul was dark.   Jesus pervades
life with light and warmth.   They saw only clouds, He
saw the sun.   They saw only chaos ; He saw loving ideas.
They walked towards the abysses of ruin, He makes souls
run through the darkness, as children through a dark room
with beating heart . . . into the arms of His Father.
This is the spirit which darts towards us from out of nature
and the supernatural world.   This it is that places our
soul in light and melts our heart !   Therefore we do not
only say, but sing that joyous revelation : Our Father !
Our Father !

"HE CASTETH OUT DEVILS BY BEELZEBUB"

" But some of them said : He casteth out devils by Beelzebub the prince of devils. . . . But he seeing their thoughts, said to them : Every kingdom divided against itself shall be brought to desolation, and house upon house shall fall." (Luke xi. 15.)

(*a*) And these were also men who believed that they were of good will, and yet this is how they thought of their Lord. Behold how dark and distorted subjective conception and feeling can be ; it can be completely interwoven with emotional elements ; it can misunderstand everything, even Christ. It is of these the Lord says : generation of vipers, poison is grafted in you ; you throw out poison from yourselves. You are convex mirrors, everything becomes distorted in you. For the recognition of truth a purified, disciplined, ordered, elevated disposition and frame of mind are necessary, for our being pleased or displeased and our sympathy and antipathy strongly influence us. Self-examination and freedom of the soul are necessary to virtue.

(*b*) *" But if I by the finger of God cast out devils : doubtless the kingdom of God is come upon you."* We cannot doubt about the work of Jesus ; He renders everyone better and nobler and brings them nearer to God. This is the finger of God in His work. If it were bad it would give itself away here and there. This is what He appropriately says elsewhere : *" The good man brings forth good things from the good treasure and the evil one evil things from the bad treasure."* " Good treasure " is the bounty which is accumulated in Him. As honey from many flowers collects in the hive, so the " good treasure " collects in us ; this is purified good-will, that is, will corresponding to aim, situation, and tasks. "Bad treasure" is the darkened, poisoned, distorted frame of mind. It is a sad treasure. What a great word is the one which says : Peace on earth to those of goodwill.

(c) "*But I say unto you that every idle word . . . They shall render an account in the day of judgement for it.*" (*Matt.* xii. 36.) The moral rule has to be asserted in everything ; words, jokes, good humour, conversation, and small talk should be the reflection of the beautiful and good soul. Frivolous, critical, sharp, abusing, cold talk is November rain which makes the forest rot and causes mud. We hate abuse, for we shall have to give account of it on the day of judgement. We loathe that unprecise, unconscientious expression which places the individuality of others in an untrue light and at one time takes away something from it and at another time adds to it. We loathe those nuances and shades of conversation which make a wedge between men, as well as gossip which only speaks of faults and frailties and with which those who practise such gossip unconsciously tickle their selfish, malignant disposition. The consciously good and aristocratic soul avoids all this ; it takes care of itself, especially by awaking goodwill toward others, so that in talk and conversation it should be neither a market-fly, a wasp, nor a scarab.

WARNING AGAINST COVETOUSNESS

"*And he said to them : Take heed and beware of all covetousness : for a man's life doth not consist in the abundance of things which he possesseth. And he spoke a similitude to them, saying : The land of a certain rich man brought forth good fruits. And he thought within himself, saying : What shall I do ? And he said : This will I do : I will pull down my barns, and will build greater. . . . And I will say to my soul : Soul, thou hast much goods laid up for many years, take thy rest, eat, drink, make good cheer.*" (*Luke* xii. 15.)

(*a*) My soul, take thine ease, be merry ! The aim of all men is the happy life. And the way to it ? Is it to eat, drink, enjoy, to banish trouble and strife . . . to live, create, act, and do . . . to work, to quarry stones, burn lime, build houses . . . to change life into a garden and put pleasure, flowers and scent into it ? Is this the way ? " Take heed and beware of covetousness, for no one's life consisteth of the things he possesseth," but everyone has to understand himself, to understand the hunger, thirst, and speech of his soul. One is not allowed to wall in the soul's prospects of eternity, to cover the stars with stucco and to break off the wings of faith and hope ; for the blind, tormented, and stifled fullness of life cannot lead to happiness. Not to possess much but to experience and live in God, virtue, trust, and love : it is on the abundance of these that life depends.

(*b*) What are we reassured by ? " *Fideles in dilectione acquiescent illi.*" Those who love faithfully and who serve faithfully for love are reassured. We have to exclude : (1) Sin. (2) Restlessness, feverish inconsistency, confusion, distrust, by strong and true discipline of our soul. We are to have diligent faith in the Lord, in big and small things. Also in our emotions, so that the pure stream of our soul should not be disturbed. We do not wish to cling to single emotions or to our dark thoughts and ideas. We strive against depression and apathy. Our soul is a moulding force and it is able to " find great peace and quiet."

(*c*) " *But God said to him : Thou fool, this night do they require thy soul ; and whose shall those things be which thou hast provided ? So is he that . . . is not rich towards God.*" God says : Thou fool ! Eternal wisdom says it, which tends and loves life and which sees the dreadful waste and degeneration of it. Only life in God can be happy, that is the life which is rich in love, truth, holiness, and moral strength. Rich are those in whom God dwells and to whom He imparts His light, beauty, joy, and strength. Let us always separate these two things : the inner world of our soul and that which surrounds us, for example, house, position, and man, and let us well feel that we are able to be light, bright, and warm in spite of these. I beg thee shape thy life thyself and do not expect others to do it for thee.

BLESSED ARE THOSE WHOM THE LORD SHALL FIND WATCHING

" *Let your loins be girt, and lamps burning in your hands. And you yourselves like to men who wait for their lord. . . . Blessed are those servants, whom the Lord when he cometh shall find watching. Amen, I say to you, that he will gird himself, and make them sit down to meat, and passing will minister unto them.*" (*Luke* xii. 35.)

Estimable, wonderful energies can develop the world of spiritual life. That may be a poor, swampy country— but it may be Canaan on the borders of primeval forest. The necessary conditions of well-developed soul-life are these :

(*a*) We are ready to die at any time, for we are prepared

concerning our individual soul-world. Is our heart pure
and does our soul side with God? We may have many
unfinished works; our family and children have need of
us; but our soul is clean; we look Jesus in the eyes with
humble trust. We also love life, we love the flowers and
forests, art and science, and the grand perspectives of the
world's development, but we view all this as the *præludium*
to eternal, beautiful life, and the "*præludium*" does not
make us forget the "*opera.*" These inclinations of ours
are only the gold-washing out of the sand, and because of
the grains of gold we do not despise the golden bars.
Oh, thou beautiful, holy, rich, eternal life, towards which
we hurry, we already experience and live it in its foretaste
here below.

(*b*) We are not to love and seek for anything at the price
of perplexity and embarrassment; neither career, comfort,
glory, and pleasure, nor betrothal nor any enterprise!
Let us love ardently and truly but every tendency and
endeavour must be subject to the will of Christ. This is
that nobility of soul, that noble unpretentiousness which
walks upon earth, but which treads the mud and does not
take roots in it.

(*c*) To do everything as well as possible, to do it perfectly. To have a sense for refinement. We have to attend
to our motives and intentions and to the straightforward,
noble way of our proceedings. To notice the many kinds
of shadows in us, the dregs and faults, bitterness and
distaste. But also to notice improvement and to enjoy
the good and noble in ourselves.

BE YOU READY

" But this know ye, that if the householder did know at what hour the thief would come, he would surely watch, and would not suffer his house to be broken open. Be you then also ready : for at what hour you think not, the son of man will come." (*Luke* xii. 39.)

(*a*) The Lord cometh, but no one knoweth when He comes. Experience proves this unceasingly ; for death does not only surprise those who have been struck by lightning or have had a stroke, but it surprises those also who die in bed. Who knows of the approach of death ? Maybe others do, but the invalid does not. Neither did the Saints know when death would overtake them. St. Francis of Xavier was preparing to go to China on the day of his death. That is why our soul has to be in order. It is not accidental death that is dreadful but death in the state of mortal sin. Therefore, at every case of death, our first thought should be : Where is his soul ? Has he obtained salvation ? How should we have fared, if we had died ?

(*b*) At the end of a " short " life death awaits us. God has measured " the number of the days," and He gave them for eternal aims. At the time of our judgement He calls up time and confronts us with it. Time is an empty shape, a receptacle ; but we have to fill it with inner life and outward activity. We have to fill it to the brim with consecrating grace, only in these divine, deep waters the pearls are born and treasures hidden ; the pure, holy, noble feelings, emotions, and actions. " *Dies mali*," the bad days, are those which contain no sunshine, no love of God.

Let us rejoice and work as long as we are healthy ; after death " there will be no time " ; or there will be a time but not one for salvation.

(c) At our death we have many graces for conversion, but the time is not at all appropriate for it ; for how weak and low-spirited the frail and ailing disposition is. Even excellent confessors cannot always help. The Blessed Bellarmine could give no help when the invalid said to him : " I do not understand thee, what dost thou say ? " In the parable of the ten virgins the unreasonable maidens offend the betrothed, by not caring about oil ; " I do not know you," was the answer. It is a dreadful word which indicates eternal midnight. To die well means as much as to die, (a) without sin, (b) having divested ourselves of our evil inclinations, (c) having acquiesced in the will of God, (d) accepting death as the punishment of God. " Magnum opus."

EXHORTATION TO PENANCE

" *And there were present at that very time some that told him of the Galilæans, whose blood Pilate had mingled with their sacrifices. And he answering said to them : Think you that these Galilæans were sinners above all the men of Galilee, because they suffered such things ? No, I say to you, but unless you shall do penance, you shall all likewise perish.*" (*Luke* xiii. 1.)

Our sinfulness. (a) It is a great grace if one feels one's sinfulness deeply, for then one sees already with the heart. Let us view our life. Is not St. Paul right in saying that he is the greatest of sinners ? Is not St. Mary Magdalen right, and St. Margaret of Cortona, or anyone who has a deeply feeling heart and a consciousness of guilt ? We

also have sins : against God (unbelief, disrespect, distrust,
grumbling, blasphemy), against ourselves (intemperance,
want of discipline, sensuality, impurity, faintheartedness,
laziness, cowardliness, selfishness), against others (malign-
ing, calumny, vain talk, envy, hate, injustice, simulation,
violence). What accusations do the Ten Commandments
of God and the Five Commandments of the Church make
us hear ? What does the missing of duty accuse us of ?
Oh, how many sins there are in thought and feeling, how
many faults concerning the Sacraments ! To how many
souls have we caused scandal ! Sins and floods of mud. . . .
" My soul does not remain in the body for it is flesh."

(b) We have to taste the bitterness and loathing of sin.
It divests us of the spirit and *the mark of beasts* comes to
the surface in us. Unbelief extinguishes our light ;
despair places us in eternal winter. Instead of the Gospel
of the soul the inspirations of the flesh, instincts, and
passions excite us. *Man becomes coarse* in his feelings in spite
of laces, perfume, and frock-coats. Culture is only a
veneer if it is not founded on morality. *The servant becomes
a rebel and insurgent* against God, without God ; but at the
same time he is the slave of another power the fetters of
which he drags about with him. Sin is poison ; it changes
blood to matter, it disfigures the face, and renders the
organs torpid ; the blood is grace, the face is the likeness
to God, the organs are virtues. In great measure sin
changes men to monsters here on earth, or it makes their
bodies rot. What an evil-smelling swamp such a soul is.
The wreath has fallen off its head. It has lost its merits.
Its guardian angel buries his face in his hands and weeps,
" *angeli Dei amare flebunt.*" The heart of Jesus is sad ; the
graces of His salvation are wasted.

(c) For the Lord what an unjust, offending hurt sin is! It is the sharpest contradiction which denies His reign, power, His rights, and holiness. . . . It is a contrast to Him and His person; as a matter of fact it is atheism. The divine soul extinguishes the sparks of its nobleness and becomes as the beast, it rolls in the mud and is distorted; while infinite perfection and sanctity dictates law, lays a claim to reverence and love and abundantly presents His graces. He educates kingly souls and they sit upon a rubbish-heap and despise Him. What will this lead to, where will it end? "They shall strip thee of thy clothes, and shall take thy fair jewels, and leave thee naked and bare, heaped with shame." (*Ezekiel* xvi. 39.)

GOD AND THE SINNER

The rôle of God and man in sin.

(a) What has God done with us? He loved us . . . that is why He created us and took us for His special children. The state of being sons of God is the content and characteristic of grace. Verily our Father is He; He bore and educated us, He taught us and loves His blood; He hears its cry; "The blood of thy brother cried out to me," He says to Cain. The prodigal sons also bear His traits and His graces and Angels accompany them. Verily we also, as soon as we were born, became the sons of God in baptism and were registered in His Book of Life. An angel accompanied us and a wonderful, bright shadow, grace; in this grace God lived; moral shadows were not yet attached to us; then our passions began to awake and we sinned for the first time and after that how often ! Our first communion, our partaking of the Sacraments, prayers, good examples and zeal opposed the corrupt surroundings, the dirty and defiled streams. How much disfigurement and how many struggles ! How often the buds of the soul have been broken, how often the pure wells of emotion and feeling have dried, and the holy fire gone out. We have become corrupted and weak.

(b) The state of the child of God does not exhaust the graces of the Lord. We do not only possess God, we also have Christ. He has grafted Himself amongst us and into us ; "*Unus ex nobis !*" . . . He came from afar, but He came ; love brought Him ; He came in disguise, in the dusk of *mysterium*. So that the feelings of brotherliness should awake in us and flourish. He gave us a mother. What did He rightly expect of us in exchange ? Innocence, purity, friendship, faithfulness ; He expected brotherly feelings from the brother ; He expected the strength of blood and the nobility of brotherliness to remain victorious in us and to find its glory in our nobility. And what has become of us ? Of our blood ? It has turned to water. Sensuality has putrefied us and dulled our senses. What has become of the child of God ? What of the Christ-face ? "*Vas iræ*, a vessel of anger." We became the unfaithful servants, the traitors of the first-born, adorable brother.

(c) Brotherhood does not exhaust the sweet connection between God and our soul. He drew us on, He adopted us to be His Levites, His Apostles, His betrothed. We remember how vocation stirred in us, how the altar attracted and drew us, how sweet attraction, ecstasy, satisfaction and union filled our memory. Maybe, He

anointed us also, maybe He affianced us to Himself!
And what became of man after this ? A worm. What
became of the child of God ? A prodigal son. What has
become of us, whom God educated with the wisdom of
Solomon in His Church, whom He guarded in a walled
garden and for whom He made His followers pray and
fast on Ember Days ? We became hireling souls. What
has become of us whom He trained to be Apostles with the
warmth of His heart ? We stabbed His heart and deserted
Him ; we turned away from Him who hangs upon the
Cross and calls after us, and when we approach Him He
takes His hand off the nail and lifts us up and strains us to
His heart, He forgives and forgets everything. Oh, how
intensely we have to loathe sin, how we have to weep over
our unfaithfulness, our downfall, our slavery and loss !
We do indeed feel our weight and feel what we are to do
henceforward so as to redound to the credit of the Gospel
and to the glory of Christ. Oh, His blood is indeed
precious, it must not be trodden on. O Lord, this we
cannot bear !

THE FIRST SHALL BE LAST

" *And there shall come from the east and the west the north
and the south ; and shall sit down in the kingdom of God. And
behold, they are last that shall be first, and they are first that shall
be last.*" (*Luke* xiii. 29.)

(*a*) The final aim is eternal life ; the immediate aim
is the Christian life on earth. All of us priests, laymen,
hermits, soldiers, merchants, nuns and married people—
all have one aim and that aim is : the beautiful, divine life.
Concerning this there is no difference between us ; where

there is soul and consciousness there the prospects open on to divine life, whether they come from the cells or the nursery. In just the same way there is no difference between us in the fact that life is not ready-made, either in the cloister or the workshop, but we have to shape and develop it, everyone according to his circumstances of life, whether we be in the world or in a monastery. And Christianity is that unity where this one mutual aim preserves us and gives us enthusiasm and where the course of regeneration, purification, and of becoming stronger and more ardent proceeds for the development of divine life ! It is a transfiguration for every human soul. Therefore there are not two kinds of Christianity, just as there are not two aims and not two kinds of Christian life. There are not two kinds of Church, of which the one is the clergy and the other the laity, not one which belongs to the priests and the other to the worldlings. We can live a Christian life everywhere and can be immersed in it everywhere. The words of the Saviour are meant for everyone: those who do the will of My Father, those enter the kingdom of heaven, and again He says : It is the will of My Father that ye be saints. Just as there are Christ-like souls everywhere, so saints exist in every vocation. That is why one can be more a saint in the world than another in a monastery, and some can come to salvation who live in the world and others to damnation in the monastery. . . . O Lord, grant that we should look with trust upon Thee ! Grant that we may feel and experience what Thou wishest us to do, that we may feel that entire, great holy aim which Thou hast set up before us. We are not second-rate Christians ; we must not want to creep into a corner of heaven ; we claim the entire Christ ; and shape our entire life according to Him. It shall not disturb us that we are not in the hierarchy of the Church, that we are neither priests nor bishops and that we do not live in cloisters! You are all brothers, is what Thou hast said; Your aim is one, one is your Master and your life.

(*b*) The means. In these there is a great difference; the circumstances of life open different ways; seemingly they point to various directions. There are those who are exclusively devoted to the care of souls in the religious orders, or profess the tending of the soul's life as their vocation in the clergy; others again lead a "worldly" life. These professions differ from each other not in their aim but in the difference of the means, and the most poignant difference is that some follow the Evangelical Counsels and others endeavour to achieve Christian life without these. Life is the aim here also as well as there; the "Counsels" only count as means. Both religious and seculars have to cultivate their soul, to meditate, to pray, to practise self-denial, partake of the Sacraments, and to love; but all these are means again and the means are valuable in so far as they help to achieve the aim. We pray, fast and check our passions so that we can live from and in the love of Christ. What is the good of means, profession, position, and occupation if we do not achieve this? What folly it is to be proud of the means; just as it is folly to disparage the means, the prayer and Sacraments, giving as a reason that only the aim impresses us! It is a great grace if we are able to live for God according to the counsels of the Gospel; but let us make use of everything in the world for becoming purer, nobler, and more at home in the feelings of Christ, that we may do the holy will of God. The aim gives value to the means, the contents give value to the shape. The modern man seeks in shape and form more consciousness, depth, and ardour ; in religiousness he urges the same ; he does well. And he can also achieve this. Even without theological science he is able to descend to the depths with Thomas à Kempis and can achieve ardour of the heart.

(c) So therefore life and life again . . . this is the watchword. We do not seek system and formality, but we seek life. We wish to educate ourselves to a serious, deep reverence toward the divine, so that we may possess deep feeling, mysterious presentiment and emotion, tender, childish faith, warm love, prayer, enthusiasm, and remorse. We willingly think of eternal life towards which we are hurrying and we long for eternal youth with the ardour of the youthful soul. We wish to become purer with great, true longing and continually to feel more nobly and purely ! All that is not pure and not divine is only semblance and disappointment. Who loves this does not live truly. Therefore let us love the eternal, true, divine life and let us obtain it at any price !

HEALING OF THE MAN THAT HAD THE DROPSY

" *And it came to pass when Jesus went into the house of one of the chief of the Pharisees on the sabbath day to eat bread, that they watched him. And behold, there was a certain man before him that had the dropsy.*" (*Luke* xiv. 1.)

(a) What unpretentious, simple, profound words these are : " to eat bread." It breathes discipline, force, and health. In Jesus life is sound and complete, it is not weakened ; nature is being satisfied but not weakened by its satisfaction. Of men on the whole it is true to say that they do not die but kill themselves by exhausting their vital force in excitements and desires and low pleasures. It is a pity that so many noble inspirations come to ruin in this way. Men are thus deprived of much pure, sweet enjoyment and many deep feelings. Their souls shrivel like the sprouts of spring in the frost of May. O beautiful life, to how many vicissitudes art thou exposed. What we need is purity, self-control, moderate food, little alcohol, and hardenihg. Let us willingly keep the fast.

(b) "And Jesus . . . spoke . . . Is it lawful to heal on the sabbath day? But they held their peace. But he taking him, healed him, and sent him away." What conception of God can there be in these heads, what small, miserable ideas and at the same time what fanaticism! Let us view the idols; what has man made of God? "He has made graven images for himself." As we view these things, deep sorrow soon changes to conscientiousness, faithfulness, willingness, and we say to ourselves: Let us take care not to make the great ideas of God shrivel. Let us be sensitive so as to notice what the Lord is and how great He is. Let us keep and hallow His feasts. If we do good we have a feast. When we do good, let us have a festive mood. Often this is not the case; what a pity it is not so!

(c) "And he spoke a parable also to them that were invited, marking how they chose the first seats at the table, saying to them: When thou art invited to a wedding, sit not down in the first place, lest perhaps one more honourable than thou be invited by him; and he that invited thee and him, come and say to thee, Give this man place; and then thou begin with shame to take the lowest place." Behold the hair-splitters of the sabbath, the proud faces, motley turbans, long caftans, and, inside, the narrow-minded malice which demands : Who sits first ? All these are mere formalities. Jesus wants morality, therefore He indicates the real longing which wishes to assert itself to the inner world ; therefore He transfers the centre from the outside to the inner world. Jesus views this low-minded squabble with sadness. He wishes us to prove effective and assert ourselves ; wishes us to take part in the work of the world, but He urges ardour and unpretentiousness, deepness and modesty. He does not despise the outer things but provides for the inner ones. He wishes force and substance to be in our lives ! We are not to achieve honour by arrogant self-assertion, but by adequate virtues ; for " whosoever exalteth himself shall be abased " ; it is God who abases and ruins them. " Though thou be exalted as an eagle and though thou set thy nest among the stars, thence will I bring thee down, saith the Lord." (*Abd.* i. 4.)

PARABLE OF THE SUPPER

" *A certain man made a great supper, and invited many. And he sent his servant at the hour of supper to say to them that were invited, that they should come, for now all things are ready.*" (*Luke* xiv. 16.)

(*a*) God has a personal connection with men and so have men with God. We are not only a combination of organs, and muscles, but individuals, and God is not only the source of strength and existence but our personal Lord and our Father. In so far as we have forces we develop them, we work and strive and, subject to the great laws of development, we do our duties. And in so far as we are individuals and souls, we believe in Him and love Him. Reciprocally, the Lord also highly values us ; He esteems us, " gives us supper," that is, He looks upon us as good friends to whom He gives joy as well as consolation. We are His children also and He has confidential intercourse with us. He makes us sit at His table and feeds us with His bread. We rejoice in this sweet connection which flatters us indeed. We gladly come together with Him, as those who partake of the " great supper." We look upon it as our duty that we belong to Him with heart and soul.

(b) " And they began all at once to make excuse. The first said to him, I have bought a farm, and I must needs go out and see it ; I pray thee, hold me excused. And another said, I have bought five yoke of oxen, and I go to try them : I pray thee, hold me excused. And another said, I have married a wife, and therefore I cannot come." What a pity that that is why they did not go to the joy of the Lord. The Lord wishes us to perform the various duties of life, but we are not to treat His invitation and our earthly activity as irreconcilable opposites. We have to hoe the soil and mould nature that we may have a life worthy of man, but the Lord is our strength, light, and treasure. Our connection with God is not altered by our physical condition, for this is His will. We are men, husbands and wives, we live in families ; but we feel ourselves to be near God and rejoice in His love. God is our Lord and we have to become the lords of the world ; He wishes it. This is what the saying " ora et labora " means ; pray and work, and when we work, let us work as such do who accomplish the will of God. Then work will not tear us away from God, but on the contrary it will help us to a stronger and more real conception of God, man, and the great world-order.

(*c*) " *And the servant returning told these things to his lord. Then the master of the house being angry, said to his servant : Go out quickly into the streets and lanes of the city, and bring in hither the poor and the feeble and the blind and the lame.*" It is a pity that man finds it so difficult to reconcile the earth and sky, work and religious life. The brave and strong ones turn their back upon God, and religious life is led by the maimed, the halt, and blind. For this is the picture of the world and the Church, is it not ? There we often see the most gifted and here there are many simpletons. But as a matter of fact this is the state of barbarism, the view of the state of violence, which failed to unite the two worlds which present themselves in man and could not create that harmony in which the spirit asserts itself in work, among machines and serious endeavour, and where the higher claims of the soul have a leading part. Therefore we place our all in the holy service of God, however gifted and strong we are, and because we love God we will not be less strong, less brave and understanding, but we will become even more so.

THE GOOD SHEPHERD

" *I am the good shepherd. The good shepherd giveth his life for the sheep. But the hireling, and he that is not the shepherd, whose own the sheep are not, seeth the wolf coming and leaveth the sheep, and flieth ; and the wolf catcheth and scattereth the sheep.*" (*John* x. 11.)

(*a*) The good shepherd is a favourite figure of revelation. A thousand years before Christ, God showed us David as a shepherd ; a brave and strong shepherd who pursued the bear and lion and fought with them. He went to the " valley of robbers " and to the " valley of the birds of prey " ; he kept night-watch by the shepherd's fire and kept the tigers, jackals, and hyenas at a distance. Ezekiel promises the best shepherd who will not be like the heartless shepherds of souls of the folk of Israel, but one who " strengthens the weak, heals the ailing, tends the sick," who walks in the wilderness and has no fear ; his zeal and love bear him on. Jesus is a brave, striving, strong-minded shepherd ; it is such a soul the Apostles need ; they have to walk, beg, seek and have no fear. The clergy can all take part in these feelings, for are not they " kingly clergy " indeed ? All can save souls, can warn them and guard them from sin, can beg them to return to Jesus, and can pray for them !

(*b*) " *I am the good shepherd, and know my sheep, and am known of mine.*" (*John* x. 14.) He does not spare Himself fatigue and sacrifice, He endures and does not save Himself trouble. His source is inexhaustible ; for it is His great heart. In the moral world these traits assert themselves ; they are conspicuous in every apostolic soul. The Apostle Paul says : " *Our* flesh had no rest, but we were troubled on every side ; without were fightings, within were fears." (2 *Cor.* vii. 5.) The apostolic soul has above all to pray much. Prayer is the breath of the ardent soul ; in it the soul sums itself up, its longings and suffering. And while praying for others is zealous itself. These hot-blooded, strong, plastic souls serve the reign of the better, serve progress and beauty. Spirituality fills them. They possess a sense for the soul. They feel the troubles of the soul and have compassion for it. This is the sense we have to develop in ourselves at every step; let us look into souls and feel their troubles.

(c) Not one, but millions, wander about in the wilderness! We must not break down under the weight of this knowledge. We would break down if we derived the motives of our ardour from the way of the world; but, thanks to Our Lord, our sources gush forth in the heights. The world is shaped according to the great ideas of God; sometimes faith and morals are overclouded, and the waste of frivolity and corruption gains ground. This we cannot help! We do not wish to complain of the waste and desert, but we wish to place an adaptable soul into it, to go there ourselves in the footsteps of " the good shepherd." The air of the moral heights and field of virtues is breathed upon us also; we walk the mystical forest-edge of contact with God, and though we see the desert our heart is not contracted. God wishes us to work, and we go and do so.

(d) The little lamb does not only go astray but becomes caught in thorny bushes. Going astray is sin and the shrub of thorns is the consequence of sin; a bush of thorns is the remorse of conscience, illness, dishonour, poverty, prison, and the anger and contempt of others. Who gets caught amongst such thorns and suffers the punishment of his sins, is to experience the love of the good shepherd. He heals these wounds also; He helps to smooth over our troubles or gives us courage with which to bear them according to His spirit and the salvation of our soul.

(e) The shepherd has two staffs—with the one he protects and with the other he drives and cares for his sheep.

At night he is the " gate " of which Christ says : " I am the gate." For he stands at the gate of the fold and scrutinizes the returning lambs with a keen, sharp eye. If he sees an injury on one of them he catches it with his crooked stick, draws it to him and rubs its wounded legs with cedar oil, and he refreshes the exhausted ones with fresh water. Shepherds of souls, priests, stand beside the good shepherd and watch how He scrutinizes and worries, how He tends and cares about every single one ; how He binds wounds and how He encourages and instigates the fatigued ones. Ye have to offer your followers oil and scented, healing ointment, ye have to give them strength of soul. Ye have to know your followers, to call them by their name and direct them. The heart of the good shepherd teaches you this. We must shrink back from helpless formality, whenever we come to realize His life-giving energy. He is the shepherd of souls, their caretaker, instructor, healer and governor.

(*f*) " *I say unto you, the joy for a repenting sinner goes before the angels of God.*" The good shepherd is not a world-weary figure ; He has divine joys. The sweetest feeling which permeates heaven flows into His soul ; it is that of strong, sublime, victorious joy. This is the way to conquer ; man has to be lifted out from the dangers of endless misery and hell ; this dark midnight has to be exchanged for glorious sunshine and damnation changed into the graces of God. Let the stars of heaven shine above souls, let peace and joy reign in us. Who achieves the like does more than artists and prophets, and greater enjoyment floods his soul than if he possessed every science and the world did fête him ; " I who know every joy tell you that this joy is not earthly, not kingly, it is the joy of the angels," and angelic joys inspire us to immeasurable perseverance and sacrifice. What a giant is such a one who can say of his followers what the Apostle said : " You are my wreath and my joy."

THE PRODIGAL SON.   I

" *A certain man had two sons.*" (*Luke* xv. 11.)

(*a*) There are two of them, sons of one father, inhabitants of one house, but two souls dwell in them, two contrary souls. To one of them the home is dear, dear are the house, the garden, the shadows of the olive and fig-tree ; the other one was listless, he was discontented with the house and with love, he laughed at his father ; this was the younger one. The soul of youth is violent, haughty, hard, and unruly ; it tears, breaks, and easily disdains. This comes partly from ignorance and inexperience of the fact that we stand on each other's shoulders and are in need of one another. We have to esteem and honour each other ; no one lives and stands alone. Secondly, it comes from cruel thoughtlessness which does not think of and weigh the load and strife of life ; it plunges into the world where it may lose all for the sake of some small pleasure. Let us be reasonable ; development is a slow, great work ; the world is not made by one man ; every one of us is a con-tinuation ; let us draw conclusions from the past and accomplish the duties of the present with a great soul. Let us believe that we are biassed in many things and that wisdom and happiness go with self-control.

(*b*) " *And the younger of them said to his father : Father, give me the portion of goods that falleth to me. And he divided unto them his living.*" The son is arrogant and exacting with his father. He was born in wealth, and considers himself entitled to a life of ease. The heartlessness of his son pains the father, but he gives the son his portion. We do not realize what we owe the Lord : we owe Him health, our five senses, and a sound body and soul. What would become of us if we were blind, deaf, and dumb ? But the more we possess the more we become conceited. And God suffers our ingratitude and does not withdraw His favours. Oh, let us be devoted to the Lord and make use of what we possess for serving His glory. If the sunlight shines into our eyes and makes the colours of nature glow—and if our soul is filled with the harmony of forms and we want to sing, then let us love, love very ardently, and be more closely attached to the Lord.

(*c*) " . . . *went abroad into a far country : and there wasted his substance living riotously.*" The son departed, he broke the bonds which unite hearts ; he wanted to be free ; his imagination drew hopes for him, and his inexperienced strength went forth to seek new professions. " To err is human," but in one thing it is not permitted to err ; one has to keep strictly to the moral order. Sometimes our soul becomes estranged from God ; as if we were in a strange land and far away from Him ; even under such circumstances let us strictly exact the accomplishment of the moral law. Man is in a strange country if he so far forgets God and himself that he commits sin. God is everywhere, but separation from Him is revealed in the depths of our conscience. How bottomless and dark they are !

(*d*) The son went to a strange land, where he was out of place—where he had no home and peace—where he was not understood ; where they did not nurse him when

he became ill and did not care about him when he felt
happy ; where he met unfeelingness and hardness. It is
a strange country where the soul grows cold and weak ;
it is a strange country where there is no love, comfort,
peace, and joy. A strange country is the country of
unbelief, immorality, selfishness, impurity, and ungodliness. This is not our native country !

(e) " *And he went, and cleaved to one of the citizens of that
country. And he sent him into his farm to feed swine.*" The
greatest treasure is man himself : his capabilities, and
forces, his graces, brain, will, disposition, faith, love,
trust, bravery, and purity ! How poor is he who has
squandered all this ! He seeks recovery ; but only partly
finds it ; he mends but will have no new robe ; he wishes
to forget but his fullness of life and hilarity will not be
refunded. How many such beggars walk the paths of the
world, the paths of defeated armies ! How easily many
part with these sublime treasures ! This is the most
dreadful waste, this sad squander of treasures. " *Particula
boni doni non te prætereat,*" do not waste even a crumb of
the divine goods. Thou art rich and wealthy ; live thy
life, that is, fill thy consciousness and soul by making use
of thy forces and gifts.

THE PRODIGAL SON.   II

" *There came a mighty famine in that country, and he began to
be in want.*"

(a) Although he enjoyed and rejoiced and although he
was stunned and intoxicated, yet his soul began to suffer
and be repelled. He felt that he had become mean and

base; the knowledge of his sin, beastliness, and cruelty overcame him; he had destroyed the hopes of his father and the sanctuaries of his youth. From his brow he had wiped away the salve of the sublime; from the arms of the loving God he came to the breast of harlots and from the throne of the immaculate, pure, strong sonship of God he descended to the trough. The stars of sanctity and idealism were extinguished in his sky, he stood in darkness, and neither honour, health, modesty, friendship, nor self-esteem could throw obstacles in the way of ruin. Amidst this decay and in this cruel night he began to feel, his heart began to awake and move him. Lovely stars, memories of his youth, the face of his father, appeared in his soul; he heard the sound of encouraging words; attachments awoke in him: why art thou in this barren, heartless misery, and even if thou hast broken away, why dost thou not return, when thou seest that thou art disappointed and hast sinned, hast become sad and miserable; why dost thou not return? is what the inner voice asked him, when a new sunrise awaiteth thee and the watching soul of thy father cries out for thee?

(b) " *And returning to himself, he said: How many hired servants in my father's house abound with bread, and I here perish with hunger? I will arise, and will go to my father.*" " I will arise," said the youth, " and return. I have to have honour, love, beauty, strength, and joy. I cannot stand it here in this soul-withering, strange land. I will not cripple my life to a curse and shame, and though I have lost much, the knowledge of my loss shall not lame my forces, and I shall do all that I am still able to do and develop all the energy and vitality there is in me." Repentance and sorrow, even if they point to the losses, will never incapacitate the holy soul from making a fresh start. God wishes us to return and live. We will do so. We will not wait till we have regained what we have lost. We do not say that we cannot return in rags, but that we will work and earn and then start. With God this " sense of honour " is an impossible attitude ; here we are only dependent on grace and we have to accept it with humility !

(*c*) " *Father, I have sinned against heaven, and before thee ; I am not worthy to be called thy son : make me as one of thy hired servants . . . His father saw him . . . and running to him, fell upon his neck and kissed him.*" And he departed and his father received him ; he did not beget him to extinguish the spark of life hidden in him ; with his love he assured him new strength and a fresh start. He was dirty, his father washed him ; he was ragged and he robed him. The father replaced the ring of affinity upon his finger and changed the accustomed house and surroundings to a festive house of harmony. This is what we need : to become purified, to regain the feeling of being a son of God, to enjoy the presence of God, and grace as a feast and as a joy. With such a mentality we cannot imagine a fresh rupture. That is why it is so important to awake to the consciousness of our dignity, nobility, beauty, and strength . . . to the consciousness of that feast which we are chosen to celebrate.

(*d*) " *Now his elder son was in the field, and when he came and drew nigh to the house, he heard music and dancing. . . . And he was angry, and would not go in. His father therefore coming out began to entreat him . . . Son, thou art always with me, and all I have is thine. But it was fit that we should make merry . . . for this thy brother was dead, and is come to life again ; he was lost, and is found.*" His brother remained

at home, he did not become a squanderer, did not cause
bitterness to his father, did not fall; he lived without
passions but at the same time without noble, deep
emotions. A narrow-minded Philistine. He did not break
away from his father but neither did he appreciate the good
fortune implied in " Thou art ever with me, and all that I
have is thine." This is that narrow-minded " goodness "
varied with a great deal of unconsciousness, which is able
to be envious and indignant, which prides itself on its
narrow-minded virtuousness and judges others severely.
This is the undeveloped, unconscious type of the children
of God ! Away with this attitude of mind; it is not worthy
of the magnanimous heart of the Father ! Let them shake
out from their soul their sleepy dullness ; let them experience the treasures of God, which are to be enjoyed in
abundance, and let them rejoice when others receive them.
All of us have an unlimited amount of graces ; let us
rejoice in them, both for ourselves and others.

THE UNJUST STEWARD

*" There was a certain rich man who had a steward : and the
same was accused unto him, that he had wasted his goods."*
(*Luke* xvi. 1.)

(*a*) The parable refers in the first place to temporal
goods. Everything belongs to God, and more or less of it
is entrusted to our hands, but it is given to us to help us
live a happy life and to show good feeling, a blissful frame
of mind, joy, and bounty to others : " *Facere amicos,*" viz.,
win the love, goodwill, and attachment of others. We
also are stewards, this is the goal the Lord has set before
us. We ought to see that the goods flow from our hands

into the hands of others. We know that all goods are more or less common property, that many have worked at these goods ; how reasonable is it therefore if we further the good and satisfaction of others with our goods. Social goodwill becomes the flower of deepest religious feeling, if we look upon our life and upon all we possess as upon stewardly goods which were given to us for the soul, the more beautiful, eternal life. " *Facere amicos . . .*" is a sublime aim ; to educate good men and by so doing to build ourselves an " eternal home."

(*b*) Secondly, we can use all this for our own benefit. The Lord has provided us with much grace and many gifts ; He has given us a position and a vocation. He has given us a greater or less share of the soil and of culture. Everything is ours : the work of epochs, the progress of history and evolution, present and past, the Prophets and saints, and the Lord Himself, He also is ours. But we are not His if we do not conquer ourselves for Him. It depends on our free will, our energy, interest, and endeavour to see that we ourselves and all we have belong to Him. It is on our initiative that everything of ours becomes the property of the Lord. Stewardship is our life ; our aim therefore is not to possess this or that, not to possess much or little, but to be faithful in what we have. Therefore the substance of life is the frame of mind and disposition, not property, rights, and donations !

(*c*) " *And the steward said within himself : What shall I do, because my lord taketh away from me the stewardship ? To dig I am not able ; to beg I am ashamed . . . Therefore calling together every one of his lord's debtors he said to the first : How much dost thou owe my lord ? But he said : An hundred barrels of oil. And he said to him : Take thy bill and sit down quickly, and write fifty.*" The steward works with the passion of self-preservation, so as to assure his life. We have to throw ourselves into our stewardship with care, interest, zeal, circumspection, and energy. (1) We have carefully to tend our soul; to work at it so that its feelings should be better and nobler; to destroy the worms, and break down the thorns. Not only to do more good quantitatively but to do more good in value and consciousness. (2) We have to take up the causes of Our Lord; His interests are the interests of the kingdom of God, of faith, morals, truth, kindness; they are the interests and the cause of souls and of the Church. These we have to notice with the instinct of self-preservation, be anxious about them, and jealously guard them. Without this the " sons of light " are shamed by the " followers of darkness."

BE FAITHFUL

" *And I say to you : Make unto you friends of the mammon of iniquity, that when you shall fail they may receive you into everlasting dwellings.*" (*Luke* xvi. 9.)

Let us collect treasures by being faithful in everything.

(*a*) " *Be faithful.*" What a lovely expression this is, much more so than : Be my servant. The word servant means little, faithful means more ; it opens up vistas of friendship . . . of betrothal. Friends and betrothed are the really faithful souls. God wishes us to be faithful, for He entrusted Himself and His treasures to us. (1) We are His servants ; (2) we have to be His friends ; (3) we may be His sweet betrothed ones. Faithfulness is nowhere so appropriate as here, where actually everything of ours belongs to Him, and where we have to serve His interests

with all that we have. We must only seek Him and that
which is His. Let us consecrate everything to Him :
work, joy, tears, longings, sorrow—life. Let us cling to
Him with our soul. " Now thou carrieth Me," says the
Lord to His faithful servant, " I am thy load." Thou
art on the way, thou art the divine carrier. Thou fightest
and strugglest in the arena, thou divine fighter, " *usque* . . .
usque ad mortem," until death. Then it is I who will repay
thee.

(b) " *Faithful unto death*." Only deep, passionate love
is capable of a lifelong attachment. The great beauty of
deep-minded souls is perseverance to the end. To persevere during a whole life-time ; this is more than to be
persevering through storm and waves, through water and
fire. These are only symbols of life ; there is more violence
and difficulty in life than in these, more pain and bitterness,
more hurts and blows. Life as well as death are mysteries.
Let us pass through them with a faithful soul. We may
have much doubt and consternation . . . but let us be
faithful . . . many things we do not comprehend . : .
but let us be faithful ; we become confused and dejected
. . . let us be faithful. Our motto must be faithfulness
till death. Loyalty is the wings which carry us aloft to God.

(c) " *And I give you the crown of life*," that is, the wreathed,
crowned life. The crown gives beauty and sublimity ;
the wreath is woven of flowers ; scent, charm, joy of life,
enthusiasm of spring, and a bridal soul go with it. It is
to thee I give the flowering, beautiful, vital, joyous life.
Thou dost enjoy it here below also, if thou art faithful,
and thou wilt enjoy it completely after thy death, when
thy soul is more free and suitable for fuller and stronger
life. The divine will ought to be to us a law imposed on

us from without. We must make it our own will and faithful, continual feeling. Thus it will belong to us and be our nature!

NOBODY CAN SERVE TWO MASTERS

" No servant can serve two masters, for either he will hate the one, and love the other : or he will hold to the one, and despise the other. You cannot serve God and mammon." (*Luke* xvi. 12.)

(*a*) Who are these two masters ? The Lord, and what opposes Him ; sublimity, beauty, strength and baseness, vileness, misery. Can there be a choice here ? No, there cannot. In the presence of God there can be only rapture— *" rapit voluptas."* He who has come to know the Lord and has seen Him, will never forget Him. But the trouble is that we see Him only confusedly and know him only dimly, so it does actually come to a choice between Jesus and Barabbas, virtue and sin, song and noise, beauty and a painted mask, deep spirituality and passion. We have so many mistakes and faults of which to accuse ourselves ; hordes of senseless, violent passions wreak havoc in us. Sometimes the depreciation of the world hurts us ; the depressions of failure weigh us down ; the riots of imagination disturb us in our judgments ; our love becomes sensual and our soul fleshly. It is difficult to reserve ourselves entirely for the great Lord! Difficult indeed, this homage we can obtain only by dint of struggling and fighting.

(*b*) The striving, engrossing power is love. We must love the one and only Lord. What an easy service is love, and what a heavy one is " endurance," the joyless bearing of burdens ! Love can adapt itself, it can stretch, be full of energy and broadmindedness. It can bear defeat without dismay. Napoleon defeated Blücher six times ; Napoleon was defeated by Blücher once, but thoroughly. Even if we are defeated now and then, we have to go on striving ; we have to do so, because we love ; we love Our Lord. Sin shall not dishearten us. The other " master," the devil, can only be endured by those who are subject to his domination ; to love him is impossible, and even endurance also becomes a sufferance, a loathing, a dread. " *Sustine*," " endure," is a heavy word ; the servants of the devil groan beneath it. Their load is the torment of conscience and the unreliable, cruel sphinx which is life. They have no real, deep joy !

(*c*) A fool is one who serves the world and not himself. We only serve ourselves, our inner value, our spiritual beauty, force, and joy, if God is our Master ! The world, that is, the opinion of others, their esteem and appreciation, is mere externality ; they are values like obsolete bank-notes ; for a time they are valuable, then they are merely paper. Semblance and iridescent refraction throw bright but bloodless figures into the void. And yet the world is imposed on by all this, for " the Pharisees heard all these things . . . and they derided him." (*Luke* xvi. 14.) Let them laugh. We have one Master, " *Deus cordis mei et pars mea*," the God of my heart is my treasure ; decay and darkness are not our masters. Therefore we consistently and strenuously serve that one Master. Oh, if thou art a singer, do not let thy vocal cords grow slack ; if a painter, do not let thy sight fail ; if a sculptor, then do not let thy sense for form grow dull ; if thou art an artist of the violin, piano, or 'cello, then do not let thy

hearing weaken ! Nor must we allow our senses, refinement, and alertness to grow weak concerning the Lord !

THE RICH MAN

" *There was a certain rich man, who was clothed in purple
and fine linen : and feasted sumptuously every day. And there
was a certain beggar named Lazarus, who lay at his gate, full of
sores.*" (*Luke* xvi. 19.)

(*a*) He was clothed in purple and fared sumptuously,
he lived a life of ease. He did not perish because he ate
well, but because he lived a life which indulged its
instincts and passions. He lived a life in which the flesh
was master ; in which the world and the instincts were
the squandering power ; a life in which God was forgotten.
Whereas Lazarus the beggar was not crushed by his
misery. Certainly, he was ailing ; he lay on the ground ;
he was not haughty ; he was accustomed to charity ; he
ate crumbs ; but God he did not forget ! Behold on the
one hand the soul sitting on a throne but stuck to the
ground, clothed in shining robes but carrying the chains
of dead loads, and on the other hand the pure-minded man
who lies on the ground but cries out for heaven, who is
sore in body but pure in soul. The earth, position, and
the flesh shall not be dead weights upon our soul ; the
body is the servant of the soul ; according to St. Francis
it is its " *asinello*," its carrier of loads. The soul dwells
in the body, not the body in the soul. Modern
prophets proclaim the liberation of sensuality, and youth
believes that it will become strong if it enjoys. Real
enjoyment is strength and the feeling of natural force which

is full of grace. Do not let us break it down, either by intemperance, and alcohol, or by softness!

(*b*) The wealthy one died, was buried, and went to hell, while Lazarus died and was carried to heaven. Jesus plainly puts the final evil and good before our soul. There is hell, which is the conquering evil; there is heaven, which is the conquering good. Here upon earth also there is much evil; its chief manifestations are sin and death. But here the blood of Jesus filters in every direction and checks evil and misery, checks the mustiness of body and soul, the sorrow and shame; but there is an evil, a definitive evil—bad will—which directly and undisguisedly defies the creative and passionately loving God. There a dreadful collision occurs, a final crushing, and rejection; this is hell. Infinite mercy accompanies man in the accomplishments of his great duties, but if man opposes and defies the Sublimity of God, then God crushes him. Lord, we believe in and adore Thy Sublimity.

(*c*) "*And lifting up his eyes when he was in torments, he saw Abraham afar off, and Lazarus in his bosom.*" When the damned one comes to himself, his consciousness is eternal agony; he remembers his life. The memories of men, graces, and sins surround him; church, cross, altar, sunshine and stars shine in his eyes. He sees his sinfulness, which developed and ended in damnation. What dreadful memories torment him! Memory makes him use his brains. What has he to consider? The senselessness of his life that ruined all, ruined grace, mercy, and love. It was easy, sweet, useful, and necessary that he should live well and in a holy way; but the time for this has passed; what is he to do henceforth? What means is he to use? What to avoid? What to beg for? The answer to all this is : *nihil, nihil*. How is he to assert his will ? He has longings and thirst ; he longs for one drop of water from the hand of the ulcerous Lazarus . . . but it is impossible for him to bring even this about. The beauty of God, the heavens, shine above him, but not for him. God is a centre, He draws everything to Him ; but this attraction crushes his soul ; this attraction is a dread to him. He knows and sees, but does not hope and does not love ; he shows no zeal for good ; he fears, he hates ; he does not repent his sins, and does not pray ; his God and his existence are " *tremor*," " *horror* " and " *dolor* " to him. This state also is a mystery ; we do not comprehend it as long as the love of what is good and the hope of happiness live in us. This also is that " other " world !

HELL. I

" *And he cried, and said : Father Abraham, have mercy on me, and send Lazarus that he may dip the tip of his finger in water, to cool my tongue, for I am tormented in this flame.*" (*Luke* xvi. 24.)

Hell also is the secret of faith ; we stand before its locked gates, and can understand it to a slight extent only with the aid of similes.

(*a*) The first is the thought of the " second death." The damned one dies again, dies a second time when death freezes his soul, his feelings, longings, and hopes, and only consciousness lives. To die means to be torn away from life, the world, sunshine, blood, home, and humanity. To be here no more. And the second death means to be torn away from God, grace, love, to be torn away from

Christ, hope, prayer, cross, good-will; to be torn away from all the benefits of Christ, from His merits, promises, and consolations. Likewise the second death is the most dreadful " state of being all by oneself." Who can endure this? Creating love has given parents, brothers, home, so that we should not be all by ourselves. Christ said: " I will be with you." He promised a consoler who would remain with us. What are we to do, being alone? To what can we set our hand in infinite space without God, without anything?

(*b*) The second thought is aimlessness. Nature and mankind pursue aims; they need an aim and keep it in eye. If they carry the aim in them then they have strength, they have life; if they lose the aim they suffer and are in want. Aimlessness is torment; here upon earth there is a partial torment such as illness, discord, fatigue, tediousness, loathing, despair—death. The soul enters the other world filled with the longing for the aim. As a stormy longing the passion for the final aim awakes in it and at that moment it wakes to the consciousness of the final loss of its aim. Everything broke down beneath it; where is it to go? What for? To whom? And why? All this means an aim, therefore it is not for such a soul. Such a state means darkness, bonds on hands and feet, and the gnashing of teeth.

(*c*) The third thought is the curse. It is with the blessing of God that creation began; God blessed every existence. Woe to those in whom existence is continued with the curse of God. We come from out of love; " He hated nothing that He created," but now He hates. Love turns to hate. We believe it, though we do not understand the psychology of the infinite. What does despised love do?

Don Jozé cries out in Bizet's opera : " It is I, I who killed her, my adored Carmen ! " Benjamin Constant writes about love : " *L'amour est de tous les sentiments le plus égoiste et par conséquence, lorsqu'il est blessé, le moins généreux.*" The Psalmist begs : Do not make me thine enemy ! We can spoil the work of God, the world of grace, and He can ruin our life and the blossoming of happiness and peace.

HELL. II

" *If they hear not Moses and the prophets, neither will they believe if one rise again from the dead.*" (*Luke* xvi. 31.)

(*a*) Jesus proclaims penitence, but also proclaims heaven, absolution, and the Gospel. Both are grave. Grave as the abyss of the Alps and charming as the bluebells at the edge of the abyss ; solemn as the night and encouraging as the star-light. Jesus places enormous motives into our life : God becomes united with man and makes a god of man, He winds the aureole of the sonship of God round the head of all of us, points to eternity, and brings the " *pondus æternitatis,*" this tremendous living force, to our consciousness. Eternity awaits you—this is what the light of the world which walks amongst us proclaims, this light which lights us also to the verge of hell. There exists happy and unhappy eternity ; let us fear unhappy eternity. " And I say to you my friends : Be not afraid of them who kill the body . . . fear ye him who after he hath killed, hath power to cast into hell." (*Luke* xii. 4.) Whom is hell meant for ? It is meant for all of us if we sin and are not converted. St. Paul fears hell, as well as St. Augustine ; the Holy Scripture does not release us from this fear.

What is more, Christ shatters every presumptuous conceit, saying : Ye are my friends, but ye can perish, if ye do not have a serious will, if ye do not strive and make sacrifices.

(b) Jesus looks upon us with the seriousness of eternity and demands sacrifice. The loss of eyesight, of wealth, sorrowful nights and prison, agony and martyrdom are as nothing to the man struggling to ensure the salvation of his soul. We have to be able to renounce every earthly good and to suffer every trouble for the sake of our soul. Let us rather step from sunshine to night, from freedom to prison, from life to death, than lose our soul. Let us therefore save the soul, let us make any sacrifice, let us be ardent, let us learn energy. Such existence has to be a striving, tiring one, fraught with great values, at the end of which eternal damnation or eternal salvation awaits us.

(c) Above the abyss of hell rises the cross. It is a warning on the edge of the abyss. It says : Do not go this way. Jesus suffers and looks at us with the final exhaustion of sacrifice ; this glance freezes us. We comprehend Thee, Lord ; we are not allowed to waste Thy blood, Thy merits and grace. What is the use of Christ and the cross if there is no hell, and likewise what is the good of Christ and the cross if still we come to hell ? It seems as if we heard the words from the cross, as if the soft voice of the Gospel would change to a roaring cyclone and cry to us : " Fight, struggle for life ; here ye are not allowed to fall ! " God also wishes us to conquer and places everything at our disposal. Therefore let us seriously endeavour to win the fight.

HOPE, WITHOUT OVER-CONFIDENCE

(a) *We have to hope indeed, but never to be over-confident.*
The flowing stream of our existence is God and His
creating will. We proceed from Him. We were His
design, His will; this is what we call creation. He imparted Himself, His existence and strength to beautiful
creation, the culmination of which is the spiritual world.
In the atmosphere of spirituality He again created a new
world which is the partaking of divine nature; the world
of grace, of the sonship of God and proximity to God, in
which we are permitted to look on God as our Father.
It is in this atmosphere that He influences us, forms and
shapes us. He shapes beautiful souls. And yet how many
shipwrecks there are in this bright world of grace! How
many Sauls, how many kingly souls, who in the melancholy
of sin end in darkness! How many Solomons there are,
wise souls like to the cherubim, who fade and are torn to
rags! Let us pray and be faithful and true in everything.
Do not let us be conceited and presumptuous, but let us
work seriously.

(b) A new grade of the world of grace and the most
beautiful realization of the state of God-with-us is Jesus.
God imparted Himself in a new creation : in Jesus. He
gives His Son to us, so as to introduce Him into our supernatural blood, our soul and home, and by so doing to
give us all. Everything already is ours : " Whether Paul,
or Apollo, or Cephas, or the world, or life, or death, or
things present, or things to come." (1 *Cor*. iii. 22.) It is
the mark of Christ's love, the kiss of Christ upon us. By
this we are grafted into God, and the Holy Ghost resides
in us. He made friends of us, but even after this it is

possible for us to perish. He made us His Apostles and we can degenerate into Judases. He ordained His martyrs to be His bodyguards and behold it was during martyrdom itself that some denied Him. He cultivated virgins for Himself and they became adulterous, wanton souls. The sad secret of all these falls is unfaithfulness. We will be faithful and true in small things ; and not give way to evil.

(*c*) Finally God imparts His glory. He carries souls up to Himself and kindles His life and joy in them. " *Merces magna nimis,*" they will have an unspeakably great reward. This apotheosis and the intoxication of souls with the infinite is opposed by eternal night and in it the dark spirits scare us ! He thrust away His defamed betrothed ones and destroyed His violated churches. He did not cast away anyone who did not himself desire it. We guard our faith and state of grace ; we will not dispute about who will be damned and who not, but we will assure our salvation with the pledge of the love of God.

THE RAISING OF LAZARUS

" *And many of the Jews were come to Martha and Mary, to comfort them concerning their brother. Martha therefore, as soon as she heard that Jesus was come, went to meet him ; but Mary sat at home. Martha therefore said to Jesus : Lord, if thou hadst been here, my brother had not died.*" (*John* xi. 19.)

(*a*) The restless, busy Martha hurries to meet the Lord and she complains : Master, thy house is orphaned : Where Thou always camest with love, there they are now weeping. Oh, why didst Thou not come earlier ? And

how can illness, suffering, and death come to the house
where Thou art at home ?   Thou lovest and yet strikest us ?
This we do not understand.   It is difficult for us to reconcile trouble, evil, and suffering with the love of God.
We do not understand this hand of iron.   We are pressed
into the iron net of physical order, and moral order also
is filled with the horror of evil will !   O Lord, we pay
Thee homage in life and death.   Life and death are our
conditions of existence, but Thou hast other conditions.
Thou sayest :   My thoughts are not your thoughts, my
ways are not your ways ;   existence is not only humanity ;
humanity is only something in infinity.   It is impossible
that everything should go according to its ideas and taste.
Lord, we adore Thee in Thy holy will !

(b) " *Jesus saith to her :   Thy brother shall rise again.
Martha saith to him :   I know that he shall rise again in the
resurrection at the last day.   Jesus said to her :   I am the
resurrection and the life.*"   There is death and there is
suffering ;   these we cannot obliterate but at the end of
the world souls will again take to themselves bodies.
Now they assume bodies through a physiological medium ;
then they will do so directly by the will of God.   Purified
souls will be strong and penetrate the body, so that the
body will be their bright, beautiful, symmetrical, lively
organ.   Even now art forms material into shape and gives
beauty and soul to the shapeless ;   resurrection will be
the real spiritualisation of matter ;   the soul overfloods it
unhindered with its spiritual beauty and strength.   This
we believe ;   we see how in hypnotism and magnetism
the soul bends the body and divests it of its nature.
What then of the final and victorious awakening ?   We also
are artists of the body through virtue ;   it is by purity,

temperance, self-control and discipline that we carry soul into our body.

(c) "*When Mary therefore was come where Jesus was, seeing him, she fell down at his feet, and saith to him : Lord, if thou hadst been here, my brother had not died.*" In the soul of the deeply feeling Mary, who is immersed in quiet grief, the news that the Master is present and is calling her, trembles like sunshine. The Master is her consolation ; she immediately falls down at His feet ; this is her place. Whether she weeps for her sins, adores the risen one, or tells Him her sorrow, she is always at His feet. How her soul bent towards the Master, how it clung to Him. This is what the true followers of Jesus do ; whether they cry or rejoice, they always love.

(d) "*Jesus therefore, when he saw her weeping, and the Jews . . . weeping, groaned in the spirit, and troubled himself. And said : Where have you laid him ? . . . And Jesus wept. The Jews therefore said : Behold how he loved him.*" Jesus loves, mourns, and weeps. His soul looks across the world into infinity : He sees our misery, but does not break down beneath its weight, for He also sees the final development, sees the glory of God. The conquering power of God embraces the world and all its troubles. For us it is good that we do not know the future ; we could not bear the foresight of our fatigue and failures. And so we go on striving and accomplishing our duty. Let us be men, be human, let us live as among brothers ; let us be able to weep and share in the troubles of others. The barbarians have no compassion ; Christian heroes can weep.

(e) "*Jesus therefore . . . cometh to the sepulchre.*" The funeral is a work of mercy ; it breathes reverence for the dead one, who robes himself in the dignity of death, in mystery . . . Let us accompany the pilgrim. His soul has passed along a long and important way towards the eternal gates ; maybe it is present at the funeral. When we bury someone let us proceed according to the last article of the Apostolic Creed. We believe in the unity of the Saints, therefore we pray for the deceased ; we believe in the resurrection of the body, therefore we honour the body in its burial ; and we believe in eternal life, therefore we hope that perpetual light will shine upon him. Amen !

(f) " *Jesus said : Take away the stone. Martha, the sister of him that was dead, saith to him : Lord, by this time he stinketh, for he is now of four days. Jesus saith to her : Did not I say to thee, that if thou believe, thou shalt see the glory of God ?* " The glory of God will triumph over all our conceptions and break all our small measures. In death it also crushes everything, the body, the figure, beauty and life. The body becomes decomposed and falls into decay. " When man dies, he falls a prey to the worms." This is the end of the glory of man and it is here that God begins to build His glory ! O Lord, let us see Thy glory, which is life ; that is what we want !

(g) " *They took therefore the stone away. And Jesus lifting up his eyes said : Father, I give thee thanks that thou hast heard me. And I knew that thou hearest me always, but because of the people who stand about have I said it, that they may believe that thou hast sent me.*" Jesus knows the deceased will be raised from death, therefore He gives public expression of His knowledge. He knows that His word creates and gives life, because God wills it so. Absorbed in the knowledge of this divine force, He lifts up His eyes.

The grave gives forth a smell of decay ; weak men, the booty of death, surround His victorious figure. He ought to be their leader. Oh, if they would believe, if they would not doubt ! Therefore He cried with a loud voice : " Lazarus, come forth." And he that was dead came forth. Faith, strength, and conviction is wanted in us also concerning the great works of God. Whether we stand above a grave, or at the altar, we must know whom we trust ; we must know that we will not be shamed. Many believe ; Lazarus, Martha, and Mary fall down at His feet : this is their unequalled, personal Easter. What a return of Lazarus and Martha and Mary, with Jesus amidst them ! Bethany, house of sweet, consoled, thankful souls. In the attachment to Jesus there is none like them. This house encloses depths, encloses souls living in ecstasy.

AT THE GRAVE OF LAZARUS

At the grave of Lazarus. We believe in Thee ! We believe the reality of the ideal world !

(*a*) The aim of progress is to subject the world to superior souls, to raise our existence above mechanism. But to achieve this, our ideals must have substance ; our ideas about God, soul, and morality must not be empty, vain reflections ! Could we endure it, if after having conquered the elements and Nature, we established infinite emptiness and nothingness ? No, we could not ; all that we mean by science and economic and social progress concerns only our exterior life ; are our interior life and consciousness to be sheer hallucination ? On the contrary, this is the true reality : our soul, our God, our eternal life. What barbarism it is to seek the value of life in money and power, in factories, markets and inns, in the formalities of life. We seek for it in the soul and find it !

(*b*) We believe in the moral order. That confronts us and commands and what it commands that is what we wish and are capable of. Our life blossoms forth from our inner world, therefore it is we who give it form; give form equally to our sufferings and joys. We hall-mark everything; what we love, that is great, what we despise is small. Our surroundings may do us much harm, but concerning these we have also to awake to the consciousness of our strength. It is from us that life, that moral strength, breaks forth; we are the artists, we are the creators. Everything we touch changes to moral force, as everything King Midas touched changed to gold. We change everything into life, into beauty. We look into our soul, as into the depths of bubbling wells, which rise and ebb. In our soul nature and grace are united, and what we are not capable of by nature we can achieve by grace.

(*c*) The soul and carrier of our moral world is freedom; it is the most original trait of our likeness to God. We take our decisions from ourselves; we will them and they exist. This creating force cannot be measured with anything, just as the ideas of Newton and Leibnitz cannot be explained from the nourishment they took, so freedom cannot be explained by physics. With this original, sovereign capability we honour Our Lord: (1) in our faith. We believe, that is, we cling to Him with free devotion in our spiritual world; (2) along the whole line of our consciousness we do what the Lord wishes.

JESUS HEALS TEN LEPERS

" *And as he entered into a certain town, there met him ten men that were lepers, who stood afar off.*" (*Luke* xvii. 12.)

(*a*) Lepers, distorted, shrivelling men, in whom the sap of life has rotted and whose consciousness is filled with agony. Joyless is their life, and they totter faintly towards their grave. There is not a more deplorable contrast than that between these living-dead and strong, beautiful, pure humanity. There are many " *lepra* " in the spiritual world ; the energy of many lives produces only degenerate life : low, dark ideas, unclean imaginations, stunned, desperate wills, ideas, whims. . . . Some are as though they could not do otherwise ; as if tape-worms were sucking their spiritual strength. How true it is that these are spiritually dead, they live in the graves of dark ideas ; their blood is as oil upon the flames of passion. Pure blood is wanted ! Do not let us poison pure, strong life either with sin or alcohol. Let us give it light, suppleness, discipline, obedience, and willingness.

(*b*) " *And lifted up their voice, saying : Jesus, master, have mercy on us.*" They beg for purification and strength ; they ask for life which is not tainted; for a soul which is not infatuated and dejected. We feel how these creatures wept and cried out to Jesus. . . . They stood afar off, it is from there that they cried out, but reverence and humility brought their cry close to Jesus. The humble, respectful soul which profoundly feels its iniquities finds its way to the healing, restoring Jesus. He gives grace which changes ideas and passions, gives confidence and initiates the spiritual reform. Do not let us doubt, but let us cry out. Already this is a strong deed, the rest will follow.

(c) "*Whom when he saw, he said : Go, shew yourselves to the priests. And it came to pass, as they went, they were made clean.*" The cleansed lepers had to show themselves to the priests ; the law demanded this. The master of beautiful, strong life places his followers under the restrictions of the valid law. Divine law helps and guards life. Therefore, however strong and beautiful is the life we lead and though we are in connection with Christ, we keep the law, we show ourselves to the priest ; we confess, and go to Holy Communion and to Mass ; we do not excuse ourselves from these duties. Jesus wishes it, we believe that it is good. Through this obedience we win life, we enhance life, we become healed, we get stronger, and we partake of the innumerable graces of Christ.

ONLY ONE PRAISES GOD FOR HIS CURE

"*And one of them when he saw that he was made clean, went back, with a loud voice glorifying God, and he fell on his face before his feet, giving thanks : and this was a Samaritan. And Jesus answering, said : Were not ten made clean ? and where are the nine ? There is no one found to return and give glory to God, but this stranger.*" (*Luke* xvii. 17.)

(a) We have to give thanks, to give thanks from our heart for the many good things we have received, which are showered upon us as the snowflakes. We cannot count them ; they fly in our faces as the breath of the forest, who knows from how many and what sort of flowers ! We will not be conceited and presuming but draw this breath in and enjoy it. Oh, how good it is to know how much good we enjoy when we are healthy and strong, when we see the light of the sky, and all our senses and capabilities are fresh and whole. And especially so when our soul is strong and supple. It is true that sometimes we lay claim to all these things and forget that they are favours. What if we had broken our leg, or badly injured our hand? What if we were blind or lame, either in our body or in our soul? O my God, we give Thee thanks for the innumerable good things, for the fragments of Thy heaven falling down upon us!

(*b*) Thanks for the many unrecognized and unused bounties! Those are like the goods enjoyed by children—they are like passing clouds! Oh, indeed, we are also children, we sleep in the lap of our mother; we also are careless and negligent souls, whose many graces accuse us of not making use of them. We draw down the clouds on us by the height of our ideas; by our ardour, humility, and the forest-breath of our absorption. We will avoid feebleness and be diligent and exact by making use of the good we receive.

(*c*) Thanks for the graces we ignore and despise in the state of sin. Those already are offended powers—the goddesses of anger. Out of the depth of this misery of ours confusion and shame confront us. *Mea culpa!* "Do ye thus requite the Lord, O foolish people and unwise? Is not he thy father that has bought thee? hath he not made thee? and established thee?" (*Deut.* xxxii. 6.) Let our gratitude be ardent and inspired by love, let it be humble and from the knowledge of our sinfulness and undeservingness and from the knowledge of the sublimity of God, let it be practical. Our life should be a "*Deo gratias.*"

THANKSGIVING AFTER CONFESSION

Thanksgiving after Confession.

(*a*) Deep souls are thankful; they comprehend that the good has to be received with the feeling of gratitude. This too is a great good. Thanksgiving after Confession is a great grace and the means of obtaining lasting effects from the sacrament. Our heart feels the immense graciousness of God's forgiveness; it feels that He has lifted the load off it which was more terrible than fetters; He has washed us in His blood; lifted us, crowned us, and glorified us. Oh, who comprehends the mysterious activity of grace which flowed into us and awoke our soul to a new spring, to eternal life? Therefore " *canet juxta dies juventutis suæ* " ; we sing the hymn of youth. It is to this that we educate ourselves exactly and faithfully.

(*b*) The sweet feeling of peace pervades our soul—the deep, sublime peace which God has promised, something of what the Prophet speaks of: " O that thou hadst harkened to my commandments! thy peace had been as a river, and thy justice as the waves of the sea." (*Isaiah* xlviii. 18.) This is what we enjoy, this is what makes our soul enthusiastic and our disposition sweet. This is what we have to give thanks for, sing, and be grateful!

(*c*) We give thanks with the deep feelings of our heart; we give our soul. God has broken the fetters of our sins; now we are free to give ourselves to Him. This act of devotion is our gratitude. The Count of Toblach had one of his enemies locked up in a dungeon of his castle and forgot about him, so that the wretched man died of hunger. The Count went to Rome to beg remission for his sin ; he had a heavy iron chain forged around his neck and feet and walked about with this till the end of his life. What joy he would have had if the angel of God had lifted this heavy iron chain off him as a sign of the remission of his sins ! What thanks he would have given ! God has lifted our chains off us ; we sing, rejoice and are grateful !

PARABLE OF THE UNJUST JUDGE

" *And he spoke also a parable to them, that we ought always to pray, and not to faint. Saying : There was a judge in a certain city, who feared not God, nor regarded man. And there was a certain widow in that city, and she came to him, saying : Avenge me of my adversary. And he would not for a long time. But afterwards he said within himself : Although I fear not God, nor regard man, yet because this widow is troublesome to me, I will avenge her, lest continually coming she weary me. And the Lord said : Hear what the unjust judge saith. And will not God revenge his elect who cry to him day and night : and will he have patience in their regard ? . . . He will quickly revenge them.*" (*Luke* xviii. 1.)

(*a*) Jesus wishes us to pray with the perseverance of deeply-feeling, distressed souls. The poor, dejected widow on whom difficulties are heaped, is the symbol of the soul. Let it beg and persevere, although help tarries ; let it strive towards the Lord, shedding tears, spreading out its arms ; and we must not let it languish. The value of this disposition does not primarily consist in receiving what we beg for ; that is often impossible ; but it consists in clinging to God, in longing for Him. For the praying soul practises its faith and hope and develops its trust, humility, and patience. In this way our disposition will be a great longing ; we breathe in God.

(*b*) The hard judge shows the feelings of a man who has turned away from God : not to fear God, not to regard men ; not to pay homage to the Lord and to be cruel to men ; not to bend the knee and to tread upon men with an iron heel. It is easy to despise man ; to look at men as dust-heaps is the temptation of the mighty ones ; but if he gives way to that temptation then his heart becomes hard as a stone and his self-esteem disappears accordingly. Let us love ourselves in every man ; our self-esteem shall impel us to raise the weak and abandoned. How much more so if we see Christ in them !

(*c*) " *I say to you that he will quickly revenge them. But yet the son of man when he cometh, shall he find, think you, faith on earth ?* " The cruel judge at last takes mercy on the poor woman ; but he does so only from natural motives, for he wishes to get rid of her. In many things God helps us by way of natural sympathy, for nature is His work and He links us to each other with the link of natural feelings. But the nobler man is, the less selfish he is, he looks upon everyone as upon his fellow-brother, and this he does true-heartedly, loves them sincerely, loves them for the sake of God and loves them in Him. This is what the world needs, this true charity. This disposition needs living faith, of which there is little in the world. There are not many clinging, longing, praying souls, for faith is scarce. Men's senses become dulled in the world ; they seem to be in a perpetual state of winter sleep. The spiritual awakening, deep vistas, the light of God, the spring of soul-life, the feeling of nearness to God, are not in them.

Let us tend the life of faith with prayer and prayer with faith. Prayer comes from faith, and faith from prayer; prayer is the wave of faith, which deepens faith anew. We believe and pray !

THE PHARISEE AND THE PUBLICAN

"*Two men went up into the temple to pray : the one a Pharisee, and the other a publican. The Pharisee standing prayed thus with himself : O God, I give thee thanks, that I am not as the rest of men . . . as also is this publican. And the publican standing afar off would not so much as lift up his eye towards heaven ; but struck his breast, saying : O God, be merciful to me a sinner.*" (*Luke* xviii. 10.)

(*a*) They went to pray, that is they wanted to sink into the depths of their consciousness, to beg God for the forgiveness of their sins, to rise to His love and grace, so that they might be filled with sunshine and strength and going back amidst men they might spread good-will and self-sacrificing love amongst their fellow-men. This is the result of prayer. The Pharisee did not achieve this, haughtiness and conceit filled him with blindness instead of sunshine and led him away from God. He forgot his sins and forgot prudent fear. The publican achieved the regeneration of his soul in spite of his sins, for his repentance was humble. He who looked at himself so as to despise others, did not see God ; he who for shame of seeing himself, cast down his eyes, saw the Lord and found His grace. Behold, we are near to the Lord in our humility ; but we divest grace and prayer of its strength if we are filled with self-conceit !

(*b*) The Pharisee is no brother but conceited and arrogant, who despises the sinner and drives a wedge between men and the law and good deeds. He does not cry from out the depths of life, for his mind is occupied with trivialities ; church-going and tithe-paying are his ideal. What formality ! We must take heed that arrogance shall not grow great from our poorly deeds. What good deeds are those which kill brotherliness, harden the heart and render it cruel ? Haughtiness and disdain exclude the good and the " good " we do in this way is only formal and valueless !

(*c*) The publican teaches us humility. He stands afar off, casts his eyes down, and smites his breast. His soul is filled with the knowledge and feeling of his own misery and he seeks the grace of God. Deep reverence for God, the altar, the church, is reflected in him ; he had no time to think of unimportant, small things. In his soul he heard the roar of infinite waves ; he had no time to attend to the chirp of crickets. He saw the final danger which threatened his hope and repentance and he cried out : God, be merciful to me a sinner. Behold how deeply the soul ploughs with the grace of God ; how the dignity of serious thought comes to the surface and teaches him reverence, repentance, self-forgetfulness without lessening his trust in God. Those who act in this way will be justified.

CHRISTIAN MARRIAGE

" *Is it lawful for a man to put away his wife for every cause ? Who answering, said to them : Have ye not read, that he who made man from the beginning, made them male and female ?*

And he said : For this cause shall a man leave father and mother, and shall cleave to his wife." (*Matt.* xix. 3.)

(*a*) The most intimate union between human beings is marriage ; it is a legal formality, but it has to be filled with soul, morality, love, intimacy, reverence, and passion. St. Paul wishes it to contain deeper and stronger contents than the Song of Songs. He says : Husbands, love your wives, as Christ loves the Church. The glow of passionate love may slowly fade away, but strong, ardent, sacrificial love must never fade in marriage. This love ensures the high moral standard of marriage. But its holy character exceedingly enhances marriage and stamps it with a divine, mysterious stamp. God reverences this alliance and places it within the radiation of his graces. Marriage is therefore a great, holy, divine idea, which enhances man and woman and imparts to their union a divine character and a holy dignity. We honour marriage as the treasure and Sacrament of Christ. We wish it to contain love, devotion, spiritual union, and friendship. Without these there is no happy home and no sturdy children.

(*b*) " *And they twain shall be one flesh. Wherefore they are no more twain, but one flesh.*" The Christian form of sexual relation is marriage. Without this, sexual relation is sinful and strays step by step to what is base because of the predominance of the sensual. The conflict between the longing for sexual union and virtue is one of the greatest that afflicts humanity. Instinct is strong and incites to the use of every means so as to be satisfied. Woman cajoles man with beauty and charm, whereas with her also not the flesh but the beautiful, noble, conscious soul ought to be predominant. Only souls are capable of the most intimate union. Therefore soul has to approach soul.

On the paths of merely fleshly desire and infatuation souls cannot meet. It is a fact that by her union with man, except in Christian marriage, the woman loses her honour and her influence over him. Man shall seek first of all soul in the woman, and the woman shall wish to give firstly her soul to man. This sentiment breaks down the vehemence of instinct and enables them to accomplish the holy will of God.

(c) "*What therefore God hath joined together, let no man put asunder.*" Marriage also has some essential requirements, which when they actually do not exist render "marriage" null, and the Church nullifies it or rather declares it as null. Further, the Church may annul valid marriage if it has not been consummated. It is a psychological contradiction to love till to-morrow, a sacrilege to be united and not to persevere till the death of each. Sacramental love renders people capable of lifelong loyalty, which is not broken by illness, nor troubled by the diminishing of sensual attachment. This the child, the dignity of human origin, also demands that it be not entrusted to instincts and feelings but to the faithfulness and devotion unto death of two souls. Sacrifice and self-abnegation is needed everywhere, and even where the most beautiful love exists there surely not only flowers but thorns also flourish. Complete devotedness also is able to suffer, strive, and persevere. Love and sacrifice spring from the magnanimity of Christian spouses. Let the sacrifice also be divine, sacramental; let it be a holy mystery, then we shall be able to bear it.

(d) "*Because Moses by reason of the hardness of your heart permitted you to put away your wives : but from the beginning it was not so.*" The basis of marriage is love; its content is the fusion of two beings, the fusion of man and woman who complete each other physiologically and psychologically ; its fruit is the child. A complete union in soul, flesh, and blood ; indeed it is one of the most sublime ideas of God. Let there not be anything therefore which separates man and woman, especially let there be no separation in faith and eternal hope. A mixed marriage is a sad married life, for the spouse is wanting in complete devotion either to the other spouse or to the faith. If he lives according to his faith, then he wishes to give the soul of his wife a share of his salvation, for it is natural that he wishes to draw the one he loves best into his faith and love of God ! It is out of such a union, based on God's will to create and on mutual respect, that the child should come ; it has to originate from noble love, pure blood, and strong health ; perversity, the heat of drink, and sensual weakness shall not approach the sources of life. He who poisons these sources is a monster !

VIRGINITY AND CELIBACY

"*His disciples say unto him : If the case of a man with his wife be so, it is not expedient to marry. Who said to them : All men take not this word, but they to whom it is given.*" (*Matt.* xix. 10.)

The psychology of the virginal souls is the noblest, for it has an aptness for the *most tender* and the *strongest* love of God.

(*a*) For the love of God is a union also, a devotion and fusion, for which virginity has the most direct vocation upon this earth. For such a soul belongs to Him : " My beloved one is mine." Further, the love of God is there where passion flames towards God and where the individuals are capable of loving "from all their heart, all their mind and all their soul." The mind turns towards the Lord in complete virginal purity ; it turns its face towards Him and its eyes shine : "*Intelligam in via immaculata . . .*" my mind is filled with light upon the paths of pure life . . . these are the "seeing ones" ; they have senses, for they possess love : : "*videre amare est*," those see, who love.

(*b*) Likewise, there is no love stronger than the love of pure hearts, for it is they who are able to love "*ex toto corde*." This is what Jesus wishes : My son, give me thy heart. . . . Rose, thou wilt be My betrothed . . . says He to St. Rose. In His turn Jesus receives such a soul with His whole heart ; He incarnates Himself into it ; He builds His altar in such a heart. It is into such a love that the "psyche," the "animus" is suffused. Let us love our God "*ex toto animo*" ; with our temperament and sensibility ; this will draw our entire being towards the heavens, "*avolare facit mentem*."

(*c*) The Lord wished to breathe the character of this virginal love into His clergy. This is the idea of the *cœlibatus*. Let the "chosen" clergy, the clerus, belong to the Lord. And the spirit of the Church felt that this befits it. Its eyes fell on the first altar of the Word which became flesh—on the heart of the Holy Virgin—it beheld the first carrier of God and saw that the duty of touching God had been entrusted to the hands of the Holy Virgin and the Church felt that its clergy must be created on this model. It is this virginal clergy which is the ambition of the Church. It loves to weave lilies into its purple cloak.

It longs for the pure souls which make an offering of life. It feels that the world is sick and that the waters of Bethesda can only be stirred by angels so as to make them healing waters. *Ecce ego . . . ecce ego . . .* behold, my Lord, here I am, I wish to be pure. Help me !

THE DIVINE FRIEND OF CHILDREN

." Then were little children presented to him, that he should impose hands upon them and pray." (*Matt.* xix. 13.)

(*a*) True parental love brings the infants to Jesus. Those parents who love in this way accomplish the most important duty of child-love. It has to be accomplished in other ways also ; we have to love, educate, and tend our children ; God wishes it : He wrote it into the heart of the parents. He wishes us to educate them sensibly and to understand the awakening spiritual world in which the child expresses itself in its good and bad qualities. The bad we break down, educate it in discipline, shape and mould it and make it love the good. Otherwise let children rejoice in frolic and play ; we must not let heartless severity and cares descend upon the soul of the child as the frost of May. To avoid the latter we work and make sacrifices ; the children shall not notice that the sweet milk is our meat and the fresh bread our hard care. They are not able to love us, as we love them ; when they grow up and have children, they will realize what their father and mother were to them and they will pray for them.

(*b*) " *And the disciples rebuked them. But Jesus said : Suffer the little children, and forbid them not to come to me : for such the kingdom of heaven is.*" Jesus loves children because of their pure soul, and we can add: He loves youth, loves the noble, pure, brave flowering of life. He and youth are for one another. He is meant for youth, because strong, divine life is seen in Him; they are meant for Him because they are flowering and Jesus also is from Nazareth, which means " flowering." Their heart swells, there is soul in them, and Jesus also introduces Himself in this way: the Soul of the Lord is upon me. What a brave, strong soul He possesses, a soul which longs to struggle. He walks " in the strength of the soul," loves mountains and forests, longs for the depth of the ocean, walks upon waves. If we draw His image well, then we cannot say that it is unfamiliar or that it contradicts our vital force and joys; on the contrary it renders them purer and nobler. To such a Jesus youth does not only return after dismays, defeats, and disappointments, but remains always with Him; rejoices with Him, amuses itself and plays with Him; for it looks upon all this as upon the divine idea and will.

(c) " *And when he had imposed hands upon them, he departed from thence.*" He did not take the children away from their parents; He wished them to be brought up fearing God, loving Him, to be brought up in good cheer and to ripen for the seriousness of life. Each one will in time find his own vocation according to his disposition, inclination, and circumstances. And for whatever vocation he is preparing himself let him do so with the consciousness that tells him that the hand of Jesus blessing him is upon him. Let not only the priest and nun feel themselves near to Jesus but those preparing for worldly professions as well as the youths entering upon marriage. Let these as well as those bear in mind that they are fulfilling the designs of God; both are led by God. Those who practise a worldly profession or those who long for married life have both the service of God as their life in front of them. It is the will of God and He will bless us for our work!

THE SPIRIT OF DEVOTION

Every child besides love has to have reverence towards God; religion takes care of the reverence for God. But just as love was inspired to *piety* by fine spirituality, so in religion it built up *devotion*. Piety is that love with which the soul embraces the Lord; devotion is that reverence with which it honours Him.

(*a*) There are many kinds of devotion. *Devovere* means as much as to hand over. Firstly man gives himself over to man ready for his service. Devotion is the devotedness of the servant for his lord. Devotion is the devotedness of the lay-sister for her dear ailing ones; she lives for them! Devotion is the winter service of the monks of St. Bernard living on the summit of the Alps. Devotion is the attachment of the king's servants who are prepared to give their lives for him. Similarly we can hand ourselves over to the Lord in different ways: by keeping the commandments, by love and faithfulness which are utterly absorbed in God. But we do not call the good, noble, virtuous life "devotion"; devotion is devotedness in the service of God, in the liturgy. This is the devotion which has built the churches and altars, this has made the dogmas flourish into feasts; it decorated the service of God with the creeping rose-wreaths of ceremony, with living wreaths; it inspired artists, brought forth grand conceptions . . . its altars smoke with clouds of incense at the *Introitus* and the *Offertorium* back to the hecatombs of Solomon and from there back again to the sacrifice of Abel. This devotion prays and sings, it steps to the altar and its *toga* changes to the *alba* of many folds, the *pallium* to *stola* and *casula* as it performs the service of God. To reverence God is our duty and consolation and this we are able to do in seclusion, as well as in public. Let us conceive the public service of God as a great interest, as an important one; let it be one of the consecrations of public life. Let us willingly go to Holy Mass and as far as it is in our power help to enhance its grandeur.

(*b*) And what shall be the character of our devotion? " *Prompta voluntas ad divini cultus actus exercendos*," willing, ardent, persevering will, attention, and devotion in accomplishing the service of God. This " prompt " will does not only build churches, but decorates and sweeps them; it enhances the splendour of the service of God; it willingly bends the knee; it partakes of Holy Communion with zeal and folded hands; it reverences the customs and functions of the Church; its eyes and face before the altar are like the everlasting light that glows thereby. A correct Holy Communion is a shining example. There is no religion where there is no devotion; devotion is the prayer of religion.

(*c*) Where does devotion come from? " *In meditatione mea* " the fire ignites in meditating souls. Where shall the willingness of the will come from? . . . " *Voluntas ex intelligentia* "; it comes from seeing Jesus . . . this sweet incorporation of all that is strong and beautiful, " *qui dulci vita inescat*," who fascinates us by His life and who is able to live so sublimely for Himself and induces us also to live for ourselves. His shadow is cast upon us ; the impression of His personality and individuality is inextinguishable and it is in this proximity that our convictions and resolutions blossom forth, we have our spring. " *Memor fui Dei et delectatus sum*," Thy remembrance is our joy and in Thy presence we become Thy " devoted " creations. We never tire of looking at Jesus as He prays on the mountains of Judea, on Mount Tabor, in the wilderness, and in the temple, and whose prayer is so sublime and so sweet that the Prophets Moses and Elias come down to Him and Angels serve Him. What sublime " assistance " ! Their soul is a flaming torch ; their heart is full of incense !

JESUS AND THE RICH YOUNG MAN

" *And when he was gone forth into the way, a certain man running up and kneeling before him, asked him, Good Master, what shall I do that I may receive life everlasting? And Jesus said to him . . . Thou knowest the commandments, Do not commit adultery, do not kill, do not steal . . . But he answering, said to him : Master, all these things I have observed from my youth. And Jesus looking on him, loved him, and said to him : One thing is wanting unto thee : go, sell whatsoever thou hast ... and come, follow me. Who being struck sad at that saying, went away sorrowful : for he had great possessions. And Jesus looking round about, saith to his disciples : How hardly shall they, that have riches, enter into the kingdom of God !* " (*Mark* x. 17-23.)

(*a*) A representative of sin-free youth runs to Jesus filled with love and enthusiasm, and Jesus looks upon him with the ecstasy of His soul. He is pleased with the youth ;

rejoices that the youth comes to Him, rejoices in the revelation of his soul, which longs for eternal life. He encourages and calls him: Approach, come nearer and nearer and if thy heart is in the right place, attach thyself to Me, thou canst become My apostle. This is the way of the Lord. Let us obey His call; transitoriness is a torture to us, it does not satisfy us; God, life, and happiness are what we want.

Incomprehensibility is a torture, also unaccomplished, aimless existence, and as transitoriness and the incomprehensibility of existence cannot be conquered by science or culture but only by faith, therefore we attach and bind ourselves to the Lord in faith. We bind ourselves to Him not as to a notion, but as to the source of existence and to the key of comprehension. It is for this reason that there are unity and fertility in our existence. For this reason we willingly keep the commandments. We wish to grow and develop, to become like Jesus. Those who go towards Him move among denials, renunciations, restrictions, move continually among "noes," but these "noes" contain a forcible "yes"; these restrictions are the limits of beauty. When we deny ourselves we break off a piece of nature for the sake of spiritual beauty and strength. This is the philosophy of renunciation.

(b) "*All these things I have observed from my youth.*" It is a great grace when God calls "*a juventute mea*" and when someone understands this call. This consciousness is heaven on earth. Let us love, reverence, and keep the commandments. The soul does not gain in substance from the outer commandments and laws, but law and commandment direct the soul and help its expressions of life to consciousness; they help to shape the inner beauty.

Law is only asserted when it becomes embodied in our own will. In this way law and morality become our property, they are something that we will and experience. In this way our benefit and goodwill become ideals which fill us, enrich us, and make us happy. The will of God is an immeasurable force and happiness and by doing it we change it into our own, into our own strength and happiness. If we wish for strength and happiness, let us accomplish the divine will. Jesus will look upon us with pleasure and will love us.

(c) " *Who being struck sad at that saying . . .*" He was sad for he looked only at the renunciation. Those who in the Christian life look only at renunciation and the fetters of the law have not yet experienced the hidden beauties in it. They see only barriers in the shapes and only denial in the outlines. But is the outline of the Madonna-face denial ? That also is a barrier, a boundary, but this barrier and boundary come from the inspiration of harmony, come from an inner lawfulness. Every form and law has to start from our will and love, then it becomes our morality. We may come into collision with our inclinations and passions—which are blind, shapeless, immoral—but this does not matter. With trusting love we encircle the beautiful shape and change it to our value and beauty. In this way we experience strength, we enjoy it and rejoice in it ; we become lordly, kingly, Christ-like. " In the heart of those who believe in Me living waters, forces and joys gush forth."

(d) " *And Jesus looking round about.*" He also was grieved and sighed : Oh, how difficult it is even for such a pure youth to wake from the mirage of riches ! Let every rich man feel that he is in danger, in the danger of frivolity, idleness, heartlessness, cruelty, envy, and conceit. He can easily be disappointed ; he believes himself to be free, whereas he is a captive ; he comes to love money and forgets that it is only given to him on trust. O my Lord, we love nothing as much as our soul and its freedom ! Who knows but that the youth afterwards became frivolous and squandered his life in luxury and idleness. To how many have riches brought evil ! Instead of living for serious work they spend their time in foolish pleasures.

THE REWARD OF THOSE WHO LEAVE ALL FOR THE LORD

" *Then Peter answering, said to him : Behold we have left all things, and have followed thee : what therefore shall we have ?* " (*Matt.* xix. 27.)

(*a*) " We have forsaken all," says Peter, forsaken our hut, fishing-net, boat, everything. Not riches, position, and rank but what might have hindered us from joining ourselves to Thee. What will therefore become of us ? Ye will be kings and judge worlds ! To renounce everything is a great deed ; who does this will be glorified and shame the world attached to the clod of earth, to inclinations and joys. We have to renounce : (1) all that leads and tempts us to sin. (2) We have to practise self-denial with the intention of promoting in ourselves spirituality, freedom, and nearness to God. We come nearer to God by the various steps of self-denial ; these are the steps of our kingly throne. Let us continually and confidently ascend them.

(*b*) " *And Jesus said to them : Amen I say to you, that you,*

*who have followed me . . . and every one that hath left house . . .
or mother, or wife, or children, or lands for my name's sake, shall
receive an hundred-fold, and shall possess life everlasting.*" The
Gospel does not only urge renunciation and devotion
where the Apostles are concerned, but urges everyone
to renounce himself for the sake of God. Renunciation
is good; breaking away from the earth is the way of great
souls. We cannot remove this feature from the Gospel.
Maybe parents, husbands, and wives take these declarations
of Christ amiss and find them pitiless, but let them not
take offence at them. We make a sacrifice of the flesh for
the sake of the soul; in life and health we likewise make
sacrifices for the sake of riches and knowledge. How much
more ought we to be willing to give up everything to win
perfection. Do not let us believe the tepid who would
draw us away from sacrifice; do not let us listen to the
syrens, to the sentimental idealists, who encourage us
" to let ourselves go and live life to the full." There is no
culture of spirit without strength and sacrifice. The longing for pleasure draws after it the degeneration of the
people. Therefore we have to educate ourselves to the
conquering of this-feeling.

(c) The supernatural life demands sacrifices still more
urgently than our natural life. Let us make these sacrifices
with the deep feeling of doing them for God, for the sake
of the Sublime. This is our glory, if we are able to give
and do anything for His glory. Great is our debt; let us
be grateful if out of gratitude we are able to offer Him
something. Dreadful and terrible is the immensity of
what we owe Him; let us feel happy, if by way of com-
pensation we are able to renounce something. The Count
of Brabant went with the army of crusaders to the Holy

Land and took his wife with him and whilst he was in
battle his wife nursed the sick in Jerusalem. After a time
he had to return to his country, but his wife asked leave
of him to remain there so as to be able to continue serving
God and the sick. " How could I leave you ? " said the
Count. " I cannot live without you." But she went on
begging him. Finally the matter came before the patriarch
and he, being deeply touched by the ardour of the woman,
also asked the Count to let his wife remain. And when
even that was of no use and the Count was still reluctant,
then the patriarch offered the Count a drop of the Blood
of Christ dried on a stone—a relic from the Church of
Jerusalem—in exchange for his wife. This had its effect.
For this treasure the Count renounced the treasure of his
heart. What is it we would not likewise do for the Blood
of Christ, for grace, for resemblance to Christ ?

PARABLE OF THE WORKERS IN THE VINEYARD

" *The kingdom of heaven is like to an householder, who went
out early in the morning to hire labourers into his vineyard. . . .
And going out about the third hour, he saw others standing in the
market place idle.*" (*Matt.* xx. 1.)

(*a*) The kingdom of God is love of work and activity.
God encourages us in this and He pays us for it. He wishes
us to work, wishes us to put our strength into labour ;
this demands strength and soul ; health and good cheer.
Enthusiasm and good cheer carry us on, give us perseverance, and ensure success. Without it life is a yoke. It is
in work that our individuality also develops. Through
work we discover the hidden treasures of life and further

the progress of the world. The fate of the idle is painful
and sad : Why stand ye here all the day idle ? The God of
force and energy deservedly accuses the idlers of their
idleness ; God forbid that this accusation should be
meant for us. But it is meant for many ! Meant chiefly
for the well-to-do women and the girls of high society who
spend their life idly or spoil it with dilettantism ; they are
bored and nervous and embittered. Let us stand in the
market of the world with a willing heart ; let us feel and
experience the many different kinds of trouble of our
fellow-brothers, and the word of God will be heard which
metes out work to us also.

(b) " *Go you also in my vineyard.*" He sends them into
His vineyard. The vineyard of God is life with its many
different professions and eternal aim. Here everyone
works in his own place, within the limits of society,
business, family, and institutions. We work for the fulfilment of the designs of God, we work for a better world.
Let us do this with consciousness ; whatever we do, let us
do it with a noble, elevated, pure idea befitting Christian
personality. We have much labour and work and
undertakings which will perhaps, as time goes on, appear
empty and useless. But let us endeavour to make good
use of our strength, so that selfishness, stubbornness,
meanness, and prejudice may never move us. Let us
put noble individuality into everything so that our
recreation may also be a moral deed. Let us do good and
let us do good well and under the title of " good " do not
let us include only fasting, prayer, and almsgiving, but
everything we do with consciousness. Let us often ask
ourselves : What are we to do now according to our best
knowledge and most noble inclinations ?

(c) By working in the " vineyard of God," by working for the fulfilment of His designs, we become His collaborators. God works in everything and we with Him ! The nobler and more spiritual the work is, the truer it is that we work with God. The most lovely work of God is man, and all the work in the world goes on in some way for him, but especially that work which directly serves the spiritual world, enlightenment, faith, moral life, and virtue. Let us attach great importance to this fact, and if we have awakened one good feeling in someone, let us believe that the world has become better by this also.

(d) " *Who went out early in the morning . . . And going out about the third hour . . . Again he went out about the sixth and the ninth hour . . . But about the eleventh hour . . .*" God calls us to work at different times ; let us be thankful for this call and faithful to grace. Do not let us complain that He called us early, that we endured the heat and burden of the day, whilst others led their life of pleasure. For are we to complain about having awakened to life and our great duties in time—and that we have so soon found substance and depth in our life—or that we have not gone astray and squandered our treasures ? This is the greatest benefit, " *a juventute mea vocasti me,*" we are happy that Thou hast called us in our early youth ! For this, special gratitude is due ! Others have been called later. But the Lord calls everyone and is ready to receive them at any time. As long as we live, it is never too late. It is not late whilst we live and even in the twelfth hour we can win eternal life. But it is a waste of time, the time we have not lived for God. If there could be a stain on the memory of the Saints, if a shadow could darken their happiness, then surely it would be the knowledge of lost time ! No one shall say : " It is too late," but shall love God and serve Him still more ardently to make up for the time he has lost till now.

(e) " *And when evening was come . . . they were come that came about the eleventh hour, they received every man a penny. But when the first also came, they thought that they should receive more : and they also received every man a penny . . . and they murmured . . .*" It causes a stir amongst the labourers who began work in good time that those who came later receive the same reward. They murmur, they are envious and rebellious. If we apply this to " heaven," which we already enjoy here below, if we love God and love that which we expect in the other world, then this murmur is senseless, for every man's share is different. That belongs to us which we have worked out for ourselves. By " work " we mean the noble, Christ-like life which comes from faith, not outward successes and aspirations. They who have shaped the Christ-like type in themselves, whether after a long or a short time, will obtain salvation. Strictly speaking, there can be no talk of equality, for every man is different. Only in the attainment of our goal, salvation, can we be equal. In the matter of depth and fire, beauty and strength, we cannot be equal. It would be a pity if, loitering about for many years, we got no further than others do in a short time with an equal expenditure of effort. And when Christ lives in us, what are we to be envious of ? Every such soul is beautiful ! Why should the cowslip envy the forget-me-not ? Let us be Christ-like ; this beauty is force and joy and life !

THE GREATER AMONG YOU, LET HIM BE YOUR MINISTER

"*You know that the princes of the Gentiles lord it over them :
and they that are the greater, exercise power upon them. It shall
not be so among you, but whosoever will be the greater among you,
let him be your minister.*" (*Matt.* xx. 25.)

(*a*) The spirit of paganism has not known and recognized
fraternity ; the instinct for power created heartless and
cruel categories ; it raised potentates to greatness which
crushed the weak and increased through their suffering
the lowliness of their minds and their hate. Power became
a yoke and the reigning force a burden and a drainer of
blood. "But it shall not be so among you"; your
greatness is to be a joy and consolation to others ; spiritual
excellence does not crush, but elevates ; those who are
powerful in spirit, help the weak. It is after this power
and greatness that we have to strive ; not only not to take
something away from others, but to be "all to all" is an
aim indeed.

(*b*) "*Even as the son of man is not come to be ministered unto,
but to minister.*" I came to serve, to serve the intentions of
God, to be the servant of the holy will of God. Let
everyone say this : the official, the business man, the
trader, the manufacturer. We have to endeavour to make
our service correspond with Christ-like faithfulness. We
have to be aware of the fact that in the fulfilment of our
duties as citizens, in our business and industry we serve
God, not only by our goodwill, but by the work which the
Lord has pointed out to us. This world is His design,
which we carry out. In this way life wins dignity and
significance. Do not let us think that we cannot carry

out our business or industry as a service for God; we can indeed. We must not believe that with this we have to serve the devil. The Christian man of business must be inspired also by the spirit of " service " ; let him serve the public according to the ideas of God ; the idea of service shall accompany him in the economic strife, so that he continue the work of God with honour, faithfulness, patience, and perseverance.

(c) " *But be not you called Rabbi. For one is your master, and all you are brethren.*" (*Matt.* xxiii. 8.) The wish for priority and power can steal in everywhere ; into clergy and apostles also. Here also man can seek his own self, and egoism may be hidden in the individuals and corporations consecrated to God. Ye shall not walk upon this track of senselessness. Apostles must forget themselves and devote themselves wholly to the service of their brethren ; they shall not wish to rise above them in dignity and titles. Ye shall not be called Rabbis, even if ye are rabbis, ye shall feel and experience that the Church, the Gospel, the Sacraments, and the clergy are for humanity, not for the reputation of individuals or orders. The Christianity of to-day has been stripped by the development of history of many of these Christ-like traits and there are few thinkers " *qui magis agit, quam agitur,*" who act independently. The flood of worldly feeling carries and sweeps away many. Lord, give us men in whom the Gospel is not word but life. Give us Apostles who do not live for themselves but for souls.

THE SONS OF ZEBEDEE

" *Then came to him the mother of the sons of Zebedee with her sons, adoring and asking something of him. Who said to her :*

What wilt thou? She saith to him : Say that these my two sons may sit, the one on thy right hand, and the other on thy left, in thy kingdom." (*Matt.* xx. 20.)

(*a*) They come to Jesus with their mother and wish to beg for something, for something that shows such a low and coarse idea of Christ and His work ; they want to sit at the side of Christ as the first ones in the earthly kingdom of the Lord. They wish to be lords, great lords such as Pilate and Herod. They appear before the Lord, filled with this longing and confident hope. It is of this lowly idea that the Lord might have said : " Your thoughts are not my thoughts and your ways are not my ways." The difference between them is that of heaven and earth ! How often does man similarly accost the Lord ; he begs for something, according to the inspirations of his silly, stupid heart—Jesus does not despise His disciples ; He listens patiently to their desires and educates them to real greatness. Let the memory of this scene accompany us in our prayers. Let us pray, but endeavour to pray in " His name," according to " His will," so that our prayers should contain sense and truth.

(*b*) Man renders divine intentio.. as well as " the kingdom of God " itself worldly ; with us everything is earthly. With difficulty we familiarize ourselves with the idea that God is Spirit and His works are spiritual, and this is our impediment. The lowly conception of the Jews about the kingdom of God has prevented their conversion. Sensual ideas estranged many in Capharnaum from the Sacrament of the Altar. What are the ideas of men about the soul, resurrection, and heaven ? The soul is not flesh, heaven is the existence in God, resurrection the spiritualization of the body. Let us carry as much spirit as possible into the comprehension of the works of God.

(c) *" And Jesus answering, said : You know not what you ask. Can you drink the chalice that I shall drink ? They say to him : We can . . . . My chalice indeed you shall drink : but to sit on my right or left hand, is not mine to give to you, but to them for whom it is prepared by my Father."* Your first care shall be that ye faithfully follow Me, says Jesus. I do not tell you what awaits you and what it is that I shall later demand of you. I will not tell you now that thou, James, wilt be the first martyr of my Apostles. I do not frighten you, but urge you on to follow Me and imitate My person, and whatever happens to you keep on saying : This is the cup of the Lord, His cup. This we will drink ; it is glory to drink it. The rest we shall see. God will give us our place in Heaven in due course. Amen !

THE BLIND BEGGAR

" Now it came to pass, when he drew nigh to Jericho, that a certain blind man sat by the wayside, begging. And when he heard the multitude passing by, he asked what this meant. And they told him that Jesus of Nazareth was passing by. And he cried out, saying : Jesus son of David, have mercy on me." (*Luke* xviii. 35.)

(a) What a piteous and frequent sight this is : a blind beggar by the wayside. He does not see the world bathed in heavenly light, neither does he see Christ. How many there are who are blind, who do not know the aim of life and strife, who do not see Christ ! Although he sits by the wayside, although he sits upon the road of warfare, and ardent, trusting souls pass by him, souls which are attached to Christ, yet he does not see them. Such a frame of mind is poorly and beggarly even when souls of value swarm around it. The way of warfare is the way of Christianity and the Apostles, and unbelief, scepticism, and immorality border its edges with blind beggars! Let us advance unceasingly! We do not sit down beside the beggars, we do not get into the ditch. We have to act. Christ leads, we follow. The beggars' song is not our song!

(*b*) "*And when he heard the multitude passing by, he asked . . .*" He does not see, but he hears; he does not walk, but the enthusiasm of the passers-by comes to his consciousness and he asks who it is who draws on and moves the multitude, who it is who is able to awake so much enthusiasm and fire the crowd. He notices how they cleave to Him, forget house and home, and follow Him. Longing fills his heart, and he says: "Oh, if I could also go with Thee, Christ, if I could but see Thee! If only striving force could be my lot instead of the wayside and inaction! If only I did not have to cling to mud and ditch and live from hand to mouth on alms and charity!" And he cries out: "Son of David, have mercy on me!" We also are to cry out and not to leave off crying. The Lord says to us also: "Follow me!" He draws us on also, He lifts us to Himself, at one time through inner inspiration, at others through nature or by force of circumstance.

(*c*) "*And they that went before, rebuked him, that he should hold his peace. But he cried out much more: Son of David, have mercy on me.*" We have to go on crying and not take heed of the world. The world quickly condemns, but also quickly praises it if sees success. We have to love our soul in such a way and so much that we are not allowed to fear even the resentment of others. And Jesus hears us ; noise and publicity do not prevent Him stopping and granting the wish of the beggar. He granted it and cured him. The beggar became rich when he saw Christ. He left his rags and the stone he was sitting on and went with the Lord, and with what enthusiasm and devotion ! " Once upon a time ye were darkness, and now you are divine light ; walk as the sons of light."

JESUS AND ZACHEUS

" *And entering in, he walked through Jericho. And behold there was a man named Zacheus : who was the chief of the publicans, and he was rich. And he sought to see Jesus who he was, and he could not for the crowd, because he was low of stature. And running before he climbed up into a sycamore tree that he might see him.*" (*Luke* xix. 1.)

(*a*) He wants to see the mighty, wonderful Man. He does not as yet think of following Him. He stands by the wayside, climbs up a tree, and looks. By this look which curiosity cast upon the Lord as upon an historical personality, Zacheus would not have been changed. He would have seen the Lord, climbed down, and would have gone on living. These unfertile ideas, feelings, and looks . . . are not the seeds of God. Even if they are initiations, they do not create a new world. How many events do we look at ; how many books are read by us ; we even awake to the consciousness of our tasks . . . there is much seeing, looking, and enthusiasm but all with a great deal of barrenness ! The cold, bright ideals impose, but do not give creative, shaping soul !

(b) " *And when Jesus was come to the place, looking up, he saw him.*" Jesus looks upon him ; Zacheus catches the bountiful glance which penetrates his soul, pervades it, and gilds it. Who could describe this glimpse ? It is the in-pouring of God and the imparting of strength. By such a glance the soul is transfigured. We do not recognize Him, if He Himself does not look at us ; therefore we beg and implore Him to glance at us, to come, to call us, He the warm, strong life which fills us and loves.

(c) " *And said to him : Zacheus, make haste and come down : for this day I must abide in thy house.*" What haste seizes him, it is the soul which breathes in him. He hurries home and breaks away from the rest. In what a new light does he see the street, men, his house and wife ! He says a few enthusiastic words here and there, and the rest is told by his glowing face. The excitement of the crowd has now become a festivity within his soul ; the Prophet is coming to abide in his house . . . He is here already. How easy it is to serve the Lord when the feeling of great reverence changes to love in us.

(d) " *But Zacheus standing said to the Lord : Behold, Lord, the half of my goods I give to the poor ; and if I have wronged any man of anything, I restore him four-fold.*" Behold he receives the Lord " joyfully " and pays homage to his sublimity with the feelings of the new, transformed man. I was a slave of money ; from now on I will not be. I have harmed others ; from now on I will make good. Only let me possess Thee, Thy love and appreciation. When bounty, beauty, strength, and life knock at our door, do not let us lock them out but receive them with joy and give way to their power. God gives immeasurably more than He takes; He demands money, flesh, and blood and gives in their stead soul, strength, and joy.

(e) "*Jesus said to him : This day is salvation come to this house : because he also is a son of Abraham. For the son of man is come to seek and to save that which was lost.*" It will be our salvation when Jesus enters and we are able to humiliate ourselves, to be enthusiastic, to become purer, to rejoice, and make sacrifices ; when our soul throbs with joy and our thoughts soar ; when our sentiments expand and when we rise to the heights of purity ! Let us make a free passage for these crystal streams ! Let no one say that he cannot do it. We are able to love, let us love therefore and make sacrifices. Let us wash and burn out the ignoble and let us believe in the good and in its strength. The friendship of Jesus reforms and saves us !

PARABLE OF THE TEN POUNDS

"*A certain nobleman went into a far country . . . and calling his ten servants, he gave them ten pounds, and said to them : Trade till I come, and he gave ten pounds to the one, five to the other and one to the third.*" (*Luke* xix. 12.)

(a) God gave many different forces and talents and more or less wealth to us. He entrusts us with them and wishes us to make use of them. Concerning wealth he wishes us : (1) To be masters ; so that not wealth and riches should possess us but that we should possess them. He wishes our money not to be a dead weight upon our soul, but a tool in our hands for the service of many. We have to be free from its magic so that we may make many free. Soul is wanted in us so that we may raise others. Trade till I come ; all this is not finally yours ; I ask you to account for it. This feeling of responsibility renders us generous and free. Let us ask ourselves if our wealth is a means or a dead weight ? Are we its slaves or administrators ?

(b) Let us make use of it firstly by practical, honourable, moral investment. To earn means as much as to invest ; but let us earn irreproachably, earn in an honourable way. To earn by way of sin and then to wish to do good is loathsome before God. (2) Let us help others with it but help with soul, help as those who collect treasure. " Thou wilt have treasure in heaven "—this is the idea which shall lead us ; value therefore the fact of giving alms, love it, and rejoice in it as in the gathering of treasure ; do it with humility, without conceit and haughtiness. It is on this frame of mind that the value of your gift depends. The eyes of Jesus glow when He sees the widow's mite. (3) Let us use wealth for ideal aims also, for churches, schools, education, and public institutions. Beautiful churches and peals of bells, sublime pictures and altars are likewise benefits to the fatigued men who seek for spirit, as bread and clothing are to the cold and hungry.

(c) Besides wealth and money man is the possessor of soul, gifts, senses, individual qualities. We have to make use of all this. We have to devote ourselves to that task which is our lot according to our position and vocation. What we are, we must live for spiritually. We seek our good deeds firstly in the accomplishment of our duties. Not in alms, in visiting the sick, in fasting ; all that is good but not the first, essential thing. First and foremost is the ordinary everyday life which has to consist of good deeds, of a correct way of thinking, of willingness, patience, etc. In the office, in the shop, in the household, we must work with goodwill, good intentions, with steadiness and perseverance. These are both individual and social good deeds. How prudent and happy are those who act in this way ! How dull and silly are those who hide the pound given to them, who do not use their talents ! Such ones weaken and dull their talents, render their life joyless, and the following words apply to them : " *To everyone that hath shall be given . . . and from him that hath not, even that which he hath shall be taken from him.*"

THE ANOINTING OF JESUS IN BETHANY

" *And when Jesus was in Bethania in the house of Simon the leper. There came to him a woman having an alabaster-box of very precious ointment, and poured it on his head as he was at table.*" (*Matt.* xxvi. 6.)

(*a*) Bethany is a dear name, full of the attractive power of Jesus, full of ardent, thankful love. Bethany is a dear home where Jesus was loved, it is the resting place of Jesus and His joy, filled with scents from the salve of Mary. How much we also love this place where Jesus was loved, and we love those who love Jesus. . . . The love of Mary became even deeper after the resuscitation of her brother Lazarus ; her thankfulness was fired by the joy of the awakened life, and so when she poured her salve upon the head of Jesus it was not oil she poured upon it but her soul, " She poured out her soul before the Lord." She loved Jesus " as her own soul " and would have given up everything for Him. " She took her soul in her hand " so that she might give it to Him. And Jesus understood her feeling ; the love of Mary shone into His soul like a ray of sunshine through the stormy clouds of His approaching sufferings, and consoles Him. He records her act in His Gospel as though to say : " Souls, this is the way ye have to love, to approach, and to touch me . . . that I may find pleasure in you."

(b) " *And the disciples seeing it, had indignation, saying : To what purpose is this waste ? For this might have been sold for much, and given to the poor. And Jesus knowing it, said to them : Why do you trouble this woman ? for she hath wrought a good work upon me.*" She spent the money for a good cause, for the most beautiful and sweetest cause. For the flowers of the meadow are not a waste, they are the art of God. Neither is the blossoming of the heart a waste ; the pleasure is worth the expense. All that lifts the soul and ennobles it, that touches the heart and gives warmth, that raises us and fills our dumb, beast-like, instinctive world with superior light and warmth, cannot be bought too dearly. Our joy in nature, art, and, above all, grace, is worth any financial sacrifice. Do not only give bread and clothes to mankind, waste a little salve upon it also ; do not give money only but oil, the oil of joy and pleasure. Let us free man from the tread-mill of banality, let us make feasts for him and render his life more beautiful and spiritual.

(c) " *Amen I say to you wheresoever this gospel shall be preached in the whole world, that also which she hath done, shall be told for a memory of her.*" So this also belongs to the good tidings of Our Lord ; the Gospel frames the memory of Mary in a glorious, eternal flowery frame. This also is the Gospel, that Jesus loves friendship and rejoices in it. This also is the Gospel, that we have to approach the heart of Jesus with such sweet love. What is the use of anything else if we are ignorant of this ? Though the Gospel starts with the preaching of penitence, and Mary has also trod this way, it afterwards announces the good tidings : Love thy Lord God with the love of Mary !

(d) " *For she in pouring this ointment upon my body, hath done it for my burial.*" What sorrowful shadows these are upon the soul of Jesus ! Suffering is already approaching ; a few days separate Him from it ; He already takes this anointment as if it was His burial service. But we know that the love of these souls served Jesus as an anointment for His struggles. With His soul He saw those whose love and faithfulness served as a consolation to Him, those for whom He suffered gladly. O my Jesus, we will strive after noble ends ; we, too, wish to be Thy consolation.

END OF VOLUME II